Metropolitan College of NY
Library - 7th Floor
60 West Street
New York, NY 10006

SURVIVING KATRINA

Metropolitan College of NY
Library - 7th Floor
60 West Street
New York, NY 10006

SURVIVING KATRINA

The Experiences of Low-Income African American Women

Jessica Warner Pardee

FIRST**FORUM**PRESS

A DIVISION OF LYNNE RIENNER PUBLISHERS, INC. • BOULDER & LONDON

Published in the United States of America in 2014 by
FirstForumPress
A division of Lynne Rienner Publishers, Inc.
1800 30th Street, Boulder, Colorado 80301
www.rienner.com

and in the United Kingdom by
FirstForumPress
A division of Lynne Rienner Publishers, Inc.
3 Henrietta Street, Covent Garden, London WC2E 8LU

© 2014 by Lynne Rienner Publishers, Inc. All rights reserved

Library of Congress Cataloging-in-Publication Data
A Cataloging-in-Publication record for this book
is available from the Library of Congress.
ISBN: 978-1-62637-044-9

British Cataloguing in Publication Data
A Cataloguing in Publication record for this book
is available from the British Library.

This book was produced from digital files prepared by the author
using the FirstForumComposer.

Printed and bound in the United States of America

∞   The paper used in this publication meets the requirements
    of the American National Standard for Permanence of
    Paper for Printed Library Materials Z39.48-1992.

5 4 3 2 1

*I dedicate this book to the women of New Orleans
who shared their experiences with me.
Thank you for helping me with my recovery
by allowing me to document your own.*

**Metropolitan College of NY
Library - 7th Floor
60 West Street
New York, NY 10006**

Contents

Acknowledgments		*ix*
1	Understanding Katrina	1
2	Theorizing Disaster Recovery and Everyday Poverty	17
Part 1: Preparation		37
3	Decision Time	41
4	Leaving Home	55
Part 2: Survival		69
5	Stranded	71
6	Shelters of Last Resort	99
Part 3: Recovery		123
7	Seeking Shelter	127
8	Living Displacement	147
9	Returning Home	167
10	Redefining Recovery	189
Appendix: Studying Hurricane Katrina as a Scholar-Survivor		*197*
Bibliography		*213*
Index		*223*

Acknowledgments

Hurricane Katrina is an everyday part of my life. Even after eight years, the ongoing loss I feel is intimate and personal. Talking with the low-income women whose in-depth interviews form the foundation of this book has affected me deeply. The storm, the interviews, the losses—all have left a gnarly scar on my soul. In response, my first and most extensive gratitude is reserved for the women you will meet—for us, all of us who survived Katrina and have been a part of someone else's Katrina research in the hopes it will prevent this type of loss in the future. I thank you for recounting your pain in the name of knowledge. I hope I have done well by you in this volume.

Professionally, many people have contributed to this work through their support, mentorship, and critiques, all with an aim of making the book stronger. Among the most notable were Martha Huggins and Kai Erikson, whose mentorship and encouragement sowed the seeds necessary to transform the research into a book. Next, I thank the women of the SSRC working group on Persons Displaced by Hurricane Katrina—in particular, Lori Peek, Lynn Weber, Lee Miller, Alice Fothergill, and Jacquelyn Litt, whose support has been essential to my success as a scholar.

In Rochester, I thank my academic friends who have been supporters every step along the way: Deborah Blizzard, Vincent Serravallo, Jennifer Schneider, Tom Cornell, Brian Barry, Jonathan Schroeder, Xiao Wang, Michael Vernarelli, LaVerne McQuiller Williams, Michael Laver, and Joanne Staskiewicz. Your feedback, comments, brainstorming, critical inquiries, pep talks, shared sample materials from your own books, and support for my progress have helped me more than words can say. Thank you, truly! At Lynne Rienner Publishers, I thank Andrew Berzanskis and the anonymous reviewers for their time and support. Their comments strengthened the work in ways I never could have imagined.

On a personal note, I thank my family for loving me throughout this process: Mom and Dad, Aaron, Stacey, Kara, Tim, Aunt Ann, Uncle Ken, Mama, Daddy, and Danielle. Thank you for listening to me talk about the project over the years, helping me along the way, and even housing me while I was displaced from New Orleans by the storm. You all played an important part in making this project happen.

Finally, to Bruce, I love you more than anything. Your support, kindness, patience, practicality, and willingness to read and review so very many drafts kept this project moving to completion. Your never-ending support and love is the very best thing in my life. Thank you for everything. I look forward to returning the favor.

1

Understanding Katrina

Hurricane Katrina made landfall on Monday, August 29, 2005. By Tuesday, multiple levees had failed in the City of New Orleans.

> Morgan: It came up all day, at one time. There were no lights, no boats. We were trapped. The water come up high, and we trapped. We can't get out. Our apartment was in the center. Nobody had lights, nobody had water. It was one neighbor hollering at the other neighbor. We couldn't get out for five days or better. We had no water, no light, no nothing. I was afraid to step down because the water was up to my neck.
>
> ... It was horrible. It was something I never experienced. I wasn't aware of this. I know God does things for a reason but—but, I never experienced it. People was yelling and screaming. Babies couldn't help themselves. I couldn't help myself. At night, you couldn't help yourself. You couldn't go to the neighbor's. You think of lighting a candle, but were afraid of a fire. Who would help me?
>
> There was no warning, and we had no water. All we heard was there was a hurricane watch, and the next thing you was in darkness. I wouldn't want anyone to experience that. I couldn't sleep, nor nothing. Wouldn't want nobody to go through it. It was horrible. Sometimes I dream, thinking I'm seeing things. I couldn't sleep for two and three days, for weeks. I'm getting over it a little, but it's nothing like home. I don't like to see it on TV. Anything about Hurricane Katrina is a reminder. Thank God I'm still here, and my mother and sisters and children still here, we made it. My heart goes to the ones that didn't make it.
>
> Jessica: So did the power go out before the storm or as the storm passed?

Morgan: When the water was rising up, everything was off. It started to lightning, and that just shut down everything.

Jessica: Do you remember what the storm was like? Was there wind or rain?

Morgan: It was horrible. You could hear the rain hitting. The wind hit the window and it made that sound, like "whoo-whoo." It was just in one corner. Then you look outside, and see the water is not going down, it's coming up, and up, and up. All that night it was raining. The rain come constantly down, and the water was just coming up.

Jessica: How were things the next morning?

Morgan: The water was up. It was just up. If you try to go down the steps, the water was up to your neck. I was scared. I didn't know what was in that water. The toilets backed up, and there was sewerage on the floor. You couldn't flush a toilet or nothing. [...] After a few days passed, you'd think the water would go down, but it never went down. The whole five days I was in there, the water was still up. The sewerage line popped and the water line bust, which was making it worser.

Jessica: How did you get out?

Morgan: The man in the boat. There was security and an army man in a boat. They was kicking the doors in to make sure the people was out. At night, we were trying to do something with a flashlight to tell them we was in there. I was scared to go down the steps to where water was. [...] How we got out? We was yelling, and a boat came by. There was all this water, and they had to pick me up because the water was so high....

Jessica: How much water was in your apartment?

Morgan: Well, it was a lot of water. That water was high. I could see it through the door when it was coming in. When that other levee popped, it was further in. Then there was a man on a boat riding past. He said that "everybody needs to get out before it gets too dark." I let them know I was there.

Jessica: Who was with you?

Morgan: My son went to try to get help. I don't know if he got trapped in somewhere. He could swim. He said, "Ma, I can make it"—he being 34 years old. He went back to try to get help. He said "If you see a boat, get in it, get on it." He was looking for that boat. Then he hollered to see if I was okay, I said "yeah." We keep in touch. I'm in here by myself. I don't want to ever experience nothing like that.

Morgan's experience is not unique. Like so many of the 51 women interviewed for this study, the details of the disaster—watching homes fall down in front of their eyes, waking up to water surrounding them, waiting days for help to arrive, facing water levels above one's head, lacking food and water, struggling to survive—demonstrate just a sliver of the traumatic catastrophe that was Hurricane Katrina. While this book focuses on the experiences emanating from the city of New Orleans, for those in other areas of the Gulf Coast, the destruction was even more absolute. According to Kai Erikson, Hurricane Katrina "was the most *destructive* disaster in our history when one considers the amount of harm it did." (italics in original).[1] "Unfathomable" barely describes the true depth of Hurricane Katrina's losses, which include 1,720 initial deaths.[2]

In response, this book has two purposes. First, it provides a formal examination of how low-income, African American women prepared for, survived through, and attempted to recover after Hurricane Katrina. Through the illumination of the intersectional relationship between poverty and disaster, this project details whether low-income women were able to successfully transfer poverty survival strategies to the context of Hurricane Katrina, and what those experiences meant for redefining the concept of disaster recovery among this highly marginalized population. This research matters because these women's experiences also provide insight into the bitter realities of continued social inequality and segregation in our society, exacerbated by the storm into instances of racial and class-based bias and violence. This book documents those experiences and demonstrates their sociological relevance.

Second, the book is written with the aim of guiding you, the reader, through the disaster experience as it is lived by survivors. While reading a book can never fully express the lived reality of such a catastrophe, it is my goal to sensitize you to the myriad of social inequalities that disasters of this magnitude illuminate, so as to provide a context in which to better understand the evacuation, survival, and recovery experiences of women with extremely limited resources. For without understanding the circumstances of the least advantaged, how can we possibly make decisions as a society that will ensure the protection of *all* our citizens when the next Katrina occurs?

Landfall

The force of Hurricane Katrina as it made landfall was less than expected. Peaking as a Category 5 storm, Katrina weakened as it approached land, and came ashore as a strong Category 3. On a scale of 1-5, a Category 3 is in the middle. However, the physical and social devastation, in combination with the storm surge, were that of something much stronger. This medium-level storm blew out windows on downtown high rises, tore a hole in the roof of the Louisiana Superdome where thousands sheltered for safety, burst levees from the pressure of the water backed up behind them, and simply flooded over others, dissolving the earthen mound that held the concrete levee barriers in place until they flipped over, releasing the deluge that was behind.[3] Roofs and walls were torn off of homes, some of which collapsed upon themselves. Trees and houses splintered, and in places like the Mississippi Gulf Coast and the 9th Ward of New Orleans, entire neighborhoods were washed away, leaving the wooden remnants scattered about like a box of matches tossed onto the ground in anger. Here each match represents the memory of a family or home lost to the storm. For those who saw the affected areas in those early months, the devastation wrought by Katrina was seemingly infinite, absolute, and simply unimaginable—a true catastrophe. No warning could prepare us for this.

As a catastrophe, Hurricane Katrina was so intense that its classification is separate and apart from that of a disaster.[4] Catastrophes include events such as the Chernobyl nuclear disaster and Florida's Hurricane Andrew—a Category 5 storm that leveled parts of Southern Dade County.[5] Hurricane Katrina, whose damages covered 93,000 square miles of the U.S. Gulf Coast[6] and devastated New Orleans, Mississippi's Bay St. Louis, Pass Christian, and Gulfport areas, covered a much wider swath of territory than Florida's Hurricane Andrew. Moreover, in the case of New Orleans, the levee breaches that followed Katrina's winds greatly exacerbated the scope and depth of the disaster in the city. Thus, the classification of Hurricane Katrina as a catastrophe results from the extensive wind and storm surge damage in coastal Mississippi, the failure of the levee system in New Orleans and the devastatingly high death toll across the entire Gulf Coast region.

At this point, most Katrina books provide a detailed account of Katrina's effects on businesses lost, the number of people displaced (over 1.5 million), and other facts and figures. I'd prefer not to do so, and direct you to read Lynn Weber and Lori Peek's meticulously researched discussion of these statistics.[7] Instead, this book is focused on the *lived* experiences of low-income African American women. As such, it seems fitting to introduce you to them and the study early, so you can come to understand Hurricane Katrina not by the numbers, but by the way it affected real people: women who simply wanted to protect themselves, their families, their children, and their grandchildren from harm.

Meeting the Women

The study's purposive sample consists of 51 women: Simone, Louisa, Olivia, Ann, Alika, Keebra, Linda, Ruth, Vivienne, Zarah, Callista, Ingrid, Aliyah, Sheila, Vanessa, Angela, Destiny, Iris, Thelma, Joanna, Jada, Ebony, Morgan, Lydia, Abigail, Janelle, Thea, Keisha, Faith, Twila, Mary, Sharon, Asia, Julia, Mercedes, Amaya, Coral, Barbara Jean, Ruby, Giselle, Eurdice, Trinity, Lillian, Savannah, Gloria, Daphne, Sarah, Perla, Althea, Regina, and Violet.[8] All are Black or African American.[9] Each woman was assigned a pseudonym to protect her identity, and those names were chosen by using a baby name website, then selecting African American baby names, then sorting them by generation. More traditional names (Sarah, Ruth, Barbara Jean, Ann) reflect older respondents. More contemporary names (Jada, Zarah, Aliyah, Mercedes) reflect younger respondents. To the extent possible, names were chosen to match the personalities of the women and/or in correspondence with their experiences (e.g., Faith, Lillian).

All of the women had been residents of the city of New Orleans when the storm made landfall, and averaged nearly six years of residency in their public housing units prior to the storm, though some had been in the system much longer. The sample was taken from lists of former and current public housing residents, displaced by the HOPE VI redevelopment of the Desire and St. Thomas communities in New Orleans. (See the Appendix for a more detailed account of the sample frame's origin.)

As a group, the mean age was just over 50 years old, making many mothers to adult children and caregivers to grandchildren whom they raised. Just eleven women had children under the age of 18 (21.6%), and another four were raising their grandchildren (7.8%). Most (55%) were single; 12% married, 16% divorced, and 12% were widowed; the remainder were separated or cohabitating. While public housing residents are often envisioned as young single mothers with many children, in the two housing sites that form the geographic starting point for sample recruitment, there was an informal housing authority policy to rehouse older women without children first, followed by families who had been long-term public housing residents, then families with small children last.[10] As a result, there are far fewer very young children among this population than might otherwise be expected.

For these women, educational opportunities had been limited during their lifetimes: 41% had no educational degree, while 47% had a high school degree or a GED. Immediately, this lack of education predisposes these women to job opportunities in the service industry of the labor market, as manufacturing was very limited in the region. Just 10% had an Associate's or Bachelor's degree. Only one respondent, a school teacher, had a graduate degree (Master's). With these low educational levels (88% with a high school education or *less*), these women are highly representative of the limited educational attainment of the broader population of the city at that time. In addition to, or perhaps because of, their low educational attainment, ninety percent (n=46) of women interviewed had earned below $20,000 in 2004, the year prior to Katrina.

Twenty-nine women evacuated themselves despite demographic characteristics suggesting they would leave at lower rates, if at all.[11] Of those 29 women, 22 women left before the storm arrived and seven women left afterwards. 26 women specifically identified family or friends with whom they left in private vehicles, while the remaining three left in their own vehicles. Among those who did not evacuate, nineteen women reported being "rescued" from their flooded homes out of twenty-one women who were stranded in the city during the storm; among them were Trinity, Lillian, Regina, Louisa, Ann, Alika, Linda, Zarah, Sheila, Vanessa, Angela, Joanna, Jada, Ebony, Morgan, Lydia, Thea, Keisha, Twila, Mary, and Eurdice. Giselle, who worked at a convalescent home during the storm and aftermath, was neither stranded nor evacuated, nor did she and her husband leave immediately after the storm. Overall, decisions about evacuation timing were determined through the engagement of narratives, defining the storm as safe or a threat, or revolving around financial concerns including the potential for job loss (a detailed discussion is developed in Chapter 3). Table 1.1 presents these descriptive statistics.

In summary, the women in this sample represent a population of African American individuals with limited incomes and finite resources, but also an ability to transform situational social capital into survival resources for themselves and their family members. Throughout the remainder of this book, their capacity for agency within the social structural constraints of catastrophe will be explored.

TABLE 1.1   Descriptive Statistics for the Sample

Variable	N=51	
Sex		
Female	100%	
Age		
mean	51.33	
s.d.	14.26	
Race		
Black	100%	
Marital Status		
Single	54.9%	(n=28)
Cohabitating	1.9%	(n = 1)
Married	11.8%	(n = 6)
Widowed	11.8%	(n = 6)
Divorced	15.7%	(n = 8)
Separated	3.9%	(n = 2)
Educational Degree		
No degree	41.2%	(n = 21)
High school/GED	47.1%	(n = 24)
Assoc./Bachelor's	9.8%	(n = 5)
Graduate degree	1.9%	(n = 1)
Income category		
0-$20,000	90.2%	(n = 46)
$20,000-$40,000	9.8%	(n = 5)
Homeownership		
No	72.5%	(n = 37)
Yes	7.8%	(n = 4)
Missing	19.6%	(n=10, all pretest)
Length of residency in pre-Katrina housing in years		
Mean	pretest = 4.74, final = 6.02	
s.d.	1.82, 7.15	

Note: pretest n=10, final survey n=41.

Studying Katrina as a Scholar-Survivor

I am a Hurricane Katrina survivor. I evacuated from New Orleans to escape the storm on Saturday, August 27, 2005 around 8 p.m., and did not return to my home for nearly six weeks. Since the moment I saw the storm headed for my city on television, I have not had a single day where I did not think about the storm, its destruction, or this study. It is exhausting. It is also imperative that this work be continued, in memory of those who lost their lives and homes unnecessarily, and in honor of the women who were strong enough to share with me what was in many cases the very worst experiences of their lives. It is from this vantage point that I engage both my training as a sociologist and my experience as an evacuee and decade-long resident of New Orleans to help elucidate not only the disaster, but the cultural significance of the events for residents. A detailed description and reflection of my role as a scholar-survivor is developed at length in the Appendix.

Collecting the Data

Telephone interviews form the foundation for the study, primarily because many respondents were displaced from New Orleans and no research funding for meeting with women in person was available. Whether using cell phones, setting up landlines in new FEMA apartments, or by borrowing someone else's phone, women found ways to contact me upon receiving one of the hundreds of recruitment letters that I sent. Only one respondent interviewed lacked her own phone and she utilized a neighbor's phone to complete the interview. (See the Appendix for a detailed account of the recruitment process, research sites, study history and context, and the author's navigations of data collection within her own displacement as a Katrina survivor.) All interviews were collected between October 2005 and December 2006.

Each interview had two parts: the first was a section of closed-ended questions on evacuation, employment, assistance before and after the storm, and demographic characteristics. The second section included open-ended questions, allowing women to describe their evacuation and recovery experiences in detail and in their own words. The first section required 5 to 15 minutes to complete while the second section typically took between 30 to 90 minutes. Responses were typed during the interview and edited after; interviews were not tape-recorded. To address confidentiality, all names in this work and other published works from the study use a set of pseudonyms. Compensation included a $20 gift card and two hotline numbers for free counseling services.

From these interviews, key theoretical questions were answered to be considered at length in this volume: Are poverty survival strategies transferrable to disaster contexts? While scholars have studied everyday survival within poverty,[12] how is that experience altered when a disaster is layered onto the analysis? How exactly did these low-income women face a catastrophe such as Hurricane Katrina, given their persistent social disadvantage? To what extent do race, class, and gender mitigate and transform those experiences? What mechanisms may become available to promote survival during a disaster, which are not available in normal daily life? The book also asks: Were these women able to recover? And, what does disaster recovery even mean for low-income, minority women, when the literature's definition of failed recovery shares the same characteristics as living in poverty every day?[13] How can you recover back to a disastrous state? The theoretical underpinnings of these questions are presented in depth in Chapter 2 for the interested reader. Now, I would like to focus the reader's attention on the experiences of Ruby and Lydia, fellow survivors of the storm. I have selected these cases to exemplify just how complex a woman's holistic disaster experience was.

Ruby's Experience

A typical woman in this study, 56-year-old Ruby had been unemployed at the time of Hurricane Katrina. Having lost her husband in 1994, Ruby moved into the new Abundance Square mixed-income housing, built at the old Desire public housing site in New Orleans. Abundance Square was located along the Industrial Canal, roughly opposite where the Mississippi River Gulf Outlet connects to the system. An opportunity for a new life, the pristine housing was high quality and comparable to apartments marketed as "luxury" in the city's for-profit housing market. With handicapped accessible units, freshly painted walls, insulated windows, and central air conditioning, the new units were sunny, appealing, and seemed to be a nice place to raise a family. When Ruby spoke with me, she explained she was among the first wave of families to move into the Abundance Square apartments. She shared her unit with six other family members—two daughters and her four teenaged grandchildren, ages 13, 15, 16, and 18. Ruby was responsible for the care of her grandchildren after their mother, her third daughter, had been murdered.

Like nearly half the women in this study, Ruby had evacuated as best she could before the storm, attempting to take her family to a small

Louisiana town halfway between New Orleans and Baton Rouge. Amid traffic, Ruby missed the exit:

> It was very stressful. We had left my house at 12 p.m. and we got ourselves going through Jefferson Parish. The people could drive in their vehicles, even with the door open. It was stressful and hot. It was 5:30 p.m. when we hit Airline Highway. We went through Jefferson Parish, then back to Airline. On the way out, I was in [my town]. I had passed [the town] by like two to three miles. Then, a hard rain came down. Then, a man on the radio said the storm would hit Baton Rouge before New Orleans, so we turned back.

Normally, this drive would take about 40 minutes. With the evacuation traffic, Ruby's journey took over five and a half hours. This slow pace for evacuation is common, and a consideration when deciding whether to shelter in place or leave. For elderly individuals, becoming stranded in a car on the highway can actually be far more dangerous than sheltering in place.

Since her first evacuation location was in the direct storm path according to the radio newscaster, Ruby returned to her son's home in a New Orleans suburb and rode out the storm there. After two days passed, the whole family went to the New Orleans International Airport, where they were stranded for a few more days until being transported to a church in a small Louisiana town near Shreveport. It was there that Ruby learned about the flooding of her neighborhood, which she described to me briefly: "I was living upstairs, but there was still water. I got 9-10 feet in my house. I lost everything downstairs and my stuff was ruined." Living in a two-story apartment which began on the second story of the building, Ruby's entire main floor was flooded, destroying her furniture and belongings. In her bedroom, located "upstairs" on the building's third story, her clothing and other things were destroyed as mold permeated anything above the flood line, growing unabated in the hot, humid Louisiana summer. Ruby lost everything except her life.

Staying in the church near Shreveport for the next two and a half weeks, Ruby and her family began to piece together survival systems during their immediate displacement. First, Ruby's daughter found an apartment with the help of the church members where they were staying. By embracing her access to situational social capital in the form of help from the church women, their knowledge, and financial resources, Ruby's daughter worked to establish housing stability for her family. Once settled, her daughter then helped Ruby to get her own apartment in the same complex and community where the church had sheltered her.

As Ruby's new apartment only had two bedrooms instead of the four her family needed, it was just a starting point, and a difficult one. In her new home, Ruby's rent increased by $82 a month compared to before the storm. Ruby also received food stamps, although her allocation was reduced from over $300 before the storm to $226 monthly afterwards because her eldest granddaughter had turned 18 and was no longer covered by the program, despite her continued dependence upon Ruby.

Ruby faced the most difficulty with her medical care, requiring medical prescriptions for blood pressure and regular screenings for diabetes. In New Orleans, her medications had cost just $18 a month at Charity Hospital; in her new home in Northern Louisiana, her medications were $259 per month. Consequently, Charity Hospital was another Katrina casualty, closed permanently by the State of Louisiana after the storm. So, while Ruby was housed, fed, and receiving medical care, her monthly costs were significantly higher for herself and her family, while her incoming assistances had decreased.[14] In this way, Ruby epitomizes the evacuation, displacement, and recovery challenges experienced by so many women in this study. She attempted to engage her poverty survival strategies in new post-disaster contexts, only to find that reliable programs like food stamps and Medicaid were no longer sufficient to meet her family's needs in other parts of the state. Ruby is like so many of the other women you will meet here—women who, after trying to rebuild their lives, managed to survive yet not actually recover to even the basic level of impoverished security they experienced before the storm.

Lydia's Experience

Lydia is the face of the working poor. A homeowner, a surgical technician, and a mother to a 16-year-old son and an adult daughter, in her 48 years Lydia built a stable life, albeit one that was certainly limited by her salary of less than $20,000 a year. Despite working in a full-time, semi-skilled position, Lydia represents families throughout the country that struggle to make ends meet on low-wage work.[15] While low-income, she is hardworking, responsible, and committed to her job and community. In fact, as flooding decimated the city, she was working at a major downtown hospital where workers manually ventilated patients as long as they could while waiting for evacuation crews to arrive.

For Lydia, making arrangements to protect her son was a top priority as the storm approached New Orleans. Taking precautions,

Lydia took the storm very seriously, recognizing the threat it posed, and openly identifying the consequences it had for her extended family:

> I put the children's birth certificates, put important papers, in a Ziploc bag. I had a bad feeling. I asked my youngest son to come with me, but he didn't want to come to the hospital. Then I saw it hadn't turned. I called my oldest brother to pick up my son, and they went to Atlanta. Then my brother after me, he stayed, and he drowned. Everybody else left. I was the only one who stayed in the hospital. There was children crying. People wanting milk for their children, and we turning them away. There was bodies floating, and people dying. I stayed until we was evacuated. Then my family called, 'cause they found my brother's body. Katrina. That's an experience I'd never forget.

As was the case during other interviews within this study, Lydia articulated many traumatic experiences in just a moment's time. Lydia's actions to protect her son reflect both a mother's responsibility to "do gender" by providing a way for him to leave town while she stayed,[16] as well as the mechanism for that evacuation—the engagement of kin-based social networks[17] that literally gave him a car ride to safety. She also described how her younger brother's failure to evacuate resulted in his death, reflecting race-based, class-based, and gender-based patterns of evacuation decision making.[18] Next, her own commitment to her workplace reflects how financial narratives become part of the evacuation decision making process (See Chapter 3). Finally, she describes the lived experience of the storm itself, demonstrating how even formal institutions such as hospitals were simply unprepared for the catastrophe that unfolded before the city and the nation. Together, this brief statement connects several themes throughout the book, demonstrating how the processes of disaster unfold and can be simultaneous and multifaceted for any given individual.

Stranded for about a week, Lydia and her coworkers pooled their food in an effort to keep themselves and their patients alive. After three days, the National Guard airdropped food on the top of the building—tuna fish and raviolis. Yet, the lack of power and an intermittently working backup generator left patients needing ventilators to perish because, as Lydia recounts, "There were people, we had to move some people on ventilators. We had to get them out. [...] They didn't have enough people to pump air into people." Over time, rescue boats finally arrived to ferry people to transportation staging grounds. For Lydia, this was the downtown Post Office, where she boarded a bus to Texas. Once there, she and some coworkers made their way to the airport, where they parted ways. For Lydia, her next step was to take a flight to stay with her daughter in Virginia Beach, where she engaged a kin-based survival strategy to help herself during this time. After a few weeks, her son, who had evacuated to Atlanta with family, also joined Lydia there.

During her displacement, Lydia quickly found work—an uncommon opportunity for many women in this study and another common survival strategy used in everyday poverty.[19] Yet, the money she earned quickly dissipated—in addition to rent on an apartment in Virginia, she was also continuing to pay her mortgage on her damaged home in New Orleans. In fact, the only formal assistance she received at that time was food stamps since she had relocated outside the disaster strike zone, even though some evacuees were receiving monthly rental assistance by this point in time.[20] In this way, her reliance on her daughter, a source of kin-based support, put her in a less opportune location to receive the federal aid which was being granted more quickly to evacuees displaced to larger evacuee centers, such as Houston, Baton Rouge, or Atlanta.

By the time of our interview in August 2006, Lydia had finally qualified for a small amount of FEMA money and a trailer. Although the trailer was delivered to her home in April, she did not receive the keys until July and was unable to move back there due to the lack of work available in New Orleans. In Virginia, she had just signed an employment contract for a year when we spoke, suggesting while a work-based path to recovery was available, it was only available if Lydia stayed in Virginia. In short, in order to initiate her own recovery, she had to live in a geographic place that itself was undamaged, since her New Orleans-based life, including her home and job opportunities, were extremely slow to return to normal. In this way, living an extended displacement became Lydia's best recovery option, reflecting a choice many women in this study had to make as they began to rebuild their lives in the face of uncertain futures.

Comparing Ruby and Lydia's experiences, it becomes quite apparent that kin-based networks are not only an important survival strategy for living in poverty, but also are similarly engaged in disaster circumstances. Throughout the book, the importance of kin (both blood and social) for saving lives through enabling evacuation, providing shelter, or being a reason to "keep it together" will be demonstrated time and time again. Often undervalued due to their financial limitations, the positive aspects of low-income networks reflect deep commitments to family and community; in many cases, help came from those who couldn't afford to assist, yet did so anyway (See the Chapter 5 for examples).

By contrast, work- and assistance-based strategies were often dismantled. Lydia's case presents a woman who was able to find work, but for many others work was an elusive opportunity, especially among those who relocated to evacuation magnets, such as Baton Rouge, Houston, and Atlanta, where the labor market could not absorb the excess workforce. Fortunately, Lydia's relocation to Virginia put her in a less crowded labor market, improving her recovery potential. Yet, the consequence of being outside the hurricane's impact zone was a restricted ability to access FEMA aid and other social assistances. In this way, geography simultaneously enabled recovery through employment, but disabled recovery through assistances for Lydia. Together both Ruby and Lydia's experiences reflect the broader myriad of challenges low-income, Black women faced as they worked to rebuild their lives with only the clothing on their backs.

The Book's Outline

The remainder of the text will present and analyze the lived experiences of female low-income disaster survivors, from evacuation to displacement, and for some, to their return to New Orleans. For readers seeking the academic groundings of the work, the theoretical discussion of poverty, survival strategies, and disaster recovery may be found in Chapter 2. From there, the book advances in three parts, in which the chapters are organized around a chronology of possibilities representing the different pathways evacuees could and did follow: from preparing for the storm to returning to, or staying away from, their New Orleans home. All pathways begin with a single decision—whether to evacuate or stay through the storm. From this moment, some paths wind through periods of stable housing experiences, while others push further into deeper displacement and uncertainty. This analysis considers each step along the way, from preparing for the storm in Chapter 3, to evacuating in advance in Chapter 4, or "riding out" the hurricane in Chapters 5 and 6, with the last often leading to being stranded in New Orleans during the disaster's aftermath. Eventually, women sought shelter in new communities, as discussed in Chapter 7, and lived through displacement, as explored in Chapter 8. Ultimately, evacuees had to decide between remaining away from New Orleans or returning home, as recounted in Chapter 9. As the accounts move further away from the storm itself, the women's narratives merge, representing many more commonalities than differences in their unified struggles and patterns living outside of, as well as within, the city of New Orleans.

Finally, out of respect for the survivors of the storm, I have worked to make their experiences the centerpiece of this book, and have moved the citations into endnotes. Doing so is a purposeful choice to make the data and analysis the centerpiece over the references engaged. In the vast Katrina literature, numerous quantitative and theoretical commentaries abound. For those looking to make sweeping generalizations, I direct you elsewhere; this sample size is too small and specific for that purpose. Instead, this book is committed to providing low-income, Black women a voice as victims and survivors of both the storm and our society's inadequate response to it. Too late came the help and too long was the suffering, as women, men, and children languished in the hot Louisiana sun, waiting days on end for water and food after being terrorized by nature and man alike. As a survivor myself, it is my hope that by reading this book, you will come to understand the texture of the experience and to rethink the meaning of Katrina for our society and for ourselves.

---

[1] Erikson 2007.
[2] Weber and Peek 2012: 1.
[3] NOVA 2005.
[4] Dynes and Rodriguez 2005; Rodríguez, Trainor, and Quarantelli 2006; Harrold 2006; Kates et al. 2006; Cutter and Emrich 2006; GAO 06-934.
[5] Adams et al. 2002; Gladwin and Peacock 1997; Smith and Belgrave 1995.
[6] The White House 2006: 5.
[7] Weber and Peek 2012.
[8] One fifth of women were in the pretest sample. The "pretest" sample refers to interviews gained early in the process, prior to the securing of any type of funding. The final survey is a modified version of the Neighborhood Change Survey, a NSF funded project to understand the evacuation and recovery experiences in selected New Orleans neighborhoods. Combining this research with the larger project allowed participants to receive a twenty dollar gift card as compensation.
[9] These terms are used interchangeably throughout the text, specifically because some women did not identify with the African American identity, and were not timid about telling me so. However, to preserve confidentiality, I do not specifically link the identity preferences to the exact women.
[10] This rehousing strategy was articulated to me verbally by an employee of the Housing Authority of New Orleans on a date I cannot specifically recall, roughly within the 6 month period prior to the hurricane (August 29, 2005).
[11] Elliott and Pais 2006: 308.
[12] Edin and Lein 1997.
[13] See Erikson 1994; Freudenberg 1997, 1993; Edelstein 2004; Picou, Marshall, and Gill 2004; Adams et al. 2002; Roberts and Toffolon-Weiss 2001; Corresponding poverty research: Wilson 1987, 1996, 2010; Massey and Denton

1993; Murray 1984, 1994; Dreier, Mollenkopf, and Swanstrom 2001; Edin and Lein 1997; Rainwater and Yancey 1967.

[14] Dreier 2006.
[15] Edin and Lein 1997; Ehrenreich 2001.
[16] West and Zimmerman 1987.
[17] Litt 2012; Edin and Lein 1997; Stack 1974; Dynes 2005.
[18] Elliott and Pais 2006; Haney, Elliott, and Fussell 2007.
[19] Pardee 2009.
[20] Miller 2012.

2

Theorizing Disaster Recovery and Everyday Poverty

The Hurricane Katrina disaster exposed the multifaceted nature of catastrophe through its social and material crisis. With thousands stranded for days and floodwaters on the rise, the magnitude of the emergency surpassed the capacity of local, state, and federal governmental agencies to respond. Despite continuous national media coverage, the arrival of food and potable water took five full days, endangering the lives of women, children, the elderly, and men alike. Through the lens of the Hurricane Katrina disaster, the social inequality, chronic poverty, and racial segregation of New Orleans took center stage in the nation's psyche, as tens of thousands of residents were seen waiting, indefinitely, for help.

Steeped in a history of inequity, New Orleans struggled to recover from Hurricane Katrina. A poorly resourced city to begin, slow recovery times and struggles with insurance companies left citizens to decide between rebuilding lives elsewhere or making their old lives work in new, challenging environments. For the poor, the loss of affordable rental housing and the demolition of subsidized public units made even a delayed return questionable as the storm's long-term displacement effects became apparent.[1] For many, the opportunity to return was largely contingent on the flooding patterns—those whose homes did not flood returned more quickly, while those living in flooded areas had to weigh their options carefully. Yet, through the entire experience, residents faced a plethora of challenges, beginning the moment the storm approached.

During this chaotic period, residents were seen as victims, but in many cases, they were also actors in their own lives, making decisions at each stage of the storm and its aftermath. In response, this chapter lays the theoretical foundation for the study's focus on low-income Black women's lived experiences of poverty and disaster. By theorizing how survival strategies function at the intersection of poverty, race, gender, and disaster, this research contributes to sociological theory by fusing diverse scholarly literatures: theories about urban poverty broadly, research about poor women's survival strategies specifically, the gender and disaster literature, and research about disaster recovery. The key intellectual thesis of the book is that existing disaster recovery definitions do not account for the experiences of the poor, much less those of female, Black, public housing residents. In response, the book asks: what does disaster recovery mean for low-income, African American women when the current research describes the failure to recover as sharing the same characteristics as living in poverty every day? How do class, race, and gender function together to affect disaster experiences, outcomes, and opportunities? Through primary data, this book will theorize the concept of recovery in a grounded fashion, making the concept applicable to a highly marginalized portion of the U.S. population.

Poverty and the Crescent City

Chronic poverty is the experiential foundation for most women in this study. It also characterizes the city at the time of the storm, as New Orleans suffered from the same urban social problems associated with high rates of poverty in other cities. These problems include violent crime (especially homicide), out-of-wedlock childbirth, high education dropout rates, family dissolution, drug-use, unemployment, and lack of services.[2] Such impoverished urban environments have historically experienced legally sanctioned racial residential discrimination, including blockbusting,[3] redlining,[4] race restrictive covenants,[5] and racial steering.[6] Such practices create and maintain the hyper-segregated, concentrated urban poverty dominant in American cities today.[7] With a checkerboard pattern of poverty, New Orleans neighborhoods would transition from completely white to completely Black in the span of just two city blocks, reflecting well-maintained social boundaries through de facto segregation.

Yet, New Orleans wasn't simply segregated—it qualifies as hyper-segregated, especially within its poorest communities and public housing projects. According to Massey and Denton, "hyper-segregation" is represented by a high score on four of five dimensions of segregation: unevenness, isolation, clustering, concentration, and centralization.[8] For African Americans, who represent the sample examined in this study, the primary consequence of Massey and Denton's dimensions of segregation is that these factors have "remove[d] blacks from full participation in urban society and limit[ed] their access to its benefits."[9] This layering of multiple dimensions of segregation results in Blacks being more segregated than any other U.S. racial or ethnic group on all hyper-segregation dimensions simultaneously. In this way, residential segregation creates and maintains barriers to full civic participation and functions to reinforce poverty and exacerbate its effects. In New Orleans, it was no different.

While segregation itself does not guarantee the concentration of poverty, among public housing residents, the priority given to extremely low-income households for participation in all programs effectively assures it.[10] For example, research on the HOPE VI initiative, a federal program to raze dilapidated housing and build new, mixed-income communities in its place, identified a nearly sixty percent poverty rate nationally among participants prior to relocation, preceding the demolition phase of the program.[11] This poverty rate was over ninety percent in New Orleans.[12] In addition to economic segregation, racial isolation is also evident in public housing, where nationally "the *typical black household* lives in a project that is 85% black, and 8% white, with 80% of tenants below the poverty level...."[13] Research by Pardee and Gotham found that in New Orleans' public housing, racial segregation was so extreme it became virtually absolute: out of a citywide public housing population of nearly *nineteen thousand* African Americans, there were just *eighteen* white public housing residents.[14] Yet, more important than the severity of hyper-segregation are the consequences that segregated communities create for families attempting to survive while living in chronic poverty.

In particular, poverty is place-bound and represents a context of disadvantage. Among the disadvantages, living under conditions of concentrated poverty creates new levels of material hardship for families; it determines access to jobs, transportation, education, credit, services, and other opportunities.[15] For example, in New Orleans, the educational system was commonly understood as having been grossly inadequate when compared to those of the surrounding parishes, reflecting common patterns among urban school districts across the nation.[16] Even before Hurricane Katrina, seventy percent of the Orleans Parish schools ranked among the worst in the state, and fiduciary responsibility for the entire Orleans Parish educational system was transferred to the State of Louisiana.[17] The consequence of this weak education system is reflected in the high percentage of adults *without* high school diplomas. Prior to Katrina, a quarter of the New Orleans adult population lacked a high school degree.[18] A second, and more revealing indicator is local literacy. A 2001 report by the Literacy Alliance of Greater New Orleans estimated that a third to one-half of all adults[19] in New Orleans were functioning at the lowest level of literacy, meaning that on a day-to-day basis these individuals are "likely to be excluded from all but minimum-wage work, [to] have serious difficulties helping their children with homework and experience barriers to full participation in the life of the larger communities to which they belong."[20]

Illiteracy blocked job opportunities in the city. Without basic reading skills, the educational limitations of nearly half of all adult New Orleanians directly translated into limited job qualifications. Reflected by the over forty percent of individuals not involved in the workforce,[21] the consequent ability to acquire and hold employment remained a challenge for a substantial proportion of adult New Orleans residents prior to the storm. In this sample, 41.2% of women were working before the storm, though most of these working women were working in low-income jobs, as reflected by the fact that only five women earned more than $20,000 per year. Again, failed access to employment opportunities created limited economic resources and tangible challenges to evacuation and recovery for many residents.

These challenges are furthered by the low vehicle ownership rates throughout the city, with 28% of households owning no vehicle. While over 70% of households do have a car, such cars among New Orleans' poorest are likely to be old and in no condition to travel long distances. One structural inhibitor to owning and maintaining a newer car is that those who are receiving state "welfare" are saddled with wealth and asset restrictions—a mere $2,000 in "resources" are allowed for Louisianans receiving benefits under the state's Family Independence Temporary Assistance Program (FITAP).[22] While a resource is defined as "possessions that a household can convert to cash to meet needs," and does *exclude* motor vehicles, educational savings, and burial and funeral insurance,[23] basic savings are counted *against* the asset restrictions, meaning money in a bank account, furniture, and anything else convertible to cash must sum two thousand dollars or less.

With such observable limits on wealth, again, chronic poverty and the FITAP program intended to curb it directly impact the year, make, and quality of vehicle that a welfare recipient can afford to own, drive and maintain, because the nicer the car, the higher the insurance premium.[24] Basically, a woman saving to pay her insurance premium every six months could easily exceed the wealth restrictions and lose her welfare assistance if her car was too new. Unfortunately, those lacking reliable vehicles often cannot use their own transportation for evacuation because older cars may not be road-reliable for the long, slow evacuation, potentially stranding them in the city when hurricanes approach. Meanwhile, as Hurricane Katrina painfully demonstrated, the city itself had not evacuated the neediest—neither those residents without their own dependable transportation, nor those too young, too ill, or too ability-challenged to even seek transportation out of the city in the first place.[25]

The rates of place-bound poverty have been consistent in New Orleans across the last four decades as well (1969 to 2009), with more than 25% of individuals falling below the federal poverty threshold.[26] [27] Even after the storm, 34.3% of African Americans are living in poverty according to the 2010 American Community Survey 1-year Estimate. By contrast, the national poverty rate during this same timeframe never exceeded sixteen percent, and was about twelve percent at its lowest.[28] As such, the poor in New Orleans face a distinct disadvantage, considering their poverty experiences are both more severe and chronic than is typical. In this manner, place and its structural realities suggest dire consequences for low-income residents who attempt to persevere in the face of a large-scale disaster.

Specifically, place predicts access to resources and being place-bound to a poor community predicts lack thereof. In New Orleans, this dearth is illustrated best in the loss of housing for the poor, as the public housing supply was reduced by half through neglect and planned destruction, both in conjunction with, and independent of, the HOPE VI housing program.[29] Meanwhile private market rental housing costs increased over the three-decade period between 1969 and 1999, such that a "fair market" rent (FMR) for a three-bedroom unit in New Orleans cost $896 a month, or approximately 335% of what a full-time, minimum wage worker earned in 2002.[30] When Hurricane Katrina hit in 2005, the New Orleans housing stock was greatly reduced by the extensive city-wide flooding—80% of units were damaged and fair market rent levels increased by 35% in a single year, further straining the economies of the least affluent.[31] Given this increase in housing costs alone, and the fact that poor families already pay almost $5,000 annually due to their limited access to affordable groceries, clothing stores, and other shopping resources,[32] how can the poor possibly evacuate for a hurricane, survive during extended periods of displacement, and then return to a city with an exacerbated reduction in housing and a precipitous increase in housing costs? Beginning in the next chapter, the women who shared their experiences with me will explain precisely how they did just that, to varying levels of success.

A final consideration for understanding the role of poverty in daily and disaster survival following Hurricane Katrina is to explain briefly the manner in which the poverty threshold is calculated.[33] An absolute standard, the threshold is based upon the food costs associated with the "emergency temporary low budget diet," a diet intended to keep a family alive for a period of about two months.[34] As Joel Devine and James Wright explain, the total annual food cost for such a diet is multiplied by three to determine the poverty threshold; then adjusted annually for inflation and family size.

The first problem with this standard is that the temporary emergency diet is not the same as the minimum adult daily requirements; it is a substandard level of nutrition if used over a prolonged period.[35] Another problem lies in the multiplier of three. When the threshold was originally determined, an average family spent one-third of its income on food costs. In contrast, "recent evidence suggests that more than a third of the nation's poorest households spend in excess of 70% of their total income on shelter alone" with food, clothing, transportation, medical, and other costs accounting for the remaining thirty percent.[36] Due to increased housing costs, even among women receiving public housing assistance and Section 8 vouchers at the time of the storm, the threshold severely underestimates the total living costs of low-income families because it is based on a national average and middle-class assumptions rather than the spending patterns of the poor, even though these are the very same families directly affected by the poverty threshold. Thus, to be poor in America is to live in nutritional deprivation, economic minimalism, and very frequently in dangerous, segregated, and isolated housing. Educational opportunities are inadequate, and literacy is likely limited. It is from this starting point that low-income women faced Hurricane Katrina.

Surviving Poverty Every Day

Given the structural confines of poverty, how do families get by on a day-to-day basis with such limited opportunities? Low-income families—whether in New Orleans or nationwide—have been shown to address their poverty and material hardship through a variety of tactics, known as "survival strategies." One of the most common strategies is to establish kin ties throughout the community, leveraging those networks to meet daily needs.[37] By creating a collective network of kin and non-kin, women are able to survive by trading resources with those in their network. Simply stated by Carol Stack:

> Whether one's source of income is a welfare check or wages from labor, people ... borrow and trade with others in order to obtain daily necessities. The most important form of distribution and exchange of the limited resources available to the poor ... is by means of trading, or what people usually call "swapping." As people swap, the limited supply of finished material goods in the community is perpetually redistributed among networks of kinsmen and throughout the community.[38]

In this manner, the community survives *together* by sharing resources, and that mechanism for survival will become an essential part of women's lived experiences during the storm and its aftermath.

In addition to kin networks, Kathryn Edin and Laura Lein's 1997 study found that low-income minority women also used other strategies to "make ends meet." Whether these women were on welfare or working, none were able to pay all their bills, often falling between one-third and two-fifths short of what their budget required. In response, these women engaged a combination of three survival strategies simultaneously to get by each month: utilizing resource networks, working, and obtaining social services. Similar to Stack's kin- and fictive-kin-based community, the networks of Edin and Lein's sample included boyfriends, children's fathers, family, and friends. These individuals frequently offered childcare, clothing, food, and diapers. This pattern of kin support is also confirmed by Elijah Anderson's work in Philadelphia, which identified the role of poor urban men as peripheral but present in the family unit, for example, bringing "Pampers" and "Similac" to the women who mothered their children or whom they were courting.[39] Among the women from New Orleans who spoke with me, many of the networks were gendered, with women providing assistance to each other. While some sons did factor into the conversations, few husbands, boyfriends, or lovers were present as women recounted their Katrina experiences.

A second survival strategy engaged by low-income mothers in Edin and Lein's study, working included involvement in legal occupations, where taxes were paid and income reported, and a combination of unreported legal and illegal work. Unreported work occurs when women supplement their income with additional jobs, but either provide a false social security number to the employer or receive money "under the table." In this way, they can receive another paycheck while not paying taxes on such money or disqualifying themselves and their families from social service programs—the final survival strategy.

Through the combination of the first two survival strategies, kin networks and paid work, women cover many of their expenses.

However, since their networks include others who also lack financial stability,[40] the collective resources are not plentiful enough to cover all the collective needs. Furthermore, some networks can drain a woman's reserve.[41] It is often overlooked that to receive help from one's network in times of need obligates one to give in times of others' need, even when doing so deletes one's own financial reserve. Additionally, Anderson noted how men attached themselves to their children's mothers for the stability of a home-cooked meal and housing, especially when his job opportunities were limited by structural economic factors.[42] Through the connection of parenthood, men can make claims on the resources women provide to their families to survive poverty.

Without consistent financial support from a man, low-income women utilize social service organizations and federal assistance programs to fill the gap.[43] These programs include TANF, food stamps, public housing, health clinics, food pantries, and local charities.[44] Of course, many programs have income caps, which task women with monitoring their incomes, being sure to decline opportunities that might make them ineligible for assistances, and ultimately, in worsened conditions.[45] Yet, even then, day-to-day problems emerge like car troubles, a sick child, or a hurricane named Katrina, any one of which can exceed the reserves of the fragile web of survival. In the first two cases, alternate strategies result: going without food, winter clothing, or medical care; having the utilities shut off periodically; homelessness, or living in shared, or low-quality housing; or utilizing soup kitchens to save money.[46] For a disaster—let alone a catastrophe—little is known on how the poor survive.

Theorizing Disaster Recovery and Everyday Poverty

In reviewing the disaster literature, the absence of studies on domestic poverty populations was stunning. While the poor are often acknowledged as vulnerable to a variety of disastrous events, it appears the boom of mainstream sociological research on poverty in the 1980s and 1990s did not extend as pervasively into this specialty. The result of this absence is a theoretical definition of disaster recovery that cannot account for the experiences of low-income women, an absence this section will explore. To better contextualize this conundrum, the section will review selected vulnerability research, then transition to a discussion of the concept of recovery.

The discussions of vulnerability among the disaster literature do provide initial insight into the effects of poverty on recovery. Vulnerability is defined as "exposure to potential harm from the effects of the disaster agent on the built environment"[47] and reflects the susceptibility of a population to the effects of disasters. Vulnerability may be exacerbated by geographical factors, such as residential location; structural factors, such as government preparedness and response; or social factors, such as race, ethnicity, class, age, or gender.[48] In this way, vulnerability can function at both the macro- and micro-levels simultaneously. Additionally, populations can be vulnerable to a disaster event and a disaster's consequences differentially. For example, upper-class Californians may be susceptible to mudslides, but have insurance to cover their losses, while low-income public housing residents may be less susceptible to an earthquake due to building codes, but more at risk during the recovery stages due to their pre-existing social locations.[49]

The first dimension of vulnerability is physical, with specific geographical spaces yielding higher levels of susceptibility to particular types of disasters than other spaces. In the Peruvian Cordillera Blanca range, the city of Huaraz sits along a river that flows from a glacial lake further above in the range. As global warming causes more of the glacier to melt, outburst floods are occurring more frequently, with the city becoming increasingly vulnerable based on its geography.[50] Yet, even when people are aware they live in a flood plain or another dangerous area, sometimes they have no choice but to live there due to their social and economic positions in the global-capitalist system.[51] For example, many residents of New Orleans knew they lived in flood-prone areas of the city, but a history of racial residential segregation prevents them from accessing housing on the city's natural levees, like the one along the Mississippi River.

The second dimension of vulnerability is linked to structural factors, such as governmental policy, risk communication, and economic development. If a government fails to warn the community of an impending disaster, or communicates the warning in such a way the threat is not perceived as serious, the affected population will be made increasingly vulnerable because of this governmental failure.[52] In the Peruvian example previously mentioned, the government failed to heed and articulate warnings from scientists about emergent flooding, causing a lack of legitimacy for the government and thousands of preventable deaths.[53] It can be argued that this same pattern of governmental ambivalence was seen in New Orleans during Katrina's approach, as delayed decision making to initiate the mandatory evacuation order implied the threat to the city was not significant.

Yet, even when emergency warning systems are in place, they may actually exacerbate risk and subsequent vulnerability, not reduce it. As

Handmer argues, emergency warnings can actually enable greater risks to be taken because:

> Development may occur in flood prone areas or in areas subject to other periodic and predictable hazards because warnings will (or rather should) trigger appropriate safety and damage reducing behavior.[54]

In this way, the warning system that is supposed to reduce risk actually encourages additional development in the affected area, and as a result, the increased population and expansion of the built environment generates greater hazard vulnerability.[55]

Among underdeveloped nations, historical patterns of development frame the context in which disasters occur, such that underdeveloped nations often suffer more extreme disaster effects than industrialized nations do.[56] In particular, Oliver-Smith's work indicates that in many underdeveloped nations, indigenous populations who would traditionally migrate to reduce vulnerability face new challenges as their countries industrialize, and the bounded nature of modern development roots them to singular spatial locations. This spatial boundedness makes migratory populations vulnerable to events like flooding or drought when previously they were not.[57] Again, similar to industrialized nations, we see development as a vulnerability factor, not a mitigating force. In short, it is the "progress" of modernization that functions to increase vulnerability, rather than reduce it.

The final dimension of vulnerability encompasses characteristics such as race, class, gender, and age, which affect the ability to prepare for, evacuate, and recover from disasters at both the individual level and as systems of inequality.[58] For example, Miller and Nigg find that income and race affect recovery separately, such that income effects are linked more closely to event vulnerability and physical damages to housing, while race effects are linked with consequence vulnerability and affect the recovery process.[59] Yet, some scholars critique the generalization that all minorities, or all elderly, or all women are vulnerable to a specific disaster *a priori*. In Fordham's work, she calls for a nuanced, gendered vulnerability analysis such that interpretations are situated within specific historical and societal contexts, meaning not all women are always vulnerable at all times.[60] In short, Fordham seeks an intersectional analysis that includes circumstance as one of its factors. Likewise, Stephen calls for the same, identifying differing levels of vulnerability among rural people of Ethiopia, where socio-economic group, social-political resources, and even the altitude at which they live all affect the ability to survive, manage, and mitigate drought conditions differentially.[61]

Addressed at the micro- and macro-levels, the concept of vulnerability is a useful tool in beginning the synthesis between the poverty, survival, and disaster literatures. Still, it is important to note that the above discussions about vulnerability do not challenge the fundamental conceptualization of disaster recovery as a process that all people, regardless of status, experience linearly. Rather, it suggests that recovery is harder for low-income populations because they are considered more vulnerable; however, it does not explore the possibility that recovery and rehabilitation among the poor may be a completely unique—or even unattainable—status.

Within the disaster literature, "recovery" means returning to the pre-disaster condition. In Couch's discussion of Chapman's natural disaster stage model, recovery is theorized as a stage during which a community seeks "resolution" toward normality—recovery occurs when communities reconstitute the old social structures.[62] At the community level, short-term responses to natural disasters are characterized by an increase in social cohesion that evolves into a "therapeutic community" as residents come together, initiate search and rescue activities, pool resources, and provide mutual support to one another.[63] Recovery is achieved by the rebuilding of the physical environment, as government institutions, schools, services, and businesses reopen and resume. For individuals, the negative effects of natural disasters are expected to be short-term, as social, cultural, psychological, and economic consequences are typically absorbed by the larger (intact) social structure.[64] The goal is to return to business as usual.

Unfortunately, these studies do little to explain how the poor are affected during the recovery stage, leaving the questions of this study unanswered. By looking at Hurricane Katrina, there are some interesting but unfortunate findings regarding recovery from displacement. First, the common conception of recovery in the disaster literature suggests returning to "life as usual," yet for those displaced by the storm, the fundamental landscape of the city was radically altered. Like survivors in war zones,[65] the city lacked livelihood opportunities, and the housing had deteriorated or was unlivable. There were inadequate public health resources and sanitation, nor any educational or recreational facilities. Affecting low-income Black women and their families in particular, hundreds of public housing units became slated for demolition, all in those early months following the storm.[66]

In this way, returning home was not actually returning to a recovery. It was returning instead to a land devastated by the flooding. Where the waters had risen, flood lines and dirt markings were left on buildings with some so high they were above the rooftops. Cars were overturned. Walls were washed away. Roofs were shredded by the wind. Schools, churches, courts, and other public institutions remained closed, keeping community members isolated from their traditional networks and daily routines. While Hurricane Katrina was a natural disaster for its wind and a technological disaster for its levee failures and subsequent flooding, the net effect of the damage on the city was catastrophic, and reminiscent of the aftermath of a devastating war.

In this context, the definition of recovery as restitution is extremely problematic when considering the long-term, irreversible effects of Hurricane Katrina, and even technological disasters more generally. Events such as the structural levee failure and toxic contamination of soil permanently alter the biophysical environment, often rendering recovery efforts powerless.[67] The negative effects of such massive technological disasters are characterized chronically, and include physical illness, pessimism about health, a sense of being out of control, fear of one's community or residence as unsafe, social and governmental distrust, and stigma.[68] When these responses fail to terminate or be remedied (by toxin cleanup or relocation), distrust and anger ensue as the community transforms to become "corrosive."[69] In short, when a community "fails" to recover, the characteristics of that community come to mirror the everyday experience of the poor in America.[70]

To summarize, low-income and deeply segregated communities are also viewed by their residents as unsafe and violent, with those residents sharing little trust in government and social services to help. With excessive rates of persistent health problems, lack of resources like healthcare facilities, quality schools, and basic public safety, the corrosive community of failed disaster recovery is the lived experience of poverty for low-income women every day, independent of the disaster. Yet, this connection is often overlooked due to the cross-sectional, large-N design of many recovery studies; studies in which income is a variable rather than a primary analytic focus.[71] This means little direct data exists to explain *how* recovery for a poor woman takes place in her life,[72] rendering our disaster recovery theories meaningless to explain her situation.

Gender, Disaster, and Poverty

Not only does theorization surrounding disaster recovery fail to examine the full range of social class experiences sufficiently, it is also lacking in its examination of gender.[73] In Enarson's recent work *Women*

Confronting Natural Disaster,[74] she argues that gender is still remarkably absent in disaster studies. Her critique of the field is merited, for "[t]his lack of intellectual curiosity is striking after nearly half a century of gender scholarship and must be challenged; it renders virtually half of human experience invisible."[75] Women's absence from disaster studies reflects the absence of knowledge regarding how they "do gender" within the confines of disasters.[76] How women perform their social roles as mothers, wives, daughters, caregivers, and emotional workers within the material constraints and among the physical destruction merits deeper attention.[77] As the glue of family recovery and community reconstruction,[78] the absence of women's lives in disaster research reflects ongoing gender inequality and their continued secondary status in society.

For minority women, their absence in the disaster literature is even more notable, reflecting continued marginalization within the discipline and society.[79] Even the Hurricane Katrina literature lacks a specific focus on Black women's experiences,[80] despite their citizenship and residency within New Orleans. Some notable exceptions to this blindness include Weber and Peek's *Displaced* volume (2012), which includes detailed chapters on the Black family as a social network,[81] elderly Black women's recovery experiences in a FEMA trailer park,[82] Black families' experiences of engaging in poverty programs,[83] and of securing housing,[84] to name a few. These detailed examinations expand the research knowledge base previously influenced by the masculinized environment of emergency response, whose male-dominated normative subculture minimizes recognition of women's recovery work and emphasizes men's labor.[85] Expanding our understanding beyond a simple gender analysis to include Black women's voices begins to transition the field to one in which a myriad of social experiences are legitimized. Just as hooks has critiqued mainstream feminism for failing to examine race and class as it modifies the gendered experience for minority and low-income women,[86] the disaster literature too could benefit from such an expansion. This book is a humble attempt to move in that direction.

Through the simultaneous lenses of multiple statuses and roles, intersectionality theory provides a pathway to conduct analyses that acknowledge the effects of each status as they interact within specific environs.[87] It requires us to acknowledge how class, race, gender, sexuality, housing, geography, and disaster can affect one's treatment and experiences. Most importantly, it views these forms of oppressions—race, class, gender, etc.—as "not separate and additive, but interactive and multiplicative in their effects."[88] In this way, a low-income African American woman will experience Katrina differently than I did, as a white, highly educated, low-income graduate student. She may also differ from another low-income Black woman, depending on her age, familial ties, work obligations, and other statuses and roles, which is where intersectionality faces a challenge navigating between individual level analyses and group level ones. Best articulated by Patricia Hill Collins:

> Intersectionality works better as a substantive theory ... when applied to individual-level behavior than when documenting group experiences. The construct of intersectionality works well with issues of individual agency and human subjectivity and thus has surface validity in explaining everyday life. Individuals can more readily see intersections of race, gender, class, and sexuality in how they construct their identities as individuals than in how social institutions rely on these same ideas reproducing group identities.[89]

At the institutional level, group identities may be conceptualized as gender-only or race-only within some contexts and transition into intersectional ones at others. There is also the possibility to have opposite meaning granted to the same constellation of statuses simultaneously. For example, being Black may be a deficit for a woman who is stranded at the Superdome, but being a woman is an asset, as women were to board evacuation buses earlier. Yet, being a Black woman at the bottom of a racial-gender hierarchy in New Orleans may make one more susceptible to rape, at the exact same moment in time.

In this way, intersectionality enables us to consider the fluidity of meaning-making and multiple realities even when the group shares a singular set of characteristics. An ideal study would compare experiences across a diverse sample, where statuses vary, to truly parse out the effects of multiple statuses working in tandem. Unfortunately, such an analysis is beyond the purview of this study and sample, due to the limited financial resources available at the time of data collection. This admitted limitation, however, is also an asset. In the absence of the narratives of those with mainstream identities, low-income, Black female Katrina survivors are allowed to move from margin to center in this work. Through expanding the disaster literature to incorporate these important voices, we can move one step further to address the concerns of hooks and Enarson, bringing women in general, and Black women in particular, into the disaster conversation.

Conclusion

In the remaining chapters of this book, I present and discuss the lived experiences of low-income Black women as they navigate the different pathways through Hurricane Katrina, from evacuation, to being stranded, to seeking shelter, to attempting to recover. Through examining the disaster experiences of women facing frequent marginalization—and who are largely absent in the broader recovery conversation—the relationships between gender, race, class, geography, and their intersectional and cumulative patterns within hierarchies of social inequality will be illuminated.

Specifically, class-based analyses will focus on the effectiveness of everyday poverty survival strategies in new disaster contexts, while race-based ones examine the role of discrimination and prejudice during Katrina and beyond. Gender-based analyses emphasize the emotional work and mothering activities women assumed, while intersectionality provides a larger frame into which all of these observations and analyses can nest.

Finally, the book concludes by returning to the important issue of redefining disaster recovery to accommodate the complex, intersectional experiences of low-income Black women, in an attempt to move them from the margin to the mainstream. Since living in endemic urban poverty shares the same characteristics that mainstream disaster research classifies as failed recovery, the recovery concept is deficient in its explanatory capacity. In response, this book attempts to reimagine that concept, to answer the following imperative question: What does disaster recovery mean for an impoverished woman when her daily life can already be defined as disastrous?

---

[1] Arena 2012.

[2] Wilson 1987; Massey and Denton 1993; Murray 1984; Dreier, Mollenkopf, and Swanstrom 2001; Rainwater and Yancey 1967.

[3] Blockbusting is a process in which a real estate agent attempts to move a non-white, usually Black family, into an all white neighborhood for the purpose of exploiting white fears of impending racial turnover and property devaluation to buy up other property on the block at depressed prices, see Gotham 2002: 25; Massey and Denton 1993.

[4] Redlining is a discriminatory practice in which neighborhoods are rated based on their risk assessments, with red being the most risky. These assessments systematically undervalued older central city neighborhoods, as well as those that were racially or ethnically mixed, see Massey and Denton 1997: 51.

[5] A race restrictive covenant is a legally enforceable contract between property owners and neighborhood associations prohibiting the sale, occupancy, or lease of property and land to certain racial groups, especially Blacks, see Gotham 2002: 37.

[6] Racial steering is a behavior that occurs when a customer's access to housing is constrained if s/he does not state any preference for a certain type of neighborhood, but is nevertheless shown housing in neighborhoods with a particular racial or ethnic composition, i.e. someone is directed to alternate housing based on their race, see Yinger 1995: 51-52.

[7] Massey and Denton 1993; Gotham 2002; Yinger 1995; Patillo-McCoy 2000.

[8] According to Massey and Denton (1993: 74), unevenness is the representation of Blacks across residential areas, while isolation refers to the physical separation of housing by race. Clustering refers to whether Black neighborhoods are scattered or contiguous, while concentration reflects the size and spread of neighborhoods—whether they are small or expansive. The final dimension, centralization, refers to whether the neighborhood is located within the urban core, or along the periphery.

[9] Massey and Denton 1993: 74.

[10] Abt Associates 1996; Gotham and Wright 1999.

[11] Kingsley, Johnson, and Pettit 2003: 433.

[12] Kingsley, Johnson, and Pettit 2003: 432.

[13] Goering, Kamely, and Richardson 1997: 734.

[14] Pardee and Gotham 2005: 9.

[15] Wilson 1987, 1996, 2010; Massey and Denton 1993; Oliver and Shapiro 1995; Edin and Lein 1997; Hays 2003; Seccombe 2007; Yinger 1995; Dreier, Mollenkopf, and Swanstrom 2001; Zhou and Bankston 1998.

[16] Kozol 2005, 1991.

[17] Huggins and Devine 2005.

[18] Census 2000.

[19] Adults are defined as individuals aged 16 years and older.

[20] Literacy Alliance of Greater New Orleans 2002: 2. Being at the lowest level of literacy also means that an individual cannot identify a street intersection on a map, or read an evacuation plan. It should be noted that evacuation maps were largely absent at the time of Katrina.

[21] Census 2000.

[22] State of Louisiana 2006. The Family Independence Temporary Assistance Program (FITAP) is the state-level implemented welfare plan, which meets the guidelines outlined by the federal Temporary Assistance to Needy Families program (TANF), while layering on state specific requirements. TANF replaced the Aid to Families with Dependent Children (AFDC) program in 1996, which was commonly referred to as "welfare."

[23] State of Louisiana 2006: II; Williams n.d..

[24] During a typical New Orleans evacuation, the traffic leaving the city is bumper to bumper, and can travel at speeds as low as 5 mph, and rarely exceeds 35 mph, until the vehicle is at least 100 miles outside the city. This low speed and "stop and go" traffic makes many older cars prone to overheating.

[25] Technically, there was an evacuation plan on record which included using school buses, but it was not implemented in advance of the storm and the

buses were flooded by the levee breaks, so it could not be implemented afterward either.

[26] The poverty threshold is established at the federal level and is applied uniformly across all states and counties, independent of cost of living and other regional expense variations, such as housing costs.

[27] U.S. Census 1970, 1980, 1990, 2000; ACS 2010.

[28] Between 1969 and 2012, the federal poverty rate was highest at about sixteen percent in 1982 and 1992, both times following a recession. The rate was lowest in 1973 and 2000. U.S. Census Bureau, Current Population Survey, 1960-2003. ACS 2012.

[29] Pardee and Gotham 2005.

[30] Pardee and Gotham 2005.

[31] Greater New Orleans Community Data Center 2006.

[32] The historical linkage between residential segregation and material hardship maintains the effects of place-bound poverty into the present as well, because to live in high-poverty urban communities is more expensive than to live in low-poverty suburbs, and in New Orleans this was no different. Based on a meta-analysis of several works, Dreier, Mollenkopf, and Swanstrom calculate the annual cost burden of living in an impoverished community to be $4,593 for a poor family earning $20,000 per year (2001). This "hardship burden" represents nearly one-quarter of an already limited income. In this manner, place-bound poverty creates a life characterized by economic challenges that disable individuals from leaving their economically disadvantaged, segregated housing, because the costs of place prevent the accumulation of wealth necessary to leave. In New Orleans, such conditions placed exceptional disadvantages on poor populations who faced the Hurricane Katrina disaster, given they had the least resources to evacuate, to be displaced, and to recover.

[33] This is important because when I teach undergraduate students in my Urban Poverty course, it is fascinating to realize how wealthy they believe poor people to be. Despite drastic welfare reforms in the late 1990's, most students fail to understand that those changes are now in place, especially the lifetime limits and the eligibility threshold of 50% of the poverty line (see Sharon Hays' work (2003) for a detailed examination of welfare reform). In this sample, no woman explicitly mentioned receiving welfare, though many did receive Social Security, Social Security-Disability, Medicare, Medicaid and food stamps.

[34] Devine and Wright 1993: 12-3.

[35] Devine and Wright 1993: 13.

[36] Devine and Wright 1993: 15.

[37] Stack 1974; Edin and Lein 1997; Domínguez and Watkins 2003; Henly, Danziger, and Offer 2005; Oliker 1995; Anderson 1989, 1990, 1999.

[38] Stack 1974: 33.

[39] Anderson 1989, 1999.

[40] Anderson 1989, 1999.

[41] Anderson 1989, 1990, 1999; Domínguez and Watkins 2003.

[42] Anderson 1989: 75.

[43] Anderson 1989, 1990, 1999; Hays 2003; Seccombe 2007.

[44] Hays 2003; Edin and Lein 1997; Domínguez and Watkins 2003.

[45] Oliker 1995.

[46] Edin and Lein 1997: 119; Erikson 1994.

[47] Miller and Nigg 1993: 2.

[48] Wisner 2004; Carey 2005; Oliver-Smith 2004; Bankoff, Frerks, and Hilhorst 2004; Cardona 2004; Bolin and Stanford 1998.
[49] Miller and Nigg 1993.
[50] Carey 2005.
[51] Oliver-Smith 1996, 2004; Lavell 2004.
[52] Handmer 2000.
[53] Carey 2005: 123.
[54] Handmer 2000: 2.
[55] Handmer 2000; Oliver-Smith 1996.
[56] Hilhorst and Bankoff 2004; Oliver-Smith 1996; Bankoff 2004; Benson 2004.
[57] Oliver-Smith 1996: 311.
[58] Wisner 2004; Cutter 2005; Miller and Nigg 1993; Fordham 2004; Enarson 1999, Collins 1998; Weber 2012; hooks 1984; Bolin and Stanford 1998.
[59] Miller and Nigg 1993.
[60] Fordham 2004.
[61] Stephen 2004: 100.
[62] Couch 1996: 68.
[63] Tierney, Bevc, and Kuligowski 2006: 58; Rodríguez, Trainor, and Quarantelli 2006.
[64] Drabek and Boggs 1968; Drabek et al. 1975; Picou, Marshall, and Gill 2004; Marshall, Picou, and Gill 2003; Kreps 1984.
[65] Frederico et al. 2007: 173.
[66] Frederico et al. 2007: 173.
[67] Adams and Boscarino 2005; Adams et al. 2002; Picou, Marshall, and Gill 2004; Freudenberg 1997; Erikson 1976, 1994.
[68] Edelstein 2004; Erikson 1994; Picou, Marshall, and Gill 2004; Adams et al. 2002; Couch 1996; Roberts and Toffolon-Weiss 2001.
[69] Freudenberg 1993, 1997; Picou, Marshall, and Gill 2004
[70] See Erikson 1994; Freudenberg 1997, 1993; Edelstein 2004; Picou, Marshall, and Gill 2004; Adams et al. 2002; Roberts and Toffolon-Weiss 2001; Corresponding poverty research: Wilson 1987, 1996, 2010; Massey and Denton 1993; Murray 1984, 1994; Dreier, Mollenkopf, and Swanstrom 2001; Edin and Lein 1997; Rainwater and Yancey 1967.
[71] Drabek and Boggs 1968; Drabek, Key, Erikson, and Crowe 1975; Picou, Marshall, and Gill 2004; Marshall, Picou, and Gill 2003.
[72] Gladwin and Peacock 1997; Klinenberg 2002.
[73] Enarson and Morrow 1998; Fothergill 1998; Enarson 2012.
[74] Enarson 2012.
[75] Enarson 2012: 22.
[76] West and Zimmerman 1987; Enarson 2012; Fordham and Ketteridge 1998; Fothergill 1998, 1999.
[77] Fothergill 1999.
[78] Fothergill 1999.
[79] hooks 1984.
[80] A review of the Katrina specific references from the bibliography of this book alone reveal the pattern, which is unfortunate as these references speak more directly to Black women's experiences than most others in the broader Katrina literature.

[81] Litt 2012; Fussell 2012.
[82] Mason 2012.
[83] Lein, Angel, Beausoleil, and Bell 2012.
[84] Pardee 2012.
[85] Fothergill 1999.
[86] hooks 1984.
[87] Weber 2010; Collins 1998.
[88] Chafetz 1997.
[89] Collins 1998: 206.

PART 1

PREPARATION

Evacuation is a peculiar aspect in the consideration of disasters. On the one hand, it is an essential tool in pre-emptive mitigation, saving lives by removing them from the threat zone before a disaster occurs. On the other hand, it is difficult to enforce, expensive for families to engage, and from a scholarly perspective, ambiguous in its definition. In fact, even Chapman's classic disaster stage model fails to incorporate this seemingly integral part of the disaster experience. For Chapman, natural disasters have eight stages: warning, threat, impact, rescue, inventory, remedy, recovery, and rehabilitation.[1] Evacuation is not included. This is due, in part, to the immediate, unexpected nature of many disasters from which evacuation is not possible, such as tornadoes and flash floods. By contrast, hurricanes are merciful in their advanced warning—often as much as a full week—yet merciless in that they often require displacing several hundred thousand people in the anticipated strike zone. Coordinating such a large population movement is a challenging venture, one based on both public policy and individual agency.

In the case of Hurricane Katrina, the storm forecasts consistently projected a Florida panhandle landfall as of midnight Friday, August 26, 2005. As a resident of the city at the time, I distinctly remember watching the news with shock on Saturday morning, at about 8 a.m., as the storm's track had shifted with a straight and narrowed path-projection cone directed at New Orleans. All day long, the local news stations emphasized the intensity of the storm, then a Category 5. Jefferson Parish, adjacent and largely south of the city, called for a mandatory evacuation. Living just a mile from the parish line at the time, I knew it was time to leave. I began to call my friends in Texas to arrange for a place to stay—they welcomed me with open arms. From there, I called my local friends and family to see where they were planning to go. Like my respondents, I engaged in the negotiated process of evacuation, even convincing one friend to leave for Baton Rouge despite his initial reluctance.

This process of checking in, talking it through, pressuring, and being pressured—the negotiation of it all—is absent in the disaster literature. So, what do we know about hurricane evacuations to date? First, we know evacuation rates vary by race and class.[2] For example, in their research on Hurricane Andrew, Gladwin and Peacock found that fifty-four percent of all households located in an evacuation zone evacuated entirely, while in the highest-risk coastal evacuation zones, this percentage increased to seventy-one percent.[3] Their analysis also revealed that Black families living in evacuation zones were two-thirds less likely to evacuate than Anglos in those same areas. In the case of Hurricane Katrina, work by Elliott and Pais found significant racial trends for Hurricane Katrina, with suburban Blacks being one and a half times more likely to leave *following* the storm than prior when compared to whites, and urban low-income Blacks to be the *least* likely of all groups to evacuate prior to the storm.[4]

Yet, among this sample of low-income Black women, nearly half of the women chose to leave *before* the storm, despite demographic characteristics suggesting they would leave at lower rates, if at all. By negotiating the decision between kin—both family and friends (social kin), women's narratives changed in a way that made them acknowledge the risk. This negotiation process also reflects the kin-based survival strategies used in everyday poverty where support from family and peers helps to keep a family afloat.[5] For others, who decided to stay, common explanations for non-compliance with evacuation orders include lack of wealth, lack of transportation, refusal to leave pets, possessions, and homes behind, medical and mobility problems, care-giving responsibilities, and disbelief of risk.[6] In the case of Hurricane Andrew, the data were inconclusive, but common reasons included lack of transportation, lack of affordable refuge, or some other factor.[7] Yet, these are all structural factors. How does agency fit into the analysis? According to Elliott and Pais, almost half of respondents reported that they did not believe the storm would be so bad, while only a fifth reported not having transportation to leave,[8] with neither finding predicted by race or class for city residents. These findings suggest that agency, in addition to structure, needs greater consideration in the literature when determining how and why people evacuate.

Gender counts, too. Since many evacuation orders specify vulnerable groups such as children and pregnant women to leave, pre-existing gender expectations surrounding care work dictate higher rates of evacuation for adult women than men.[9] During Hurricane Katrina, the results were mixed: work by Haney, Elliott, and Fussell[10] found gender to be the strongest and most consistent predictor of evacuation, while Zotti et al. found low-income pregnant women evacuating before, as well as after, the storm had passed.[11] While men are often considered the decision makers for emergency evacuation,[12] Peek and Fothergill found that during Hurricane Katrina, mothers were the most common individuals choosing the location and when to leave.[13] In relation to this study, these findings suggest that gender matters, but women are not always vulnerable—instead, they have agency, even within a crisis. For low-income African American women, this is even more the case, as their pre-storm lives require a level of self-advocacy and familial responsibility often established in the absence of a husband.[14]

A final consideration in understanding how low-income women evacuate may be that extended warning periods redefine the decision making process into a social interaction between multiple individuals based on a consensus-interpretation of the danger and risk, independent of the objective threat.[15] By this logic, the same communities that provide social support and kin ties to low-income women for daily poverty survival might also be acting to either promote or inhibit evacuation, since the decision to leave, like survival resources more generally, becomes communal. This collective interpretation is supported by Drabek and Boggs' work, which found encouragement and insistence by family members to be a statistically significant predictor of evacuation prior to the Denver flash flood.[16] In their study, almost a third of surveyed families received warnings from relatives, while three-quarters evacuated in units including extended kin. Ultimately, well over a million people left the Gulf Coast region prior to Hurricane Katrina.[17]

Building on this finding, Dynes argues that pre-existing social capital, such as Stack's kin networks, creates a type of consensus formation process regarding the severity and threat of a storm, and is founded in the obligations individuals hold to friends, family members, and coworkers.[18] This consensus encourages evacuation because "behavior during the evacuation phase is prefigured by normal daily routines and action choices are guided by obligations that existed prior to the disaster situation."[19] In this way, I hypothesize that if the family unit or kin network decides to leave, an individual in that network will likely go as well. In this sense, the idea of "all our kin" may extend well beyond daily poverty survival and into the realms of disaster evacuation.

In response, Chapter 3 reveals the process of decision making among women as they made sense of the potential risk the storm might bring. For some, the storm was "not that bad" and could be weathered safely at home. For others, Hurricane Katrina posed an imminent threat, which required evacuation. Yet, how did some women conclude the storm to be safe enough to stay, while others did not? This chapter examines the role of family members and friends, to show that "safety" and "risk" are negotiated conceptualizations; in short, danger is not inherent to the hurricane, but instead conditional upon the perceptions of the evacuee, their friends, and family.

Chapter 4 explores how during the evacuation many families formed a "caravan of kin"—a long evacuation train of cars connected by social networks—to assure that no one was left behind. This chapter demonstrates how women who lacked the money to evacuate would join the caravan of kin, allowing them to ride with family members, stay in hotels, as well as access food and other resources. In return, they gave what they could, whether it was food, child care, or a working car. Yet, in some cases, the caravan failed, as kin outsiders were left behind. Together, these chapters examine the preparatory stages of a disaster—how warning and threat are interpreted and managed.

---

[1] Couch 1996: 69.
[2] See West and Orr 2007 for an overview.
[3] 1997: 64. Gladwin and Peacock report this as a low-rate of compliance. The standard compliance rate expected by emergency managers is 80% compliance according to Waugh (2006: 16).
[4] Elliott and Pais 2006: 308.
[5] Edin and Lein 1997.
[6] Waugh 2006; Cutter and Emrich 2006; Fussell 2005; West and Orr 2007.
[7] Gladwin and Peacock 1997: 71.
[8] Elliott and Pais 2006: 309.
[9] Enarson 2012: 111.
[10] Haney, Elliott, and Fussell 2007: 83.
[11] Zotti et al. 2011.
[12] Enarson 2012: 112.
[13] Peek and Fothergill 2008.
[14] hooks 1984.
[15] Gladwin and Peacock 1997: 56.
[16] Drabek and Boggs 1968.
[17] Nigg, Barnshaw, and Torres 2006: 113; Weber and Peek 2012: 1.
[18] Stack 1974; Dynes 2005.
[19] Dynes 2005: 6-7.

3
Decision Time

In the eight years since Hurricane Katrina, many have asked nearly the same question: Why didn't people evacuate the city before the storm? While the decision to leave in the face of a major hurricane may seem obvious to outsiders, the reality is that hurricanes are part of the history and culture of New Orleans to such an extent that residents only evacuate selectively. The logic for this decision develops from the fact that nearly every year a tropical storm or hurricane will pass through the city, causing minimal damage and lots of hype on the news. These smaller storms are part of the culture, as seen by the alcoholic drink named "The Hurricane" or the quintessential hurricane party. Over time, one develops a sense for what level of risk one can safely sustain. For myself, I would shelter in place for a category 2, but would evacuate for a category 3 or higher, for fear the hurricane would intensify as it approached land and shallower, warmer waters. For others, that line was less clear, especially given the tendency of storms to weaken rapidly once they moved on shore.

During 10 years living in New Orleans, I evacuated for three storms—George, Ivan, and Katrina—and sheltered in place for countless others whose names I have forgotten. For a New Orleanian, tropical storms mean very windy, rainy days, and often businesses and schools are not even closed. It's essentially the equivalent to a "snow day" for schoolchildren in colder climates. With stronger storms, one of the major determinants of evacuation is one's sense of risk. In the last few decades before Hurricane Katrina, several "big ones" had missed the city, leaving barely a scratch—just a tree branch here or there, but no flooding. In fact, had Hurricane Katrina lacked its powerful storm surge, it likely would also have been a distant memory by now. Only in the face of the massive flooding and poor emergency response was Katrina dangerous. In the absence of that history with other storms, residents were ambivalent about—and even adverse toward—evacuation.

This chapter demonstrates how low-income women came to define the threat of Hurricane Katrina through a process of narrative creation, one negotiated through interactions with kin networks. First, women created narratives of the storm as safe or dangerous for themselves based on their resources and situations—in other words, the social structures within their lives. Other narratives also affected how they viewed the storm, such as financial narratives. Next, these narratives were challenged or confirmed with family members, who negotiated the women's interpretations with different sets of evidence, offers of shelter and transportation, or basic appeals to logic and emotion, to find that when the storm's severity and threat were defined collectively within kin networks, evacuation became a viable and necessary option. Ultimately, these interactions affected women's evacuation decisions, transforming the decision making process from an individual act into a communal one, as negotiated by the members of the kin network.

Within the negotiation itself, women used narratives of "safety" to minimize their perceived risk and justify the decision to stay through the storm. By contrast, narratives of "threat" also functioned to acknowledge risk, presupposing evacuation in most cases. This process of negotiated narratives suggests that low-income women were not, in fact, mere victims of their socio-economic status—poverty alone was not keeping them from evacuating.[1] Low-income women were empowered actors who chose through a collective process whether to evacuate or remain to ride out the storm. Certainly, chronic poverty makes the "how" more complicated, yet, almost every woman in this study reported that she could have pooled resources with kin to access transportation and enable evacuation. Sadly, many simply elected not to do so, under the logic that Katrina simply wouldn't be that bad.[2]

Narrating the Storm as "Safe"

On Saturday, August 27, 2005, Hurricane Katrina was a dangerous category five storm on a direct path to New Orleans. Residents of New Orleans were encouraged to partake in a voluntary evacuation, and in parishes[3] surrounding the city, many were required to do so. On Sunday, the day prior to landfall, the city's Mayor called for a mandatory evacuation, though at that point in time, the storm had already weakened. Despite Mayor Nagin's increasingly dire warnings throughout Saturday and Sunday, many women who spoke with me did not initially perceive that they were in danger.

Especially among older respondents, Katrina was "just another Betsy"—a big storm that would cause some flooding, but nothing severe enough to merit leaving home. As Twila, Zarah, and Eurdice's comments demonstrate, narratives about safety framed their decisions to remain in the city for the storm:

> Twila: I stayed because I done been through a hurricane, and it was a bad hurricane. Because I'd been through them before, so I didn't think nothing of it.

> Zarah: I thought it wasn't gonna be that bad. It was just wind and rain at first, it wasn't bad. Nothing had blown off; everything was okay, until the flood came.

> Eurdice: I said "oh, it wasn't going to be nothing but a little rain and wind." The following day, that water was coming up, and I got really, really scared. I still can't believe it. The water kept rising higher.

Using a narrative of the storm as "safe" minimized the storm's risk and justified the decision to remain in New Orleans. While the local news stations would run specials on the risk of hurricane-related flooding at the beginning of each hurricane season, women like Twila viewed Katrina as comparable to any another storm as it approached the Gulf Coast. This logic is clarified by Zarah, who cavalierly points out that until the storm surge burst the levees, Katrina *was* like any other big storm—lots of wind, but nothing to fuss over. In the absence of experiences of genuine devastation with prior hurricanes, or alternative interpretations of the storm as threatening, these women put themselves at great risk by believing their own narratives of safety about the storm.

Consistently throughout the sample, women narrated the storm as "safe." When I asked women how worried they had been before the storm, not even one-third of the sample stated they were either "worried" or "very worried." And these women were not unique in their attitudes. In a random sample of 1,510 Red Cross assistance recipients, Haney, Elliott, and Fussell found that of those New Orleanians who did not evacuate before Katrina struck:

> ... nearly half stated that they did not evacuate because they did not believe the storm would be as bad as it turned out to be. In fact, nonevacuees were five times more likely to cite this reason than a lack of money or transportation, and less than 5 percent cited a lack of proper warning for failure to evacuate.[4]

This high level of disregard for the storm's risks translated into disastrous outcomes. For even when the option to evacuate *was* available, many women who spoke with me chose to stay in New Orleans, albeit in the safest place they could. In short, narratives of safety function to prevent evacuation and directly endanger people's lives.

Considering Alternate Narratives

As women created narratives to guide their assessments of danger, their evacuation decisions were impacted by material considerations such as expense and job security. Of the sample, only Ebony stated money specifically as a reason for staying, while most stated that they just didn't think the storm would be so bad, including sixteen women who left in advance: Lillian, Savannah, Althea, Alika, Zarah, Callista, Sheila, Vanessa, Thelma, Janelle, Keisha, Twila, Asia, Mercedes, Amaya, and Eurdice. Nine working women elected to stay in New Orleans through the storm. Of those, six reported work as the reason they remained: Alika, Vanessa, Lydia, Thea, Amaya, and Giselle. Faith would have stayed, had she not been fired immediately before the storm. No women cited health as a reason to stay, though one woman left due to health concerns: Violet.

In the context of chronic poverty, some low-income women assessed risk using a financial narrative: could they afford to go? For Ebony, her chronic poverty stifled her capacity to leave New Orleans with her adult son because the cost of evacuation was too expensive for her to afford:

> Jessica: Did you stay in New Orleans because you couldn't afford to go?
>
> Ebony: Yes. I had no other choice. I couldn't afford to go. If I had money, I would have been gone. I didn't have no transportation. My son didn't have enough money to not go to work. He had a car, but no gas. It's like you ain't got nothing.

Through the financial narrative, money determined access to transportation, gas, food, and shelter by transforming the decision to remain into an obligation independent of safety. With limited social and kin networks, Ebony could not "pool" enough money and resources to evacuate as many women did, nor could her son risk losing his job. By engaging the financial narrative, Ebony's decision is focused on the realities of her poverty survival every day, not on her safety from the storm. Elaborating on this reasoning is Sarah, who explains how the financial narrative factors into one's decision to evacuate:

> With Hurricane Ivan, more people left than this time; New Orleans barely had a sprinkle, so a lot of people feel it's wasted money and are not gonna want to leave. Nobody took Katrina as serious as it was! And by it's being the end of the month, a lot of people didn't have that money to leave. We had to pull our money together to go.

Evacuation expense represents a significant consideration, costing around $300 for gas and food for a household and increasing when hotels are required. Among this sample, the modal annual income category was $20,000 or less, meaning that even if a household earned $1600 per month (near the top of the income bracket), a modest evacuation expense of $300 would represent nearly a fifth of the family's monthly income. Similarly, as monthly income declines, the proportional evacuation cost burden increases, further discouraging evacuation.

A second form of the financial narrative, job security, emerged to justify a woman's decision not to evacuate. At the time of Hurricane Katrina, 21 of 51 respondents reported working, representing 41.2% of the sample. For these women, they had to decide whether the evacuation from New Orleans was worth the possibility of lost wages or jobs. Vanessa elected to ride out the storm, believing she would be able to go to work after it passed. Like so many women who engaged a narrative of the storm as "safe," Vanessa was "not at all worried" before the storm. Instead, she focused on the financial narrative to justify her choice, while ignoring her family's requests to leave:

> Sunday they had called and said the hurricane was coming. I just didn't think it was coming. My entire family evacuated except me. I thought it would pass over so I can go to work.

Work was an important part of many women's lives, with commitments to the workplace running deeper than simply a need for financial security could justify. For Giselle, remaining in the city was actually a moral decision she and her husband shared, volunteering to stay at the upscale elderly home where they both worked. Giselle's social ties at her job were the deciding factor to stay because "the residents, they were more like family. I developed a relationship with them. The thought that it'd be such a big storm—I wanted to help them get out safe."

Unlike others who stayed based on a narrative of safety, Giselle acknowledged the storm's risks: "Thank God I understood the damage a category 5 would do. And listening to people who dared not to move, saying it wasn't going to be bad. I was horrified. This was a real eye opener." Giselle's work was a way to serve her community and support her social network, by caring for elderly kin outsiders whose families had left them behind, despite the strong sense of risk she felt prior to the storm. In this way, work prevented her evacuation, but not due to the financial narratives of others.

Illustrating the complex circumstances in which women created their narratives is Faith, a 911 operator who was scheduled to work during the storm. Torn between a financial narrative of job security and a second narrative of the storm as a legitimate threat, Faith faced an impossible dilemma: take her sons out of the city to safety or lose her job on the spot.

Jessica: How did you decide to evacuate?

Faith: Well, I wasn't really planning on evacuating. I was essential personnel, so I couldn't leave. I had planned for my kids to leave with my parents. But they grandmother left before everybody, so my kids couldn't get out. I lost my job for taking them out the city. I had to take them out.

Jessica: That's a difficult choice, to risk their lives or lose your job.

Faith: My employer gave me a sob story. They say "what you gonna do for the city?" But you can't take your kids to work, and you can't leave them at the house by themselves. So, I told them "I will go to Baton Rouge and come back. I have a badge, so I can get back in." But they said "No, we'll call you,"[5] all the while I'm answering 911 calls. So I went home and got my kids. I enjoyed my job, but they wasn't working with me. They wouldn't let me start an hour late on a 22-hour shift, just to get my kids to safety.

For Faith, her kin network failed her by leaving without her children, forcing her to choose between their immediate safety and her need for long-term employment for the family's overall survival. At the cost of being fired, Faith narrated Katrina as a legitimate threat that merited the rejection of the financial narrative in order to protect her children. Likewise, it is possible that her boss also entertained a narrative of legitimate threat, realizing that firing Faith would save three lives in the face of such risk. This is unknown, but those working in emergency management were most likely to narrate the storm as a threat, as did Faith despite her offer to return to work out of a sense of duty.

Thus, for working women in this sample, each assessed Katrina's danger relative to both the economics of evacuation as well as a sense of duty to their employers, grappling in the process with the choice between long-term survival and the immediate threat to their lives and well-being. Both evacuation expense and job security structured low-income women's decisions to evacuate New Orleans in powerful ways. Through a balancing of each against the perceived danger of the storm, individual women weighed their well-being against the narratives they created. This internal conversation helped to shape an evacuation decision that was later challenged or supported by significant others within each woman's social network.

What is most notable, however, is exactly how few women in this sample stated that money prevented them from evacuation, because lack of wealth is a major reason for not evacuating, along with lack of transportation, refusal to leave pets, possessions, and homes behind, medical and mobility problems, care-giving responsibilities, and disbelief of risk.[6] Yet, among low-income African American women in this sample, potential job loss and disbelief of risk were the primary inhibiting factors.[7] Unexpectedly, only Ebony specifically declared she could not afford to leave. For others like Sarah, Vanessa, and Giselle, the commitment to keeping one's job prevented evacuation, while the actual cost to evacuate did not. Similarly, had Ebony's son not feared job loss after the storm, it is conceivable they too might have been able to evacuate.

The Collective Narrative

So how exactly did women come to change their minds about the severity of Hurricane Katrina's risk? Fortunately, women's singular voices were not the only ones in conversations about evacuation. Women exist within social networks and their resources are connected to those ties, and this was especially true in New Orleans.[8] Within a disaster context, evacuation is a negotiated process—kin networks can promote or discourage evacuation,[9] and those kin ties both changed the narrative of Katrina's risk and enabled evacuation from it.[10]

Among these women, kin networks functioned to enable evacuation in two ways—first, by altering a woman's individual narrative about the storm's severity; and second, by offering a material, tangible evacuation option through the network.[11] This option was achieved by pooling resources from network members such as cash, food, transportation, and shelter to allow the entire network to evacuate, whereas an individual member could not have. By broadening the conversation to include new narratives, actors, and resources, evacuation became an available alternative for women, as kin networks created group possibilities that altered the parameters of the individual evacuation decision. Perla, Thelma, and Ingrid illustrate this transition:

> Perla: Really, I had been hearing about the storm a couple of days. I didn't give it too much thought. The kids called, said it was a Category 5. I told my husband we should go. My husband was sick, real sick. I grabbed three pieces of clothing for myself, my grandbaby, and my husband.
>
> Thelma: I wasn't planning on evacuating. I never drank water, but I had stocked up on bottled water and canned food. I didn't think to prepare to evacuate. It wasn't until my granddaughter called that I decided to leave.
>
> Ingrid: I have a brother, if he don't say move, we don't move. My brother, he say "it's time to go. We don't be able to stay," and we go.

Callista also explains:

> Callista: The most, that I can say is, initially.... Due to the information on the news, I didn't take the hurricane seriously. Then on the day of the hurricane.... I saw how much damage, and the power outage, it had done. It was devastation.
>
> Jessica: How did you decide to evacuate?
>
> Callista: My brother contacted me. He called me telling me to get out.

As the narrative of the storm as "safe" dissolved under pressure from family members and friends, it was replaced by a new narrative: the storm as a "legitimate threat."

This narrative transformation from "safety" to "threat" occurs through a process involving what I refer to as "threat legitimation"—a redefinition of risk as negotiated by family and friends. Through threat legitimation, the women interviewed reshaped their assessments of safety and danger, reframing their decision to evacuate based on kin negotiations and the emerging risks following the storm. This was especially the case for women who evacuated late, like Callista. Once the risk was transformed into a "legitimate threat" and the narrative of safety discarded, choosing to evacuate became much simpler.

Illustrating how threat legitimation and its preceding negotiation unfold are Sarah and her aunt. Sarah, very worried about Katrina's danger even before the storm had hit New Orleans, begins:

> I was focusing on the hurricane—Thursday, Friday. I was still going to work, but on Friday I was ready to get up and get out. That's when I got very worried and I wanted to go.

But, of course, the decision making process was neither as linear nor as singular as Sarah describes it. In those important days before landfall, Sarah and her family negotiated the evacuation decision, calling each other often "to see who could go with who," ultimately making a plan to leave Sunday morning. Sarah subsequently described the process to me:

> I talked to a lot of people at work before the storm. They weren't sure which way to go. I told them that if the storm goes this way, they needed to evacuate. When I talked to my aunt, she said "God is gonna take care of me." Then I said, "But, if he's giving you a warning, you need to leave."

At that point, Sarah explained, her aunt decided to evacuate with the family. She then added, "We had to pull our money together to go."

For Sarah, evacuation decision making was a process between herself, her co-workers, and her family. Like many evacuees, pre-existing social capital guided assessments of evacuation possibilities,[12] reshaping a narrative of safety—in her aunt's words, "God is gonna take care of me"—into a legitimate threat: "if he's giving you a warning, you need to leave."

For 84-year-old Janelle, it was the women in her kin network who shifted her personal narrative of safety to one of threat. Initially Janelle stated, "I had said I wasn't gonna leave, cause about two or three years before then they said there'd be a hurricane and I went to Houston, and I thought that's what this would be like." With storms like Hurricanes Ivan and George setting a precedent of "near misses" in New Orleans, this logic was founded in lived experience. However, at her daughter's insistence, Janelle reluctantly left—but only after negotiating the decision: "I said I was gonna stay, yes. My oldest daughter, she say 'oh no, you going' and she was sending her daughter, and I should get a few things. She had sent her daughter there." Ultimately, Janelle's willingness to concede to the possibility of Hurricane Katrina's risk reflects her acceptance of the storm as a legitimate threat; a concession which saved her life:

> Then my daughter called and said we were leaving and to get my things together. She said she was sending her daughter over to get me. She came here and got me, and I left with just two or three things. I lost everything. I was so worried about if I lost all my usher clothes. I had just bought a few new suits to be an usher, and they were all ruined. Everything was ruined.

While the women in Janelle's network interpreted Katrina as a threat, her sons did not, reflecting gendered patterns of risk perception.[13] With conflicting interpretations within Janelle's broader network and experience with false calls in the past, her reluctance reflects the negotiated nature of evacuation decision making, as one weighs experience against information and kin pressures.

Janelle's reluctance also demonstrated the important fact that not everyone will succumb to pressure to evacuate, even when kin can enable that evacuation. Janelle continued to describe her two sons' experiences staying behind:

> One of my sons say he wasn't leaving, and he stayed. [The other son] said he was going to stay too, but he wasn't at home. My one son, he said he was sleeping, then he woke up because he felt something cold. Then he realized it was the water, and he had to jump up and leave. [My first son] was over by his cousin's house, then he left by them and went to Mississippi, after the water was up by him.

While both sons survived the storm and were able to later reunite with Janelle, they did so at the risk of death by drowning. They also influenced Janelle's decision making process, which would have resulted in her own death if their narrative of safety had prevailed over the risk narrative of their sister and niece. In this way, the full kin network—not just immediate household members—all play a role in how women assessed the risks of Hurricane Katrina. While the gender connection in decision making is clear in this case, it should be noted that some men also perceived the storm as a legitimate threat, as Callista's previous comment demonstrates. Determining what factors statistically predict why some individuals perceived the storm as threatening and others as sustainable merits deeper investigation than this data can provide. This chapter will next engage a qualitative examination of those instances where the kin network failed to convince members to leave.

Resisting New Narratives

Just because evacuation decision making can involve multiple voices does not guarantee that the narrative of threat will prevail. A woman's own narrative of safety can still be maintained in the face of network pressure to evacuate. For Louisa, her individual narrative kept her in the city during the storm, staying in a downtown hotel where her adult son worked. This "vertical evacuation" kept her safe initially, but after the first day, she received a call from her other adult son insisting she evacuate to his home on the city's Westbank because the floodwater in New Orleans was rising. As Louisa explains it:

> A lot of people just don't want to go. I stayed where I was.... I would have never gone, but the children said we not staying there this time. My son went to look at the floodwater, came back and said "Water's coming on Claiborne." He said that, and I threw a few things in a bag and left.

Through conversations with loved ones, Louisa's narrative of safety was redefined to acknowledge the threat, legitimize it, and encourage evacuation from the flooding city. By negotiating the evacuation with her second son, she connected herself to new resources, including food, shelter, and transportation out of the city. In this way, evacuation negotiation both encourages evacuation as an option, while also making it viable through pooled resources.

Yet, negotiating narratives is no guarantee a woman will change her mind. While Hurricane Katrina was catastrophic, other strong storms in the past have been very threatening, only to have little lasting impact on the city. These false alarms during prior experiences make it easier to resist pressure from family and friends to leave. For 28-year-old Alika and 76-year-old Ruth, the safety narrative was not altered by kin negotiations, with the result of placing them each in very dangerous circumstances:

> Alika: It was the same day as the evacuation order.[14] [...] I was at my job. They let us go home early. My mother said, "We have to evacuate," but I didn't think it was that serious. We went to the Superdome, and then there go Katrina. It was like a hell-hole ma'am; Excuse me, but it was hell. I talk about it every day.
>
> Jessica: So you were at work when you found out?
>
> Alika: Yes ma'am, they had to relieve us early because it was that serious.

Ruth chose to stay in New Orleans despite her fear:

> Ruth: Well, I was really scared, to tell you the truth, but I didn't show it. The Lord, he make a way for me, one way or another. I stayed home. I didn't know where to go and I had nobody to bring me out of town. My son, I didn't know where he was. My son's out in the East. The storm just got so strong, so I decided I'll stay in my apartment. Other people were here in they apartments, and I went downstairs and talked to them. It got so I had no water, no food, or electric, and it was time to get up and move.
>
> Jessica: Were you alone or with family?
>
> Ruth: My daughter and grandchildren came over here with them. They was in here, then we all walked to the Superdome.

Upon returning to her home after the storm passed, Ruth found her roof caved in. Yet, the threat of Katrina wasn't enough to encourage an evacuation prior to the storm's landfall. From enabling evacuation through a narrative of legitimate threat to creating a false narrative of safety, women made their decisions within an interactive process that linked the outcomes of multiple lives to one another. Unfortunately, just because women negotiated their decisions with others did not guarantee an evacuation. In fact, sometimes the narrative of safety was the one to prevail.

Conclusion

Throughout this study, low-income women's narratives about the approaching storm's severity guided their initial decision making processes. They created narratives of the storm as "safe" in reaction to the information at hand, experience with prior hurricanes such as Betsy, as well as in relation to their own obligations to work. These decisions were individual and active, *and* were simultaneously occurring within the confines of structural constraints—work requirements, family expectations, and poverty survival, to name a few. Had businesses closed down for the three days surrounding the storm, hence eliminating the risk of job loss, the power of work as a social structural constraint would have been reduced, enabling evacuation. Similarly, had the city engaged its evacuation plan, filled buses and trains with people in advance of the storm, or closed the Superdome as a Shelter of Last Resort, the narrative of threat that city officials claimed would have been more powerful. In this regard, narratives reflect both individual decision making, as well as social structural reality.

Yet, the effects of social structure do not always guarantee a negative outcome. In fact, the social structure of the kin system—of family and friends—and its inherent obligations disempowered the structural confines of poverty, to instead promote a path to evacuation. Once narratives of safety were negotiated with kin actors, there was an opportunity to alter the final decision and encourage evacuation. Since each woman was embedded within a social network, pre-existing social capital came into play as Hurricane Katrina neared and other voices joined the conversation. Like Dynes[15] and Drabek and Boggs found,[16] the women here demonstrate how pre-existing social capital set the parameters of evacuation decision making, while such material realities as income, shelter, and health status were considerations, rather than structural determinants.

Gender also matters, though to what extent it surpasses other factors such as race and class is questionable among this sample. During Hurricane Katrina, Haney, Elliott, and Fussell found that it was "hardworking and religious black men who stayed behind to look after property and maintain employment in the face of a recurrent hurricane threat."[17] Most notably, these were the individuals who formed the "social core of the Gulf Coast region, not its margins."[18] Similarly, many low-income women in this study also made the choice to stay based on the financial narrative and concern over job loss and their long-term survival needs. In other cases, women remained because Hurricane Katrina was not perceived as a legitimate threat. While evacuation resistance based on job loss concerns could be addressed through job-protection policies, mandating evacuation among those simply unwilling to leave is a far greater challenge in future storms.

Most importantly for our theoretical understanding of evacuation, the competitive narratives of kin transformed decision making into a process—a social interaction between a woman and her kin. Through a woman's kin network, narratives about safety were translated into narratives of threat, or vice versa. While other narratives existed, safety and threat dominated the discourse. As such, the transformation of a sense of safety into legitimate threat through kin network negotiations was an important mechanism to promote evacuation from the city both before and after the storm passed. Ultimately, far more than material realities influenced a woman's decision to remain in New Orleans or evacuate from Hurricane Katrina. Kin mattered, too.

[1] This finding contradicts research which suggests low-income individuals were too poor and/or lacked the transportation to leave. When embarking on this project, I expected to confirm the poverty hypothesis, and was genuinely surprised to see how few women stayed behind due to lack of money or transportation. How women worked around those limitations to evacuate successfully is discussed in the next chapter.

[2] This was the case for more affluent residents as well. See Haney, Elliott, and Fussell 2007 for a statistical analysis.

[3] Counties are referred to as "parishes" in Louisiana. Orleans Parish is identical to the boundary lines for the City of New Orleans.

[4] Haney, Elliott, and Fussell 2007: 82.

[5] Researcher note: Faith was fired on the spot.

[6] Waugh 2006; Cutter and Emrich 2006; Fussell 2005; West and Orr 2007.

[7] See also Haney, Elliott, and Fussell 2006.

[8] Stack 1974; Anderson 1989, 1990, 1999; Dynes 2005; Domínguez and Watkins 2003; Boteler 2007; Zakour 2008.

[9] Dynes 2005; Drabek and Boggs 1968; Behan 2007.

[10] The next chapter examines how kin networks enabled evacuation through the caravan of kin.

[11] 29 women evacuated themselves. Of those women, 22 women left before the storm and 7 women left afterwards. 26 specifically identified family or friends with whom they left in private vehicles. The remaining 3 left in their own vehicles.

[12] Dynes 2005; Litt 2012.

[13] Enarson 2012; Fothergill 1996; Stockard, Stockard Jr., and Tucker 2007/2011; Drabek 1986: 328.

[14] Sunday, August 28, 2005.

[15] Dynes 2005.

[16] Drabek and Boggs 1968.

[17] Haney, Elliott, and Fussell 2007: 86.

[18] Haney, Elliott, and Fussell 2007: 86.

4

Leaving Home

Evacuating before a hurricane is an extremely stressful event. It requires packing for an immediate trip of at least three days duration, finding a place to stay on very little notice, coordinating the departure with family and friends, and spending several hundred dollars unexpectedly for food, gas, shelter, and any other needs that emerge. For Hurricane Katrina, the evacuation experience was even worse. On Saturday, August 27, just two days before landfall, Hurricane Katrina was a Category 5 storm—the most powerful category on the scale. Category 5 storms have winds over 150 miles per hour, can tear entire roofs from homes, and can demolish those same homes with wind force alone.

What is most intimidating about a Category 5 storm is that there is no worse possibility. With a Cat 5, one simply has to pack as if everything one leaves behind will be gone because it very well may be, as tens of thousands learned in New Orleans. As that possibility invades one's thoughts while preparing to leave, the foreboding winds and gathering rainclouds intensify the sense of danger felt.[1] At the same time, the evacuation process becomes a form of pre-emptive mourning; because loss will be inevitable, one prepares for it. The only unknown is how bad it will actually be. So, residents evacuate and pray for the best in a situation they know will be bad. They leave, and then they wait.

As hundreds of thousands took part in this mass evacuation, many used their families and friends to help them make the departure actually happen.[2] Regardless of the destination, there is a comfort in knowing that loved ones are on the road and nearby, sitting in the passenger seat reading the map, in the next car on the road, or in a string of dozens of cars carrying an entire social network to safety. Through the "kin caravan," many women were enabled to evacuate who otherwise may have lacked transportation or money for basics such as gas, food, or a motel room.[3] The caravan also brought the network group together as a team, fighting against the storm, as was the case for Thelma, Asia, and many others. Implicit in this relationship was the shared group belief that evacuation would be a temporary experience that would end with everyone's return home after a few days. Through such a belief system, several families in this study became strongly bonded and highly inclusive as they helped each other to evacuate. As explored in the previous chapter, low-income women's evacuation experiences are enmeshed within kin-based survival strategies,[4] as individual members offered each other material support to ensure the groups' survival within the kin caravan.

This chapter explores the lived experiences of those low-income women who evacuated in advance of the storm, with particular attention on the way women engaged in kin-based assistance to promote their evacuation and survival. "Evacuation" is conceptually defined as the process of departing from a zone threatened by disaster or a place in which a disaster has already occurred.[5] Of the women in this study, 22 evacuated in advance of the storm, problematizing the common assumption that a lack of resources prevented "the poor" from evacuating. In fact, based on this sample, nearly half of all low-income women were able to evacuate independently, or in caravans of kin, where the collective fiscal capacity of the caravan offsets the financial disadvantages of individual women and their immediate households.

By contrast, women without the resources to leave or who came to a consensus that they would be safe during the storm faced dire circumstances: they left New Orleans late, going through the long and arduous experience of evacuating after the storm had passed, or they remained to wait for help, stranded, making their way through rising water to a "shelter of last resort"—the New Orleans Convention Center or the Louisiana Superdome.[6]

For the 22 women who left in advance, their evacuations were not easy. With only two days' warning before the storm, highways were clogged with traffic by Saturday afternoon and stayed that way as Sunday saw the city's first-ever mandatory evacuation order. As an evacuee, such traffic leaves one fearful of being stuck on the road when the storm approaches. Even two days out from landfall, the wind begins to pick up, and out of season breezes precede the impending hurricane. Driving along, one can feel the "bump" of wind gusts threatening as one seeks safety. After about five hours on the road, one tires of driving and the effects of exhaustion become apparent as the erratic swerving of surrounding cars increases. Especially at night, anxiety, combined with the need for sleep, competes against the emotional urgency of the evacuation. There is no stopping for an extended time or even to rest because the storm threatens from behind. Instead, all there is to do is to drive, and drive, and drive. Coffee, soda, caffeine, fear, and eyestrain create headaches and nausea, but the evacuee must keep driving to stay alive, to protect one's family. Evacuation is a genuine act of survival.

The Kin Caravan

Emerging from the negotiated evacuation decision making process, the kin caravan is the material mechanism that enabled evacuation for many low-income women. As those who communicated with trusted others found a new narrative voice that encouraged evacuation, engaging the network also provided tangible, pooled resources that rendered evacuation viable. This option emerged because while low-income women do not have a lot of money readily available, what they often do have is family. Just as family functions to help them survive living in poverty every day, kin became enablers of evacuation during Hurricane Katrina. Through the kin caravan—a portable version of the kin-based survival strategies that poor women activate in their own neighborhoods—women pooled food and water, secured and shared transportation, and split costs for short-term shelter, such as motels. So effective was this approach that over a third of families (n=19) used it to evacuate, some in groups as large as 100 people, including Trinity, Daphne, Sarah, Perla, Althea, Violet, Simone, Olivia, Keebra, Vivienne, Callista, Ingrid, Destiny, Thelma, Abigail, Janelle, Faith, Asia, and Mercedes.

One of the most notable characteristics of the kin caravan was its impromptu nature. For Thelma, her original evacuation plan was actually to shelter in place, seeking higher ground with her daughter, and then her granddaughter. However, once the narrative of threat was embraced by her granddaughter, the creation of a caravan of kin emerged rather rapidly:

> Well, at first, me and my daughter—my youngest girl—we was going to go by her complex because she was on the second and third floor.[7] My other daughter's house is flat, and she was in New Orleans East, so then we decided we were going to my granddaughter's in the East because she is also on the second and third floor.[8] Then, my granddaughter—she called Sunday morning, about 5:00 a.m. in the morning, and said "We leaving town. Get your things together and we will come and get you."

> It was her mama and dad in her car, and her two kids. I rode in a car with a friend of hers. She got me in her car. I took clothes for three days. At the end of the month I get my medicine, so I got insulin and

left. Not sure how many hours it took us from the highway, but it was bumper to bumper. First, she said, "We going to Baton Rouge." We just kept riding and riding, and stopping on little stops when we can.

Thelma's granddaughter altered the narrative of safety to one of threat. In a material way, the granddaughter also enabled evacuation by offering a ride from the city and a place to stay once they found a final destination. The pooling of resources created tangible opportunities to maintain their safety and well-being as Katrina threatened New Orleans.

Describing her evacuation in detail, Sarah left New Orleans in a caravan of three cars, after her family had convinced her that it wasn't safe to stay in New Orleans. Through telephone calls to her kin, Sarah's perception of the risk shifted to threat. Once this new perspective on the hurricane's risks crystallized, Sarah and her kin network wasted no time in leaving:

> I wasn't in the storm, but I know it had to have been God that made it possible for me to leave. I left with my sons and their children. We didn't think the car would make it. We had no gas money—everybody pulled together. We came to Tennessee, my other son went to Atlanta, then my car broke on him. It broke in Atlanta.

Despite her employment at the time of Katrina, evacuating alone was beyond Sarah's means. Through pooling resources with her sons and grandchildren, Sarah was able to provide the car, while her sons put what little money was available into gas, though this was very minimal. Together, they were able to evacuate as a caravan, making it safely to central Louisiana, then on to Tennessee where Sarah had settled at the time of our interview.

On the whole, Sarah's evacuation was reasonably smooth, except for the immense traffic jams that her kin caravan faced getting out of New Orleans. For evacuees, traffic was a major barrier to getting to one's destination, with drive times taking anywhere from two to five times as long as normal. Layer on the fear of running out of gas,[9] or that the storm might turn towards your selected evacuation pathway, and the slow pace of departure becomes exhausting both physically and emotionally, as Sarah described of their Sunday evacuation:

> Well, we left the day before the storm. We left around 12 o'clock to go to my sister's house in a small town north of Natchez, Mississippi. It's usually about three and a half hours to get there. It took us fifteen hours. Traffic was bumper to bumper, and *it was hot*! We had two kids with us. When we left, we didn't expect a long trip. We had a bunch of

food and put some in each car. We had sodas, food, and other things in different cars, but our car had nothing. We had frozen food and clothes. We went out on Airline Highway—we followed my auntie in her car.

Once we crossed Carrollton Avenue where it intersects Airline, we hit traffic. From Carrollton on it was backed up, bumper to bumper. I watched the traffic and it was so slow. It was so hot and we were so thirsty! The traffic was so slow that I was able to get out of the car, buy cups of soda and cups of ice at a gas station. I paid for it and got back to the car and the cars had only moved like six yards. That's how it was the whole way. You'd stop for five minutes, pull up two feet, stop for five minutes, pull up two feet, and stop again. It was like this all the way there.

The traffic was the most traumatic thing, being afraid of being out of gas. We were all out of gas and we got the kids and stuff in the car, when we made it to a service station. We could buy gas, but the store was locked. People were stopping—to use the bathroom. They wouldn't let you use the bathroom. People were going behind the station—there was a lot of space back there. People went to the bathroom behind the store! I thought that was terrible. That's how it was; they were only selling gas. That was my most devastating experience.

While Sarah and her family had brought food and sodas for the drive, these resources were not sufficient to last for the slow evacuation to her sister's house. Yet, despite the hassle of a 15 hour drive to central Louisiana, the alternative would have been worse: flooding with no safe escape from her Section 8 apartment in New Orleans. While Sarah and eleven of her family members had to sleep on her sister's living room floor for a few days, they were safe, sheltered, and fed—all through the collective resources of Sarah's kin network. Sarah's experience also demonstrates her ability to engage situational social capital, as her sister hosted her, her sons, and their children for their initial evacuation. While Sarah's sister wasn't part of Sarah's regular assistance network, with the threat of Katrina looming, new opportunities for kin-based assistance developed in response to Sarah's unexpected need.

In some cases, the kin caravans were quite small, often just a handful of cars leaving together; in other cases, they were quite large as extended families connected in the days surrounding the storm. For Asia, a 51-year-old grandmother, her sizable kin caravan coalesced unexpectedly:

> Asia: It was unexpected. We left Saturday. We were worried about our family.
>
> Jessica: How worried were you?
>
> Asia: We were worried, but not too much. I thought it would be like the other ones and we'd just turn around and come home.
>
> Jessica: Who did you evacuate with?
>
> Asia: My son-in-law, and like 50 of them other people, including my daughter, her four kids, and one of my brothers.

While the narrative of safety so dominated Asia's thinking that it kept her from initially evacuating, the narrative of threat among significant kin in her network resulted in evacuation.[10] Enabled by the kin caravan, the pooled resources put 50 people out of harm's way, reflecting the expansiveness kin caravans can have.

For Vivienne, she first left New Orleans in a single car early Monday morning, the day of the storm, with her mother, her niece, and her daughter. Staying in a hotel in a small city north of Houston that night, she watched the storm's aftermath unfold on television. Over the next few days, she was in constant contact with her extended kin, including another niece: "My niece, she owns her home in Baton Rouge, and they left also. They wound up being in Galveston, TX, and we were communicating with them through the phone in the hotel…."

Once Vivienne's niece had returned to Baton Rouge and checked her home, she invited the extended kin network, including Vivienne, to stay.

> My niece got her house together, then she come back to where we at in Texas, so many of us.[11] Her husband's mother, his family, they went to Galveston with her. When she left and came back, she came to our part of Texas, where it was my immediate family, my brother and his wife, and her mother and aunt.

At this point in time, the caravan emerged and began to roll, as family members reconnected to head back to Louisiana to stay with Vivienne's niece in Baton Rouge:

> Vivienne: It was a caravan, a pile of people.
>
> Jessica: How many people were in the caravan?

> Vivienne: Like 60-something people, a lot of them my sister-in-law's family, but we all did leave together. In cars, trucks, in vans.... We all in Texas [now].

Together, this caravan pooled group resources, helping each other in the weeks following the storm. Here, the kin caravan didn't develop for the initial evacuation from New Orleans; it developed as people moved between places while evacuated. For Vivienne, caring for her blind mother, her eleven-year-old daughter, and her sixteen-year-old niece,[12] the kin resources of the caravan and the shelter options it provided allowed her time to figure out a longer-term survival strategy for her immediate family members. Eventually, that strategy became to move back to Texas where a friend of hers had settled.

Another common characteristic of kin caravans was their temporal nature. Vivienne's caravan broke apart quickly as members went to new destinations to establish temporary residences while displaced. After just two weeks, Vivienne herself left Baton Rouge because, "It was overwhelming, you couldn't get anything done.... I had to get out of Louisiana to get some help, even after I got some food stamps." Hence, to leave Louisiana meant Vivienne would gain access to better social support, including assistance from FEMA and the Red Cross, as well as a housing voucher and food stamps. In working to secure longer-term stability, Vivienne exited from the kin caravan to engage an aid-based survival strategy for her family's extended displacement.[13]

The kin caravan was welcoming in its nature. Among women who spoke with me, it was common that when the kin caravan rolled, it collected as many kin members as it could.[14] Ingrid's evacuation experience demonstrates this quality:

> We was on the highway 22½ hours.... When we left, one followed another one to pick people up. They had not a dime in their pocket. We had nine cars on that highway, with sisters and brothers, nieces and nephews, great nieces and nephews....

Here the kin caravan performed an important survival function by providing real, material support to kin as they engaged a traditional, network-based poverty survival strategy[15] in an innovative way by making it mobile. For without the pre-existing network ties, those with "not a dime in their pocket" would have been denied the ability to get to safety before the storm.

This helping ethic was especially important considering what the actual evacuation experience consisted of: waiting out uncertainty in painfully slow traffic to stay a few days in severely overcrowded motel rooms, evacuation shelters, or in relatives' homes. As Ingrid continued the interview, she described the evacuation drive in greater detail:

> Jessica: How long were you on the road?
>
> Ingrid: 22½ hours! Traffic was backed up. Oh my Lord, Jesus! It was so backed up! People was breaking down and one of our vehicles broke down. It was a long, hard ride.
>
> Jessica: Was traffic moving?
>
> Ingrid: It was slow. It's sometimes like you pick up a little speed, 20 or 35 miles, then next time you might be riding at 10.

Once a caravan arrived at its destination, the entire kin group found itself crowded into shelters, motel rooms, or a friend's or family member's house. For Ingrid, her husband, and their kin caravan, the final destination was her son's modest home: "There was like 65 of us in a 2 bedroom. We were sleeping on floors, wherever. Anywhere you could sleep, you slept." In this case, the caravan of kin provided transportation and shelter for Ingrid, her husband, and over 60 additional kin members. It permitted them to leave before the storm as a group, while having the added security of extra transportation if a car broke down during the evacuation, which one did. While the evacuation destination, Ingrid's son's home, was excessively crowded, everyone in the group was safe and sheltered while they waited to learn of Hurricane Katrina's effects.

The final characteristic of the kin caravan is that it reflects the ability of low-income, Black families to work together with others in their kin networks as a system, for the purpose of saving lives. Across this sample, kin caravans collectively moved approximately 330 individuals to safety, which is 6.5 times greater than the sample size. Despite difficult conditions, kin caravans enabled evacuation, pooled resources, and illustrated how many low-income women could evacuate despite having few personal resources to do so.[16] This ability to engage situational social capital in the face of catastrophe suggests that low-income African American women are far more resourceful than they are often acknowledged to be. In part, this resourcefulness may be founded in the patterns of community-based childcare that hooks describes as occurring in Black communities, where neighbors and people in the community contribute to the raising of children in addition to their parents.[17] In the disaster setting, these linkages of care contribute to provide food, transportation, or shelter, with kin caravans composed of family, friends, and neighbors meeting immediate needs in the face of the disaster, where the federal, state, and local governments failed to do so.

Finally, while women are often at the center of this carework,[18] men, too, have important roles. As the lived experiences of Sarah, Thelma, Asia, and Ingrid demonstrate, sons, brothers, and in-laws called for evacuations, provided transportation, and offered up their homes to provide shelter from the storm similar to women. A deeper examination of men's roles in the evacuation process is unavailable with this data set, but should be considered in future research on the role of kin networks and caravans during evacuation. Next, the limitations of kin networks will be explored.

Left Behind

Kin networks are neither universal nor impervious to dysfunction because they include outsiders to the group. As research has demonstrated, kin systems can support and encourage an individual just as easily as they can undermine individual-level social mobility, pressure individuals into bad choices, enable drug or alcohol abuse, refuse membership to outsiders, and deny access to the group's resources.[19] Six women stated they were left behind by kin or had nowhere to go: Ann, Ruth, Angela, Iris, Julia, and Coral. For Ann, a middle-aged woman caring for her grandson, weak connections to her kin network meant that she and her grandson were left behind by the larger kin caravan.

> Looking at the TV, the traffic leaving the city, I got scared. Family members hadn't offered me a ride. I have a sister, they left in a truck; they coulda took my grandson and myself. My brother drives a limo, so some of those wealthy white folks he knows put him up in a house in Texas.

Unable to evacuate New Orleans with siblings, Ann and her grandson sought safety at her daughter's high-rise public housing unit in the city, engaging a different branch of her social network. Together, they waited out the storm in the concrete building.[20]

For Destiny, her kin caravan consisted of multiples of kin and friends: "Me, my mama, my two brothers, my brother's girlfriend, my boyfriend, my children, my niece, and her children" all left together in three cars. Destiny's group departed "Saturday after we watched the news and how it would be with the water." Safely outside the city when the levees burst, Destiny described the evacuation itself to me:

> Most of us had little children. We had to drive in three cars, there were 26 of us. As we watched what happened, it was hurting. We saw people we knew drowning—actually seen it on the news.

Seeing your friends die on television was a startling and devastating aspect of the storm. Even when safely sheltered, losses like Destiny's hurt evacuees from a distance as loved ones perished in the flood.

What made this experience even more traumatic was Destiny's father's refusal to evacuate New Orleans with the caravan. As powerful as group solidarity and pressure could be to encourage evacuation, it could also fail, especially in the face of self-imposed gender role expectations. Specifically, women take warnings and advisories more seriously, while men are more likely to stay behind.[21] As her kin caravan went through New Orleans picking up friends and family, Destiny's father refused to leave:

> It was awful. My daddy stayed, and we didn't have a way to get him back with us. [...] The phones went out; power was out. The phones went out so I couldn't contact my daddy to see if he safe. He used somebody's cell phone and wind up calling up somebody who could take him somewhere and my sister knew where it was, so that's how he came to be with us.

What factors might have influenced Destiny to leave, and her father to remain? For Destiny, the need to evacuate went beyond her responsibility to care for her children, as she stated, "I think I probably still would have left. I think it was because of what they said about the water." Here, Destiny is attributing her decision to the severity of the storm, rather than her role as a mother; yet as a woman, she is more likely to take those threats to heart.[22] In this way, Destiny's and her father's decisions both reflect gendered patterns of evacuation, even as they each made independent decisions whether or not to evacuate with the caravan of kin.

Ultimately, Destiny's father survived: access to sporadic power allowed him to telephone members in his kin network who evacuated him from the city after the storm passed. Despite a cavalier attitude in advance of the storm, Destiny's father changed his mind as the threat and risk of Katrina's aftermath became self-evident. This relinquishing of gender expectations freed him to put his safety above all else, albeit only after he risked his life by choosing to stay behind to maintain his masculinity, as did Black men throughout New Orleans.[23] Though belated, by reuniting with a different branch of his kin, Destiny's father received help from his family in the face of ongoing displacement.

Conclusion

For many women in this study who chose to evacuate, the kin caravan provided additional assistance with transportation, food, water, and temporary shelter, enabling more women to leave when their personal circumstances prevented them from doing so on their own. Through the provision of tangible, material assistance, the kin caravan was an essential survival resource for women in the days preceding the arrival of the storm. The caravan was welcoming and temporal, though not infallible. In some cases, family members were left behind. While the concept of the kin caravan is not unique to Hurricane Katrina, it does demonstrate that low-income families engage this process as a situational survival strategy, just as more affluent classes do. Without the economic capacity to evacuate as single individuals, families and friends pooled funds, vehicles, knowledge, and resources to render evacuation possible. In this way, the kin caravan represented unified teams of networked, low-income individuals working together to survive the storm.

What is most important about this finding is that low-income, urban families are often assumed to be largely restricted by the structural or psychological effects of their poverty, suggesting evacuation would be beyond their material means.[24] However, when compared to prior evacuation research, the reactions of the families to Hurricane Katrina presented in this chapter parallel mainstream disaster threat responses seen within the disaster literature in general, and Katrina specifically. For example, cross-sectional research by Drabek and Boggs found that families were instrumental in encouraging evacuation prior to a severe flood in Denver.[25] Similar to low-income Katrina families, Denver families called each other on the telephone, confirmed the warning of the forthcoming risk, and left together in evacuation units.[26] This finding also parallels Litt's work on Katrina, who found that just one woman within a social network has the power to initiate the evacuation of an entire caravan of kin.[27] When Miss Joanne insisted her daughter Wendy spend the storm in Baton Rouge, she said: "tell the people, whoever's bringing you, that whoever they got behind them, bring everybody over."[28] This simple invitation to "bring everybody" resulted in 54 individuals who survived the storm.

Another consideration is the assumption that low-income networks are limited to the low-income community. While beyond the scope of this dataset to test this formally, many of the women referenced homeownership, stable employment, and transportation access among family and friends in their extended kin networks. This suggests that the broader kin network spans across multiple social classes, creating the availability of enhanced social capital in a time of crisis. Reinforcing this tentative conclusion of access to situational social capital is Bankston's evacuation experience, where the similarities in how middle-class distant kin can open up evacuation opportunities are documented.[29] What differs across race and class, however, is the quality and duration of assistance available. While Bankston describes how being part of a white, affluent family provided shelter in golf-side condos and summer homes, low-income networks provide guest beds, floor space, and couches (often in the strike zone), as discussed at length in Chapters Seven and Eight.

In this way, low-income Black women in this study engaged in an evacuation caravan as did members of other social classes, yet simultaneously, it was through the pre-existing networks that enable their poverty survival strategies that those caravans formed. However, their disaster networks are not completely synonymous with the everyday survival networks—in fact, extended kin, particularly those outside the neighborhood, often became the "Miss Joanne" to initiate evacuation. Women in this study described a capacity to engage situational social capital—limited, emergency assistance on a temporary basis (i.e., the duration of the hurricane). In this way, low-income women's networks have multiple branches, some of which are used every day and others that are only accessible when the right circumstances allow.

---

[1] Pardee 2007.
[2] Pardee 2009; Litt 2012.
[3] Pardee 2009; Litt 2012.
[4] Dynes 2005; Edin and Lein 1997; Stack 1974.
[5] *Evacuation* was operationally defined by several indicators, including: "How did you evacuate the city? In your own or a family member's car? A friend's car? By some other means?"; "When did you evacuate from the city?"; and "Were you rescued?" If "yes," "how many days [after Katrina had hit]?"; "When you first left New Orleans, did you go to a shelter, hotel/motel, family member's house, friend's house, or somewhere else?" These questions identified the role of economic structure on evacuation decision making. Other indicators included: "When did you first learn about Hurricane Katrina?"; "Before anyone knew what would happen, how worried were you? Not at all

worried, somewhat worried, worried or very worried?"; "Did you evacuate before the storm?" and "How was your initial evacuation experience? Could you describe it?"

[6] See Part II of this book to understand these women's experiences; Idakula 2007.

[7] The daughter's apartment had a second-floor entrance and was two stories tall, making it located on both the second and third floors of the building.

[8] The granddaughter's apartment had a second-floor entrance and was two stories tall, making it located on both the second and third floors of the building.

[9] See Behan's discussion of running out of gas for Hurricane Rita, 2007/2011:181-182.

[10] It should be noted that neither the final decision to evacuate New Orleans, nor the operation of a kin caravan were democratic: Not all voices were equal in the decision making process. In fact, it was often those offering the help—whether transportation or housing—that held greatest influence because they simultaneously resolved monetary issues discouraging evacuation. Additionally, both men (n=7) and women (n=6) were reported in equal measure as encouraging evacuation, and many respondents (n=6) made the decision themselves and for their families.

[11] Other members of Vivienne's family had also evacuated to the same part of Texas as she did.

[12] Vivienne's mother had legal custody of Vivienne's 16-year-old niece, making Vivienne the de facto caregiver now that her household was combined with her mother's.

[13] See Chapter 8 for a discussion of living in displacement.

[14] Litt 2012.

[15] Edin and Lein 1997; Stack 1974.

[16] Common explanations for failing to evacuate include lack of wealth, lack of transportation, lack of affordable refuge, refusal to leave pets, possessions, and homes behind, medical and mobility problems, care-giving responsibilities, and disbelief of risk (Waugh 2006; Cutter and Emrich 2006; Fussell 2005; Gladwin and Peacock 1997: 71).

[17] hooks 1984.

[18] Fothergill 1999; Enarson 2012; Noel 1998.

[19] Domínguez and Watkins 2003; Anderson 1989, 1990, 1999.

[20] See Chapter 5: Stranded.

[21] Fothergill 1996; Enarson 2012; West and Orr 2007; Haney, Elliott, and Fussell 2007; Stockard, Stockard, Jr. and Tucker 2007/2011.

[22] Fothergill 1996; Stockard, Stockard Jr., and Tucker 2011; Drabek 1986: 328.

[23] Stockard, Stockard Jr., and Tucker 2007/2011; Haney, Elliott, and Fussell 2007.

[24] Wilson 1987, 1996; Massey and Denton 1993; Murray 1984, 1994; Dreier, Mollenkopf, and Swanstrom 2001.

[25] Drabek and Boggs 1968.

[26] Drabek and Boggs 1968: 446.

[27] Litt 2012.

[28] Litt 2012: 171.

[29] Bankston 2011: 29.

PART 2

SURVIVAL

Hurricane Katrina was a huge storm. In the days preceding landfall, its cloud cover spanned the entire width of the Gulf of Mexico. Its winds were so powerful that it was classified a Category 5 hurricane just as city residents were beginning their evacuation planning. Downgraded to a Category 4 days later, it approached the Gulf Coast, initially targeting the Florida Panhandle, only to shift to Mississippi and New Orleans that Saturday morning. On Monday, August 29, 2005, it made landfall. Downgraded again to a Category 3, Hurricane Katrina was still a very powerful storm. In fact, for some time, many evacuees thought Katrina had made landfall as a Category 4, since that was her status as they hurried to make their final arrangements and locate a safe place to stay.

Once the storm made landfall, Hurricane Katrina's threat became undeniable. Its winds ripped across the city, blowing out windows on high-rise hotels that were designed to sustain extra winds. It tore roofs off of houses, leaving crawlspaces exposed, and allowing rain to invade the contents below. It splintered large limbs from huge Southern Oaks, humbling these proud trees in their old age. In Grand Isle, its winds whipped so fiercely, it stripped the bark from the trees, drowning their roots with saltwater. In its wake were left dead, bleached, tree-shaped carcasses to remind residents of its apocalyptic power for months to come. Driving its storm surge from the Gulf onto shore, it forced those same salty waters toward the city through the narrow levee channels of the Industrial Canal and Lake Pontchartrain, bursting their concrete panels through pressure and overtopping.[1] In Mississippi, Hurricane

Katrina washed away buildings, restaurants, and homes, mocking their futility to survive its wrath with a 30-foot storm surge. Only parking lots and concrete steps remained—all else was splintered to pieces and washed away. Devastated landscapes stood in place of neighborhoods.

Still, Katrina's effects extended well beyond its flooding. In New Orleans, a city where much of the housing stock was built before the 1930s, old wooden homes were susceptible to termite damage, weakening their protective abilities in the face of driving winds and rain. With power lines down and service interrupted, storm preparations proved futile, since any food requiring refrigeration would last three days at best. Include rainwater and sewerage backups into the streets, and it was not long before the city's water supply was contaminated and undrinkable. Without power to cook, even frozen food would go to waste, and any food stored on flooded floors of homes was completely eliminated as a source of nourishment. The days following Katrina were a threat to the lives of everyone who was stranded in New Orleans.

The next two chapters analyze the lived experiences of low-income Black women stranded in New Orleans during the storm, those frequently marginalized by society[2] and vulnerable as a result.[3] Overall, 21 women from this sample were stranded by the flood waters: Trinity, Lillian, Regina, Louisa, Ann, Alika, Linda, Zarah, Sheila, Vanessa, Angela, Joanna, Jada, Ebony, Morgan, Lydia, Thea, Keisha, Twila, Mary, and Eurdice. 19 women were rescued by the U.S. Coast Guard and other rescue teams, including private citizens. Seven women were able to leave on their own before the flooding overtook their neighborhoods.

Within this context, women engaged in, experienced, and witnessed acts of courage and kindness, as well as violence, inhumanity, and viciousness. For many, the days spent stranded caused a lasting trauma, one evident in the sound of the women's voices as they recounted their experiences during our interviews. This trauma was caused by the massive loss of life occurring before their eyes, the feelings of helplessness and despair as they waited indefinitely for help, and the incivility of interactions with militarized assistance providers such as police and National Guardsmen. Hurricane Katrina brought out the best and worst of humanity following its impact, all the while altering the lives of women and their families in fundamental, permanent ways.

---

[1] Freudenberg et al. 2009.
[2] hooks 1984; Collins 1998.
[3] Bolin and Stanford 1998.

5
Stranded

> Ebony: After the storm was over, I was ready to go home, but the kids wouldn't let me go home. The night of the storm, I spent that night at my granddaughter's. If I had went home when I wanted to, I'd be drowned. The entire house was covered with water.

Ebony, a 57-year-old grandmother with a disability requiring a walker to move, sheltered in the safest location available among her kin network connections—her granddaughter's St. Bernard public housing unit, located on the second and third stories of the aging brick building. Encouraged to stay an extra night by her family's narrative of the storm as still threatening, her life was spared by this decision. That Monday night Ebony truly believed the danger had passed. At the time, the localized rainwater flooding was "not over our ankle."

How quickly circumstances changed. Just hours later, when she took a break from helping her granddaughter clean the apartment where she stayed, the view from the balcony was different and devastating—the London Avenue canal had ruptured; the deluge had reached them. Ebony recounts the rapid changes:

> We couldn't carry anything; it came up on us so fast. It wasn't the flood, the flood was over. The water was not over our ankle. I was on the balcony looking. Then I went to help my granddaughter to clean her house. Then I went to the balcony again, and the water was pouring over the project, into the house that quick. So how are you supposed to get a house full of people out? People was having seizures. Then the boats come by, and tell them they can't come get them, because they too sickly.

The complex faced extensive, rapid flooding, which rose to devastating levels on the order of twenty feet or more in a matter of just a few hours. Trapped in their homes, residents were stranded. With water up to the balcony, Ebony's family waited for rescue as boats repeatedly passed them by:

> The boats, the rescue boats wanted folks to come out to St. Bernard Ave., so they would take you to the bridge. But the water was so high from the bottom of the St. Bernard project, the water was up to the balcony and steady coming up. My granddaughter's bedroom was on the third floor, and the water started climbing. So, how are you gonna walk through that to get to St. Bernard?
>
> Jessica: Do you think they left people behind on purpose?
>
> Ebony: Yes, they left people intentionally. Yes they did, they left them intentionally. And talked to them badly. How you feel if your mother is trying to get to safety and they tell you, "We come back," and they never come up? How you feel if you want your children to be safe and they can't carry them because they say too many people are on the boat when they only have 3 of 12 on the boat? You wouldn't wish that on anybody! I'm grateful. Me and my granddaughter got out by the skin of our teeth.

The unwillingness of those in boats to aid the stranded contradicts our general understanding of post-disaster response, where community members come together to help each other.[1] Rather, it reflects the emergence of a corrosive community, one in which the disaster serves to splinter the ties in a community, to devastating consequences.[2]

In New Orleans, race and class factors were shaping the response, as Ebony explains how that corrosive reaction developed, in part, out of economic opportunism:

> So many people got drowned. I was seeing people calling for help, and help was right there, and they couldn't do anything 'cause you needed help. It was the saddest thing in the world to see people do what was so selfish. They had boats and could get you and they didn't. They didn't have time to help you. Some, they was with boats, trying to get $20 or $30 dollars to get you to the bridge. If I had twenty or thirty dollars, I would have been gone.

Through the act of charging survivors for boat rides to safety, the flood became a mechanism for exploitation of the vulnerable. For low-income families in the St. Bernard public housing complex, their class status and resulting lack of wealth meant they simply had to wait, and watch, as boats passed them by to rescue more affluent survivors with cash on hand to pay for a ride.

While helping behavior did occur in the storm's aftermath as well, especially among low-income neighbors attempting to help each other, this unwillingness to help by more privileged, and often white, responders occurred in a variety of locations and circumstances, from rescue boats, to evacuation gathering points, to the Superdome and Convention Center. How the response manifested and the ways in which it was experienced by low-income Black women is discussed at length in this chapter and the next. For Ebony, her family was eventually taken by boat to an overpass, where they were left to wait indefinitely. She described her experience to me:

> I'm telling you it was devastating. I don't have the words to describe what we went through. You cannot imagine having to stand up, having to stand up from 9 a.m. to 2 p.m. in the afternoon on a hot bridge, with no socks on; on a hot bridge, with no water. We did get water from under the bridge, but there was so much chlorine you couldn't drink it. There was nowhere to sit except on the ground, which was soaking wet. Imagine needing a walker, with a heart attack, and having to stand like that? It was the most devastating thing.

Her own one-story home completely submerged by the water from the levee failures, everything she owned destroyed, and stranded on a bridge, Ebony suffered a massive heart attack without knowing it. Confirmed later by her doctors, it was clear Katrina had aged Ebony well beyond her years. During the interview, Ebony sounded far older than her age, which made much more sense when she shared the severity of her health concerns—that her doctors had told her that her heart was actually half dead.

In the face of true trauma, Ebony's experiences provide a starting point for understanding how the disaster was actually experienced by low-income Black women. In some ways, Ebony's experiences being stranded were commonplace—many faced floodwaters and crisis as the levees ruptured, including wealthier families in the Lakeview neighborhood. Yet, to be told you could pay for a ride to safety reflects the way that social class factors into the experience, as responders spoke badly to the stranded, degrading them in their desperation. Other themes emerge as well. For example, as soon as the storm's winds passed, traditional gender roles resumed, as Ebony cleaned the apartment where she stayed, a form of reciprocity for providing shelter, and an act that must have been physically challenging given her poor health status. As the remainder of the chapter demonstrates, even as racial, class-based, and other forms of discrimination manifested amid the crisis, the work of doing gender and meeting other role expectations were maintained.[3]

Overall, the vast majority of New Orleanians faced floodwaters that invaded their homes, damaging or destroying approximately 71% of all housing units in the city.[4] For some, the levees' collapse created an immediate, dangerous, deadly wave of water that overtook houses, splintering them into pieces and drowning those unfortunate souls who happened to be inside. For families living further away from levee breakpoints, the flooding was a slow terror that rose inch by inch to overtake streets and sidewalks, then steps and porches, until it finally consumed windows, then entire homes. For Vanessa and Regina, the water entrapped them, forcing them to await rescue by the National Guard, just as 41% of the sample did. For Joanna, Twila, and others, living in areas distant from the broken levees allowed them to leave late, but safely. For all the women involved, fulfilling their roles as care workers for their family members including aging parents, brothers and sisters, or scared children and grandchildren was a top priority, even as the disaster was happening before their eyes.

Exposure to Danger

Regardless of whether women and their families prepared for the storm in advance by gathering food and water, or relocating with kin to the safest shelter available to them, few who stayed in the city for the storm were truly prepared for the experience. Thea was not prepared, not at all. A 53-year-old married woman who rode out the storm, Thea had no prior knowledge of Hurricane Katrina. Early Monday morning, she awoke expecting to go to work, when instead, the storm was bearing down upon the city. Thea explained her experience to me:

> It was a horrible experience. I got up that morning about 4 or 4:30, but I was not expecting the storm. I made breakfast, and at about 5:07 the lights went off, then they came back on, then they went out three more times. By 5:30, 6:00 a.m., the wind was picking up, and I had gassed my car for work, but it was so bad I just had to stay home and eat what I had. So I took some cans of food up to my bedroom and watched from upstairs. The water was rolling so fast I couldn't do nothing. Water was just pouring in, through the cracks in the window, under the doors; anyway it could come in, it did. I watched the water rising. It came up so fast, I thought it looked just like the water from the 17th Street canal. Then the boats came to rescue us. They had helicopters, too.

Stranded in her public housing unit, Thea's only option was simple: to wait for rescue teams to save her life. Eventually, Thea and her neighbors were evacuated to a bridge where she waited in the intense heat for a bus to take her from the city.[5]

The severity of the storm surprised most New Orleanians, regardless if they evacuated or not. First, it was common knowledge that the levees were designed to withstand a Category 3 storm. At landfall, Hurricane Katrina *was* a Category 3 storm, meaning the levees should have held. Second, after so many false calls for storms like George and Ivan, the power of Katrina was amplified by the devastation of the social aftermath to a point where it seemed unbelievable, almost surreal. It was true reality, unfolding before the eyes of the stranded and millions of others who watched families on rooftops, begging for rescue in the United States of America.

Third, the narrative of safety women engaged in making their decision to stay echoed through the accounts of the stranded. So many of the women I spoke with told me how they just didn't think "this thing could be *that* bad," including Vanessa, whose apartment was very close to the Industrial Canal:

> Vanessa: Well, see the reason I stayed—you know New Orleans people, we thinking this thing, the storm, is gonna pass over. I hadn't been watching the news, so I got up, and started cooking. Then, the lights went off and my son, the one that's dead, he said, "Come see the water." By the time we got there, there was no water. [...] He said, "Come see the water" and this time we could see the water. My window was facing a train track, we're watching and watching, and about two seconds later the water came over the train track and knocked the train car off the track. Then the water came up over the van in about five minutes. We just knew then. The phone was still on then; we called the Coast Guard, but they never came to get us.
>
> The water was clear at first; then the water was black with fish and all kinds of stuff. It was horrible, horrible. Everybody who was downstairs, they had to leave then—both the upstairs and downstairs apartment. The people downstairs came upstairs, 'cause the water was over their ceiling and up to our floor.
>
> Jessica: Were you upstairs?
>
> Vanessa: On the second floor. The water came like a wave and it knocked a box car, a chemical car, and we was choking. We could see some kind of chemical stuff on the water, and we was running, coughing and crying, and we just start praying. The water was at the door then.

Unsuspecting, Vanessa, like so many others, went from riding out the storm to scrambling to safety as the floodwaters rose with a fierce rapidity, consuming her community in just several minutes' time. Without a moment's hesitation, Vanessa and her son ran downstairs to gather her neighbors, a family with three small children living directly below. By bringing everyone upstairs to her two-story apartment for safety from the flood, she and her son saved their lives.

> Vanessa: We heard a loud explosion between 7:00 and 7:30. I don't know what it was; they say it was the levee, and that's when the muddy water came in, about that time.
>
> Jessica: So there was an explosion, then the wave came?
>
> Vanessa: I heard the explosion; well, I was in the kitchen, and I'll never forget it. It was like between 7:00 and 7:30, my son was in the window, and he told us to see the water, but when we got back there, we didn't see the water. We watched and watched and watched, and within a few minutes the water came.
>
> Jessica: How high was it?
>
> Vanessa: About ten feet. We was panicked, trying to get everyone together. We were trying to get everybody in one house. They were hysterical over there, and they had three little kids under the age of seven, like seven, five, and two. We were trying to plan about what to do with the children. After the rain stopped, we got together and came out on the porch. That's where we stayed.... The water stayed up for like a day, then it slowly went down. That Monday, that Tuesday, there was no more water, and it went down by that Tuesday.

In the crisis, Vanessa's first instinct was to save her neighbors' lives—an act of helping that reflects a commitment to community regardless of her poverty. In fact, helping in a time of disaster is a common activity,[6] and Vanessa typifies many of the women I interviewed who consistently helped others when they could. In stark contrast, the media focused so heavily on stories of looting and violence that the public representation of the storm was of an urban war zone filled with enemy combatants, instead of an ongoing disaster and humanitarian crisis in which many more people were trying their best to help.

Evacuating Late

As women did everything they could to protect their families, they often took great efforts to stay at the safest shelter available. Yet, in the face of such a powerful storm, this "safest shelter" approach did not always prove to be safe at all. Homes located near levee failures were susceptible to flooding, as families were trapped in them until rescue boats and helicopters arrived. Homes in dry areas risked wind damage to their roofs and windows. As power failed, families had to wade through backed-up sewerage and floodwaters seeking food and better shelter, or an exit from the city altogether. Amid all of this, no woman expected to be stranded as she was, or to face the challenges she did. For a very small minority (n=7), geography spared their homes and selected shelters from severe flooding, permitting a delayed evacuation following the storm, as was the case for Louisa, Sheila, Joanna, Twila, Julia, Amaya, and Coral.

At 43 years old, "Jo" had experienced some of the worst New Orleans had to offer. For her, the city's deep poverty, racial segregation, excessive murder rate, and devastating violence were all part of her everyday experience. Growing up in the projects, she observed community violence in a direct, personal way. Like so many public housing neighborhoods, New Orleans' public housing was composed of vast communities of isolated, dilapidated, repetitive brick buildings, with large interior courtyards and streets that stopped once a project began. To drive in or out, most sites had just one or two main roads that were stretches of a quarter or half mile, without any cross streets. In each of these vast complexes, the feeling of separateness, segregation, isolation, and abandonment was undeniable. They felt much like a defunct college campus, with a substantial spatial presence in the overall urban landscape, a massive and sprawling sense of size, yet uniquely a separate universe, much as the designers of these housing complexes intended them to be.[7]

Yet, unlike a college campus, the predominant feeling within New Orleans' public housing was insecurity rather than safety; the housing was tired, the windows were often broken or boarded up, and the cars lining the roads were old, damaged, and rusty. The men and women loitering around looked exhausted, some angry. Through Jo's description, one can begin to see why:

> Between seventh grade and age thirty, I seen like 150 people shot—one execution style, and shot right there at my feet. But I block that out of my mind. I feared that storm more than I felt fear ever living in the projects…. It's like a nightmare I'm not getting over. It's the same

way I look at it, ma'am. How can you be in a project and see killing and not be disturbed, but you more disturbed in a hurricane? I seen shooting since the seventh grade, it's like it was normal to you. I didn't have no fear of that, I seen it, but I didn't feel it, I blocked it. But the hurricane, it's 24/7. It is always pitch-dark. It was like, like a nightmare.

Despite being "tough" out of necessity and capable of handling more than most Americans can imagine, none of Jo's experiences prepared her for the hurricane and the threat it posed to her family. The winds, rain, and sheer power of the storm were completely unexpected to her. In a small house in uptown New Orleans, Joanna and her siblings gathered at her mother's place before the storm:

That Monday, when we got up to brush our teeth, the whole ceiling came down and it destroyed the whole room. [...] The windows were shaking, and the ceiling came down in my mom's room, then my brother's room, then the sitting room. And the wind blew the door off the hinges. Then, a tree came and knocked off the side part of the house. [...] It was like five of us, my mama's daughter, her brother, his wife, and my sister's kids. It was like the rooms was collapsing. One collapsed that morning, one in the middle part of the day, and one at night.

In the "safest" location available, Jo was trapped with 12 other family members, forced to ride out the storm in a wooden house that was literally falling down around them. Gathered together to pool resources like so many other families, Jo's entire family was stranded in the remnants of her mother's home.

On Wednesday, as water began to collect and rise in their uptown neighborhood, the family decided to attempt an evacuation after Jo's nephew began to have seizures. Hearing her brother's car alarm go off, Jo and her brother went outside to investigate, falling into dire circumstances:

What happened that night—my brother had put the car on higher ground and this young sixteen-year-old guy put a gun to his head. He wanted the radio from his car. We heard the car alarm, and I told my little brother that someone was by the car, 'cause we heard the alarm. We went out, and had a flashlight. Then the boy told me that if I didn't put the flashlight down, he'd blow his brains out. So we went back inside. My mom said we had to go.

Yet, leaving the collapsed, damaged house was no easy task with a sick nephew, young children, and floodwaters all around. Jo described how they created a makeshift raft to keep the children safe from the floodwaters:

> We took the closet doors off the hinges and had the nephew of seven months and nieces and nephews—they like seven years old—on the door, 'cause they couldn't walk in the water. We walked out through the water, and tried to get gas. When we tried to get gas, someone was demanding 20 dollars for each gallon. We was walking some more, walking some more, got to Napoleon, and this man, he got gas. My brother had to drive us across the river so we could stay at my sister's. Then we called my sister who live out of town, and she came down and get us in pieces, some of us, then drive back, then get some more people.

Using her sister's house as a launching point, the family only made it to the city's Westbank in their initial exodus from New Orleans. Still, it was far enough to put them out of the imminent danger they faced in their own neighborhood, and near enough for Jo's other sister to drive down and collect them "in pieces," taking them back to her home outside the city. In this way, extended families enabled evacuation after the storm and provided safe shelter outside the city. In Jo's case, her sister even became the transportation outside of the city, illustrating just how deep the personal connections between this family's members were, despite their poverty and unfortunate decision to stay for the storm.

Yet, the decision to stay was common, and fifty-seven-year old Twila evacuated to her daughter's brick apartment in the city. Twila initially felt secure there, describing how she made the decision: "We rode it out in my daughter's house. I felt that I'd have been safe in the brick. Hers was brick. But mine didn't get any damage, but hers did." In fact, Twila's daughter's bedroom ceiling caved in, forcing the family to ride out the storm in the living room. Over time, her power went out, leaving the home hot and crowded with Twila, her daughter's family of four, her other daughter, and a two-month-old grandchild. Together, the group waited amid the damage, hoping the water outside would recede. Without power, it is unclear if Twila knew the levees had broken, since the city was susceptible to several feet of flooding anytime a massive rainstorm passed through.[8] She explained how the flooding was at first:

> That Tuesday we couldn't do anything. They had water, about two feet. Then that Wednesday, we went to my house because I have a gas

stove and could light it with a match, so that's what we did, but the lights was still off.

Arriving at Twila's home, they found no flooding and were able to make plans to evacuate late, using her daughter's car.[9] After being contacted by Twila's cousin, who offered a place to stay outside the city, "All seven of us left in one car to Lafayette.... My cousin had called us and told us to leave and come over there." Quickly, they packed the car and took Highway 90 West to leave the flooded city. Through pooling their resources, Twila's family enabled survival by helping each other through the uncertainty of the storm and its immediate impact. While her daughter provided transportation from the city, her cousin offered a place to stay for all seven family members, demonstrating the importance of kin networks for post-storm survival. As a family, they evacuated on Thursday, three days after the storm.

While unlivable conditions encouraged many residents to evacuate late, for Sheila, it was an incident of police brutality that caused her to leave the city. Living in a neighborhood without flooding, Sheila stayed in the city because she believed she'd be safe. With poor health overall and limited cash on hand, evacuation was a risk unto itself:

> Sheila: It was terrible.... The car, it didn't have any air, and we was falling short on cash, it was just terrible. [...] I didn't think it would be as bad as it was.
>
> Jessica: How was the storm itself?
>
> Sheila: It was okay, we was just was riding it out.... I stayed at my house.

After several days passed, Sheila's advanced diabetes became an emergent threat to her well-being. With stores closed indefinitely, and her insulin supply running low, Sheila was becoming very sick:

> I take insulin, and I ran out of insulin. Then I was—I had to really leave, 'cause I was assaulted by a police officer. [...] What happened was, my son and his friend got a car, and it didn't belong to them. They went down by Walmart. They was trying to get me some insulin. The cop thought I had keys, which I didn't, and he hit me twice, knocked me down, was choking my son, and had a rifle to my son's head. It was a big ol' mess. The friend took a chance with the car and left. The neighbors, they started hollering at the cop, and his partner was telling him, "Don't hurt that lady."

This encounter, which is mild compared to confirmed violence and murder experienced by other survivors in those early days, reflects the militarization of a humanitarian crisis by the New Orleans police, a pattern that was perpetuated by external first responders as well. More importantly, there would have been no need to steal a car and look for insulin in the first place if the City of New Orleans, State of Louisiana, FEMA, the Red Cross, and other service agencies had a functional disaster plan in place before the storm, or had response plans for the days afterwards to provide people with needed medicines. In the absence of appropriate medical care, Sheila's son broke the law to save her life. Soon thereafter, Sheila evacuated with her son to a relative's home in Texas, where she was finally able to get the healthcare she required, including treatment for the injury sustained when the police officer assaulted her, "I wound up going to the doctor for an infection in my eye. My vision was worse from glaucoma, but it was no problem. My vision is worse now...."

As if being assaulted by an officer was not sufficient to punish Sheila for stepping out of line to save her own life, when she returned to New Orleans, a neighbor reported to her that the same policeman had looted her home:

> When I did get back, the police had stolen from my house, and a neighbor seen it, so I filed complaints. It was terrible.... When I returned, the same police as when I left, they ramshackled my house, threw my syringes, cut up my sofa, saying it was a crack house. They spray painted the front of the house, and broke the glasses. They stole my son's leather jacket, and his PlayStation 2. They took everything out of there, 'cause nobody really was in our neighborhood.

Ultimately, the storm itself caused Sheila no direct trauma. Instead, the violent attack by the police coupled with the looting and destruction of her home and furniture were more upsetting than either the winds or flooding had been.

Sheila's experience was not an aberration. In such a limited sample, it is extremely telling that six other women (Ann, Alika, Jada, Mary, Sharon, and Giselle) also reported harassment or violence perpetrated against them by first responders and police in the days following the storm, as will be further documented in this chapter and the next. As low-income women of color, they were targets for harassment, violence, prejudice, and racism at the hands of those same individuals whose jobs were to serve and protect them, reflecting the ways pre-existing social inequalities shaped the lived experience for marginalized populations during the disaster.[10] For the women of this study, the heroes became the predators, making the terror of Katrina about much more than wind, rain, or massive flooding.

Mothering in the Storm

Children are an important part of many families. They provide a sense of playfulness and joy, and can be the glue which gives a family purpose. Amid the thousands of works written on Hurricane Katrina, the voice of children is largely absent from the conversation. One notable exception is the work of Alice Fothergill and Lori Peek,[11] whose focus-group interviews with child survivors help remind us that children, too, were among those affected by the storm. In this study, the focus is on mothering through the disaster. Nine families had children or grandchildren who remained in the city through the storm, three of whom you'll meet here: the families of Zarah, Regina, and Mary. Perhaps one of the most heartbreaking aspects of the aftermath was women's inability to provide the basics like food, water, and shelter for their children and grandchildren amid the chaos of Katrina. As best they could, Alika, Aliyah, Sheila, Jada, Lydia, Keisha, Mary, Amaya, and Coral worked hard to protect their children from the vulnerabilities created by floodwaters, collapsing buildings, hunger, homelessness, violence, sexual assault, comprehensive trauma, and inevitable fear. Many others, such as Zarah and Regina, had grandchildren, nieces, or nephews under their care. For many, this was an exceptional challenge as hours turned into days and resources ran low.

Zarah, a 57-year-old grandmother, spent the storm at her home with seven family members, sheltering together as so many families did. Also, like so many others, Zarah felt the storm wouldn't be anything like it was, a reasonable assessment given her actual experience with the rain and wind. Reflectively, she explained: "I thought it wasn't gonna be that bad. It was just wind and rain at first—it wasn't bad. Nothing had blown off, everything was okay until the flood came, you know?"

In her home, Zarah hosted her daughter, her two small grandchildren (ages 1 and 2), her teenage granddaughter, her son and his girlfriend, and her brother. Stranded by flooding that was "neck deep" outside, water had entered the home and settled to the height of Zarah's knees where it remained without going down. Everyone was eventually evacuated by helicopter on September 5, 2005.[12] In the meantime, the family was crowded in Zarah's home, wading in the toxic soup, doing what they could to make things bearable for the toddlers. Zarah described their efforts to care for the children within the context of the disaster:

> I sure wasn't ready. The cans we did have, we ate that. We was using the bathroom, pouring water out of buckets, to keep the odor down. We was sprinkling Windex on our hands to sanitize our hands. I had three grandchildren there too, in the house.... I keep 'um mostly on the sofa, but they was walking in the water too; it was in the house....

> My daughter flagged the helicopter. She put a sheet outside to get the helicopter to get rescued. It was a white spread. She had marked on it, "HELP! Have babies in the house." [...] They didn't come until Labor Day, you know, Sept 5th. The boats and stuff had been passing, and we was still hoping the water would go down. We'd rub water on the kids, to keep them cool. We used Vaporub to help them sleep. We was fanning them with a board, cardboard, to help them sleep. It was miserable and hot.

As guardians and caregivers, Zarah and her daughter prioritized the care of the children, which they used as an appeal for help on the sheet Zarah's daughter created to catch the attention of the Coast Guard helicopters. Being protective mothers and grandmothers in an extremely catastrophic context was a role these women willingly accepted, regardless of their own ongoing sense of loss and trauma.

These acts of caring were common among women as they lived in the uncertain, dangerous, and unsanitary conditions created by the failed levees. Like Vanessa, who reacted to the levee break by gathering her neighbors to her apartment for safety, Regina's pregnant daughter became the focus of similar acts of caring by neighbors in her community. At 45-years-old, Regina was a mother and grandmother who worked fulltime as the supervisor of the housekeeping department at a local hotel. Like many other families, hers decided to spend the storm at her apartment, which was located on the second floor. Overall, this was a good decision, since Katrina's wind and rain seemed of little consequence to Regina:

> We slept through the Storm. Sunday night my daughter come over with her kids, and she wanted some collard greens—she's pregnant. I made her the greens, and then we went to bed. When we woke, Katrina had passed. We slept through it. I lived on the second floor, and the water was up when we woke. It was up to just below the second floor. We got scared. My daughter started pacing, and then she started having labor pains.

With her infant grandson on the way, Regina was able to communicate the situation to her neighbor through the community's impromptu system of "hollering out"—they would literally yell to each other to make sure everyone was okay. Relaying the news that her daughter was in labor, her neighbor responded by creating a makeshift raft to seek help for the expectant mother and her soon-to-be newborn baby.

> Regina: My neighbor, he took the door off his fridge to use as a boat. He got in and started off, but as he got to the gate, the fridge flipped. He got on top of a van, and from there the rescue people saw him and got him. Then they came by and got my daughter with the guy from the van.
>
> Jessica: Were there any more boats?
>
> Regina: Nothing. An hour later a helicopter flew past, but there was nobody come by to pick anybody up. There was just the paddle boat that my daughter was in. They was volunteers, strangers. They just had a boat with paddles. It wasn't an airboat or anything like that.

Through the helping behaviors of a neighbor and complete strangers, Regina's daughter was transported to a hospital, where she had a safe delivery of her newborn son. From there, she was evacuated to Texas, where it took a few days for Regina to locate her and reunite the family.

Until that reunion, Regina and the boys were stranded in her flooded home for several more days. Listening to the radio for updates, they began hearing stories of the damage and new threats emerging across the city. In those early days of flooding, entire houses were washed away by walls of water from levees that had burst, sewage was backed up into the floodwaters and homes; drowned, dead, bloated bodies were floating down streets; and plumes of fire shot up through this toxic soup where gas mains had burst. To stay safe from this apocalyptic scene, Regina kept the kids indoors, closed up, despite the sweltering heat:

> It was Hell. It was Hell. From my apartment building, which is right off the Boulevard, I couldn't see the Walmart. I couldn't see nothing no more. I had my grandkids—we didn't know how the water was getting up. We shut the doors. We heard on the radio that the gators from the Zoo got loose. We were scared to open the doors. We didn't know what would happen. My grandkids were so hot, I was wiping them with towels to cool them off. We were afraid to go outside, even though it was so hot.

Desperate to leave, with no information on her daughter's well-being, Regina waited and waited for help to arrive. After several more days, Regina's hopes were raised when City Councilman Oliver Thomas passed by in a boat, proclaiming help was on the way:

> Regina: Oliver Thomas passed by on a boat and my grandson hollered to him. He said "We be back, little man." He didn't come back. It was two or three days later when a helicopter came by. [...] They was red and white. [...] They had a basket and wanted me to get in, but I wouldn't leave my grandsons. They took them too, and a neighbor. There were five of us in the helicopter. They just dropped us off in a field. [...] They took the sick to another place. They had that brown bag military food. [...] It was the worst thing that ever happened to me. We was living outdoors. We had to sleep in an open field. We was like those people at the border.
>
> Jessica: Illegal immigrants?
>
> Regina: Yeah, we could have just gotten shot out there....

For Regina, the entire situation was traumatic—from the flooding of her neighborhood, to her daughter's unexpected labor, to being stranded indefinitely and then left in a field with her grandchildren and a few MREs to survive. From the moment the water rose, her family's lives were in the hands of complete strangers, from the boat of humanitarians who took her pregnant daughter to the hospital, to the Coast Guard who picked her family up and took them to safety. Regina was powerless to protect her family against the flood, except by keeping the door closed so the alligators couldn't come in. Stranded by the water and strained by her inability to meet her own role expectations as a caregiver, the pressure was tremendous.[13] As was the case for so many survivors, the storm's aftermath of flooding and the official reaction to it was much worse than the winds and rain of the hurricane itself.

Throughout this project, acts of caring permeate the interviews with women, even among relationships that were far less intimate than the connection of kin. Despite their poverty, people in the communities where these women lived came together to help each other[14] in the exact same ways we expect disaster survivors will,[15] contradicting both the media portrayal of the city's residents as exclusively lawless, and portions of the poverty literature that underestimate the humanity and interconnected nature of social networks in poor urban communities that can simultaneously be dangerous, isolated, individualized places.[16] Perhaps the most telling aspect to be noted in these experiences was that the accounts of help from neighbors and strangers are plentiful. At the same time, when the dataset is considered as a whole, the accounts of direct threat by strangers are predominantly limited to shelter environments like the Superdome, whereas the accounts of direct threat by police and National Guardsmen are more frequent. From the standpoint of low-income Black women,[17] they were much more likely to be traumatized, assaulted, hurt, and threatened by the individuals sent to evacuate them than by other survivors, reflecting their marginalization in society, as perpetuated during the disaster.

Surrounded by Guns

For so many women, had the levees held, there never would have been a need to rely on the government or perfect strangers for help, rescue, food, water, or shelter in the days following the storm. Without the massive flooding, people would have returned home, stores reopened, jobs and businesses continued, with just a short pause that soon would be forgotten. However, the inconceivable nature of Katrina's technological devastation forced dependency upon the stranded, and in response, women did what they could to hold just a small piece of control and agency whenever possible. For Mary, a 44-year-old grandmother, this meant enacting care work by sheltering her grandchildren from the sight of floating, drowned bodies as they were evacuated from her apartment by boat. She began her story by explaining the family's experience with the storm's passing: four days stranded, with no water or electricity, in a home with broken windows and rain-saturated furniture, walls, and ceilings:

> Oh, the wind was blowing hard. Water was coming in the window, and it broke the windows. We was huddled in the hallway. Water came in the roof, and you could hear the wind tearing the top of the roof off. We watched all the rest of it, then it died down, and we laid back in bed. Water was coming from everywhere. Lord, where water come from like that, I don't know, but I know Katrina didn't do that. We had water to the second floor. We had to go underwater to get into the boat.

Mary's experience with her family reflects the challenges of living in uncertainty in the days following the storm. Stranded on an upper floor, Mary and her kin were lucky to have elevation on their side. Yet, for days on end they waited, relying on pure faith that help would come, evacuating them from the dilapidation Katrina created in their home. Amid shattered windows and leaking ceilings, Mary kept her focus on helping her family as much as she could by cooking meals at home, maintaining her gender role despite everything. Four days passed until they were rescued, and when they were, they had to swim underwater to get out of the building to get to the boat. Drenched in the city's toxic soup, Mary struggled to protect her family as best she could, reflecting women's common practice of gender-role maintenance, even in the face of disaster.[18]

Mary became especially vigilant in her protective actions as she and her grandchildren were being evacuated from her apartment, paying close attention to her surroundings and distracting the children from the death that was floating just yards away in the murky floodwater:

> Rescue men took us in a small boat, and took another family. The kids were scared. People in the water drowning, Miss. We made the kids sit in the bottom of the boat to not see. There were bodies floating in the water, people on top of roofs. We was on top of City Park, that's how high that water was. Miss, that was something....

Evacuated from her home, Mary and her family were left to stay on a bridge, waiting in the heat for the federal government to rescue them from the city itself:

> We went to a bridge—we was on Jefferson Highway. We was on a bridge waiting for buses. We waited for a day. There was a lot of people. People was just falling out, they packed like sardines. And it was stinking, 'cause everybody sweating. It was a mess. A mess, Miss. Then a man come, but he didn't have a CDL license. He must of had a license because he was working for this company, so they sent him to drive. When we got to Baton Rouge, the police drew guns on us, and said we wasn't going anywhere until the head man came. They said they gonna arrest the man and everything. They had him on the wall, handcuffed, with their guns drawn. When we pulled up to the gas station, the police came with guns out, and made everybody get off the bus. Man, did they hate all us. Then another bus, a greyhound bus came, and then they took us to Houston.

Ultimately, Mary and her grandsons had to rely on a civilian acting privately to evacuate her and others from the city. This man drove a bus to the city, found a location where people were gathered, and took them to safety in Baton Rouge. This man was a hero to those on the bus as he took them from danger, preventing them from dying of heat stroke and dehydration. Yet, in America, a country of rugged individualism and self-sufficiency, he was rewarded with rifles and arrest for saving human lives. While the federal response took five days before it began, civilians were present with boats and buses helping people get to safety much sooner. By contrast, the chain of command for the federal rescue response was contested, unclear, and ineffective. This delay and lack of leadership by FEMA meant help was not only slow to arrive and disorderly; it actually threatened the lives of storm survivors, as Sharon's experience will illustrate.[19]

Sharon was a 58-year-old woman who spent the storm with her granddaughter. Living on a Section 8 housing voucher before Katrina, Sharon was located on the Westbank, the part of New Orleans across the Mississippi River. For several years she worked for a local non-profit agency, and lived in one of the large public housing projects located near downtown before moving to a private apartment. Her home survived the storm, but had extensive roof damage—enough so that the building was torn down as part of the city's recovery.

Despite the loss of her home, during our interview, Sharon's focus continually returned to the poor treatment of evacuees as they waited for buses to take them to safety. Within just five minutes, Sharon began to describe the scene:

> We saw the police standing with guns. So then we said "Excuse me, where are the buses to take people out of the city?" They told us where to go. We walked down, and then got in line. My daughter wanted to leave, but I wanted to stay. Then when we got down there, there were tons of people under the bridge. They was in bad condition, with some people going into attacks because they sugar was high, or low. They had baskets, and there were thousands of baskets under the bridge. We all waited. We still gonna wait, cause you couldn't leave before they go on a bus. It was a long time before we was finally able to get on a bus.

Under a bridge in the neighborhood of Algiers Point, thousands of evacuees had gathered seeking transportation out of the city. Sharon described to me how there were babies in baskets, elderly people, and first responders. Another common sight in this scene of desperation was the presence of guns—lots of them:

> There were tons of National Guard, and the Parish police was surrounding us with guns. At one point, the mall caught fire. This old guy crossed the street to urinate behind the bushes. He accidentally stepped on a boy's head, and the boy kicked him, drugged him down, slammed him and said he would set him on fire!
>
> While this was going on, the policeman stood back, then set his gun off. People just ran. They were screaming, and hollering, and the

police was holding guns on us. They said "if you don't show us who has the guns, we won't call any more buses." They finally realized no one in line had a gun, then they settled down to call the buses back to pick up people. We was just trying to get to safety. I said "You almost gave me a heart attack." I wanted to go home but I was afraid I would be shot.

By Sharon's account, the threatening police officers didn't realize it was one of their own who shot the gun, causing them to hold evacuees *at gunpoint*. This failed communication by the squad, and aggressive behavior on the part of the officer firing in the first place, provides insight into how a humanitarian disaster was transformed into an escalating crisis. In fact, the shot had more severe consequences than simply the mistreatment of evacuees. At the nearby mall, the fire department refused to put out a fire, saying they were shot at. Sharon explains how this one bullet caused a chain reaction of fear:

So, the fire department said they were shot at, and that the Oakwood Mall was on fire, and they couldn't fight it because they were shot at by the crowd. But the mall was on fire because the workers was trying to cook and fix something in the mall. We was by the bridge near the mall, but no one in the crowd made the shot, it was a cop.

In the context of uncertainty, evacuees were blamed for violence they didn't initiate. Between the heat, the rain, and rampant stories of looting,[20] the post-storm situation was very tense, and small misunderstandings escalated exponentially.

One of the consequences of the escalation of misunderstandings for evacuees was that the environment under the bridge itself became a new source of trauma. Evacuees were held hostage at gunpoint, unable to leave despite being at greater risk from the first responders who were there to keep them safe. Returning to this experience later in the interview, Sharon provided an even deeper description of the fear she felt for herself and family as they were effectively imprisoned by the police:

The police, they was shooting at people in the dark. It was horrible. [...] Then we stood under the bridge for hours and hours, and I have never looked down to see so many barrels of guns. I thought they'd shoot us like a firing squad. They was hollering, screaming, cursing. They hands was shaking, like they ready to shoot them. I'm afraid to go back, 'cause if a storm come, I don't want to be in that situation again.

How could this incivility happen in a situation predominately defined by need, not violence? When asked "Do you think your race mattered?," Sharon replied:

> Yes. Truthfully speaking, there was very few whites, I don't even know where they were. Very few white people under the bridge, because they have cars. Even in the shelter, there was very few white people. Very few. In the church and shelter, there was only one white person. And she was helping out. I'm in a daze, just like you. I seen very few white people. I don't know whether they evacuated in a different area, but there were so few, you could count them on your finger. They weren't by the bridge, or in the shelter with us. And Spanish too, there were very few. And it was thousands of people. When we hit the causeway, they wanted people in certain areas. The middle group was for elderly people. When I went, it was really, really dark. They had those elderly people there, but they didn't take care of the elderly at all. It was a shame. Some were in wheelchairs, some had Depends diapers on, but they hadn't been changed in days. They was like clinging on to life.

Between the militarization of the relief effort and the failure to meet basic needs of care for evacuees, Sharon was audibly saddened as she remembered her time stranded within the city. In fact, in the absence of massive flooding at her home, the treatment she experienced by the police while stranded was more upsetting to her than any of the rest. Here is a woman whose apartment building was so damaged the entire structure was torn down, yet throughout our conversation, she reflected mostly on the severity of mistreatment as she and her kin patiently waited for help to arrive. Summing up the desperation of the environment, Sharon shared the story of a man having a mental breakdown before her eyes:

> They were dropping people off like bundles of trash. There were grown men laying on the ground, and one man, he just cracked. He had laid down, and a friend told him to get up for him to not get stepped on. The man broke down to a child state of mind.

The Aftermath of Incivility

As this chapter concludes, there is one last story to present that reflects the deep need for a conversation about civility, respect, and the dignified treatment of disaster survivors. The women, children, and men who survived this storm faced atrocities that I hope you, the reader, will never have to overcome in your own lives. They watched as family members drown, as roofs were torn from their homes, as walls collapsed around them. Many New Orleanians died—trapped in the attic crawlspaces as the water overtook them, with no hatchet nearby to break through the roof to safety. Dead bodies were floating down streets. Homes and lives were demolished in the immediate wake of the storm. These realities are devastating and the losses they caused require us, as a society, to seriously consider how we treat those who have been to Hell and back. They are not prisoners, deviants, or criminals; they are average people experiencing a disaster. Katrina survivors are citizens of our nation.

Giselle's story represents the epitome of what should *not* happen to a storm survivor after a tragic catastrophe. As a married homeowner, Giselle is remarkable for her ability to rise above the challenges her poverty created throughout her life. Prior to Katrina she had found success, security, and independence. A former public housing resident, Giselle had been working at a retirement community for seven years at the time of the storm, along with her husband. Recognizing the seriousness of the threat, both had volunteered to work during Katrina to look after the elderly residents whose families left them behind—a common occurrence during Katrina.[21] Giselle explained how the facility was affected by the storm:

> It was an upscale community, so it was funny to me that with people being more fortunate, you'd think three or four days before the storm they would get family and be transported or whatever. [...] The assisted unit was full during the storm. They were all bedridden. They was abandoned by their families, but not by the employees.

Stranded within the facility by choice, Giselle, her husband, and their co-workers tended to several hundred residents, completely shut off from the outside world: "We were just looking out the window, and it looked like the Wizard of Oz. I hate to even daydream about. It was really bad once the water shut down.... There was no water, no power, no nothing. No telephone, no cell phone usage. Everything was completely dead." Fortunately, the storm caused minimal damage to the building, although the residents were suffering; the loss of water meant dehydration was a concern, bathing was not allowed, and some elderly went as many as 18 hours without a diaper change. As the National Guard began to enter the city, some police and firemen took Giselle and other employees to the ransacked Walmart in the Garden District, where they received food, water, and adult diapers for the residents of the retirement community. Together with her husband, Giselle stayed at her workplace until the residents were completely evacuated, monitoring the storm with battery-powered radios and televisions from the residents' units. In those early days, Giselle learned from CNN of the death of someone she knew, as well as other losses around the city:

> We borrowed one of the residents' TV-radio, and were able to put batteries in that. We could see the news at night, and there was a set of kids, between six and seven years old. They were seen on the camera, and they drown. They were floating on a piece of wood. I couldn't talk, I couldn't smile, I couldn't laugh. I was just thinking about people dying, and dying, and dying. It was unbelievable.

> There was a dead body on the street. Right on the corner of Jackson and Magazine. It laid there for 6 days. I thought she got struck by debris. But my husband said she got hit by a car. They buried her on the corner, right there. I lived there. I love reading and was always in the bookstore. Then on Time-Life, CNN, it turns out it was somebody I knew my whole life. But when you find out, it's like—it was the lady I'd always see at school. I never looked for her, so I missed her. I rode around past her [dead on the ground] for a whole week. She laid there like a bag of potato chips. It was bothering.

After two more days at her workplace, Giselle and her husband returned home to check on their house in the city's Westbank neighborhood. During their short ten-minute drive, they were nearly carjacked, as two men used a family to crowd the street in an attempt to force the car to slow down. Travelling in a caravan of two cars, Giselle's husband sped up, creating a space for them both to escape. Giselle recounted their escape:

> When we left, my husband and I had a group talk. He explained to me, in detail, that once we were on the road, "Do not stop unless I say stop. If I turn, turn." He said if he speed up, I should speed up. I didn't understand why until then. I came to a corner, it was like 4th and Tchoupitoulas, and there were four Black women, and a bunch of kids between them, like two to ten, the whole group was ten or eleven people. They seen the car, and started screaming. I started to slow down, and my husband just goes on, like he's out of control. He started blowing the horn. Then, out of nowhere, there were two guys waiting to carjack us. They used a family of people like the bait, so once we be stopped, they'd carjack us.

From the safety of their home in Algiers Point, Giselle and her husband planned on staying in the city, buying a generator, and a small air conditioning window unit to mitigate the heat. Grieving the loss of her friend and trying to understand everything that happened, Giselle described the city at that point in time:

> It was so silent and dead, you could hear the looters. They were just everywhere. You had this unsecure feeling. I couldn't fall asleep at night. We stayed until the 11th of September. We felt fortunate and didn't want to go at first, but that got hard and I wanted to get out. [...] It was so quiet. It was dead silence. I could hear people cough a block away. I missed the sounds of the bus, you know, the engine on the bus. My biggest fear was men. I didn't trust the police, or the National Guard. We made out more fortunate than most.

Considering the help the police had given Giselle while working at the retirement home, I asked why she was so fearful of the men, especially the National Guard. As an upstanding citizen who helped save the lives of hundreds of elderly men and women abandoned by their own families, I was surprised she had felt so threatened by those individuals sent to save her. Yet, her experience as a hardworking, self-sacrificing homeowner and storm survivor speaks volumes to the inappropriate aggressiveness exhibited by many first responders against the citizens of New Orleans. Giselle explained:

> Giselle: There were rumors of women being raped in the Superdome. Lots of rumors about being raped. I heard it was guys in police uniforms offering assistance and them being the hardest criminals. So I'm thinking, "Okay, what now?" And then there was the National Guards. I didn't talk to them. My husband would greet them. I felt no sense of security, but at my house. I didn't trust nobody. One National Guard said to come to the truck and get ice. I was so hot and thirsty, but I refused to accept ice.
>
> Jessica: I know I felt uncomfortable with the weapons. Did he carry any weapons?
>
> Giselle: It may be that, too. My second night home, I had an ugly run-in with the National Guard. They didn't realize we lived here. They was yelling, "Hey you, come here! Let me see your face! Come here!"
>
> Jessica: So they were very commanding?
>
> Giselle: Yes. I said "I live here." After that, he was so rude. He yelled, "Get inside, inside! You need to get inside. Sooner or later you gonna be put out of this town!" It was the same thing with the policemen. I heard on the news that the police were robbing stores. But you didn't know if they were police or someone else in a dry cleaner's with stolen

uniforms. So, who is who? I know for a fact the cleaner's was ransacked. So many uniforms were on the racks. Imagine what can happen when they stolen people's clothes! What criminal didn't take police uniforms?

Reports of police officers looting stores were commonplace after the storm, and while Giselle's fears about stolen uniforms may seem extreme, her observations on the demeaning behavior of police and the National Guard are consistent with those of Sharon and Mary.[22] They are also corroborated by Ann, Alika, and Barbara Jean at the Superdome, to be discussed in the next chapter. Fueling much of the vitriol in first responder interactions seemed to be a deeper sense of racism and classism, both home-grown[23] and imported with the relief workers themselves. In this regard, Hurricane Katrina didn't just expose existing racial and class-based cleavages within New Orleans or broader society; at the level of micro-interactions it became an experience in applied racial violence, where empowered first responders could threaten, intimidate, hold hostage, and even murder stranded civilians, as seen with the Danzinger Bridge incident. Offenses such as stealing food, or even a car, became meritorious enough to constitute the threat of death under Katrina's extraordinary circumstances. This reality, reported from a multitude of women with a myriad of experiences, is simply unacceptable.

Reflecting on the media images of New Orleans during the aftermath, the image of two young, Black men with a shopping bag of what looked like belts, being held at gunpoint, comes to mind. While looting certainly transpired, limited attention has been given to what was stolen, and why. A bag of belts may hold up oversized clothing for families whose own clothing was drenched with floodwater and other toxins. They may be used to slow blood flow to a leg or arm with a deep cut. In normal circumstances, stealing is unnecessary, but would you really stand by waiting for days, watching your children starve and dehydrate, with a grocery store full of food just across the street? In a crisis, people make compromises to survive. These survival compromises are the decisions we make when faced with no better option in extreme circumstances: a woman breaking into a bar to get fruit juice for a child, a husband accelerating his car to force pedestrians from the road to protect his wife from being carjacked, or a woman looking the other way as her son steals a car to find a store with insulin to keep her alive. A survival compromise is a choice made out of desperate need, not vindictiveness. It is not something one takes pleasure or pride in doing. It is simply the choice one has to make when the only other alternative is death. For many in the flooded city, survival compromises are all that got them through: looting for food, water, clothing, blankets, and medicine to stay alive.

For years now, people have asked me about the looting, offended at the post-disaster disrespect of private property. This is a form of demonizing survivors. Yet, very rarely does the conversation shift to demand an answer to what seems a more obvious and more important set of questions to pose: why weren't water, food, clothing, and medical supplies in place *before* the storm even hit? Why weren't there food trucks for hot meals waiting and ready to go in Baton Rouge, Lafayette, or Alexandria, ready to descend as soon as the roads were clear? Why weren't MREs ready to go in a warehouse with helicopters stationed across the state, out of the strike zone yet close enough that supplies could be lifted to the city in under two hours? Why wasn't there a predetermined rendezvous point in the city arranged for the day after landfall where stranded survivors could go and have food, medicine, or cots waiting? Why weren't we better prepared *as a nation*?

Conclusion

In the midst of catastrophic disaster, three major patterns of behavior emerged to frame the experience of low-income Black women. First, we see that traditional gender roles are maintained and continued, regardless of the devastation happening all around. Gendered behaviors of mothering, through care work enacted by cooking in the absence of power, or protecting children from seeing dead bodies, or relieving suffering using whatever resources were available all reflect how gender expectations permeate our lives, even when the world falls apart around us. For the men who stole cars to find insulin, or created refrigerator boats to flag down help, gender also increased their risk as the expectations to be providers played out in dangerous ways. In this regard, disasters in motion occur on gendered landscapes.

Second, low-income communities do have social capital and network ties that function as a resource for help. Kin networks provided resources—for the women in this chapter, network ties both receive and give help, as the experiences of women like Vanessa and Sheila demonstrate. Despite a disciplinary legacy of viewing low-income communities as dysfunctional,[24] their strengths also need to be acknowledged. As more affluent responders charged victims for rides to safety or simply passed them by altogether, it was the residents of some of New Orleans' poorest communities who were helping each other to survive. In the face of death, network-based survival strategies continued to be a mechanism that poor women, their families, and neighbors engaged to survive.

Third, while race, class, and gender all mattered in the experience, race was arguably the most powerful status in shaping the experience of the stranded, especially in regard to the formal response by emergency institutions. The police, National Guard, and other rescue groups formalized racism, classism, and sexism into their operating procedures, as evidenced by the treatment of survivors. Racism explains the actions of holding victims hostage at evacuation gathering points, physically beating them, threatening them, and aiming guns at unarmed civilians. This pervasive racial hatred, which boiled over during Katrina's aftermath, transformed a traumatic situation into a military maneuver, where victims became combatants—the enemy in an ongoing racial war.

Finally, it is almost as if the disaster planning for the city assumed such catastrophe *a priori* that there would be no need to manage any survivors at all. Yet, as we mitigate disasters, we not only create the capacity for catastrophe,[25] we also create the potential for partial or incomplete disaster. For example, Algiers Point had limited damage overall. With a response plan in place, food and other services could have been established there by Tuesday, if people knew where to go. Eventually such services did arise precisely due to the lack of flooding, but with forecasting becoming ever more accurate, why didn't the federal government gather supplies beforehand, storing them at the perimeter of the strike zone for quick infusion into affected communities in any state along the Gulf Coast? Are we so inept in our disaster preparations that we cannot comprehend that a Category 5 storm will require food, water, and medicine, wherever it lands? Are we so fragmented as states we cannot acknowledge that the federal government needs to step in quickly at a certain threshold of destruction? Rather than blame the victims, perhaps we need a deeper examination of the government's role in this catastrophe. After all, Hurricane Katrina's approach was no surprise for FEMA; there was ample warning of the storm's size, strength, and potential for destruction.

---

[1] Drabek 1986; Tierney, Bevc, and Kuligowski 2006: 58.
[2] Freudenberg 1993, 1997; Picou, Marshall, and Gill 2004.
[3] Fothergill 1998, 1999; Enarson 2012.
[4] HUD 2006: 23. Later damage estimates by the City of New Orleans were reported on the local evening news to equal 80% of the city's housing stock.
[5] It is unclear from the interview where her husband was at the time.

[6] Tierney, Bevc, and Kuligowski 2006: 58; Rodríguez, Trainor, and Quarantelli 2006.

[7] In New York City, Robert Moses purposely designed public housing to be separate from the surrounding communities by refusing to continue cross streets from the urban grid. This design component, known as "superblocks" was commonplace in public housing projects across the nation. Only in designs since about 1990 do you see the reinstatement of cross streets. However, in the Desire/Abundance Square community in New Orleans, prior to Katrina, the cross streets that would reintegrate the redeveloped community to the full urban grid were blocked off by concrete construction barriers, keeping the newly built housing isolated to form an "island" of quality housing within a section of town that was deeply impoverished.

[8] The pumping stations were commonly known to be able to handle two inches of rain for the first hour, then just one inch afterwards, meaning that a stationary storm with several inches of rain per hour would cause water to collect and flood low-lying parts of the city. In 1998 as an undergraduate student, I remember a rainy day in which five hours of continual heavy rain caused the entire Tulane campus to collect at least 4 inches of water, and Willow Street to gather approximately 2-3 feet, creating a "river" on which students were floating with their inflatable furniture. By comparison, the majority of the city received somewhere between 4 feet and 10 feet, with one Interstate underpass collecting so much water a school bus was stranded in the dip, with water covering its windows.

[9] During rain events, including hurricanes, it is commonplace to park your car in places that are elevated, including the neutral ground (the wide dirt medians on all major boulevards), neighbors' driveways, or even on sidewalks. Also residents tend to learn where a street's high spots are and utilize them effectively.

[10] Enarson 2012; Enarson and Morrow 1998; Fothergill 1998; Wilbon Hartman 2007/2011; Idakula 2007/2011.

[11] Fothergill and Peek 2012.

[12] Hurricane Katrina hit on August 29, 2005.

[13] West and Zimmerman 1987; Fothergill 1996.

[14] Stack 1974.

[15] Tierney, Bevc, and Kuligowski 2006; Freudenberg 1997.

[16] Massey and Denton 1993; Wilson 1987, 1996; Murray 1984; Dreier, Mollenkopf, and Swanstrom 2001.

[17] Collins 1998.

[18] Fothergill 1999; Enarson 2012; Enarson and Morrow 1998.

[19] The notable exception was the Coast Guard, which was quick to bring in helicopters and rescue baskets, putting the preservation of life above the importance of a military chain of command and absolute civilian control.

[20] Tierney, Bevc, and Kuligowski 2006.

[21] Idakula 2007/2011.

[22] See also Idakula 2007/2011; Stohlman 2007/2011.

[23] Wilbon Hartman 2007/2011.

[24] Wilson 1987; Massey and Denton 1993; Murray 1984; Dreier, Mollenkopf, and Swanstrom 2001; Rainwater and Yancey 1967.

[25] Freudenberg 1993.

6

Shelters of Last Resort

In New Orleans, there was a commonly understood tradition surrounding hurricanes and the Superdome. While city officials would make repeated public announcements that the Superdome would not be opened as a shelter during the storm, in truth, for Hurricanes George, Ivan, and Katrina, the building was used for exactly that purpose. Titled "the shelter of last resort," this language was meant to discourage would-be evacuees from staying in town, while accommodating residents who could not afford to evacuate or had medical needs that made evacuation more dangerous than riding out the storm. Residents were required to bring their own food, blankets, clothes, and water, but aside from that, they had the ability to be sheltered in a spacious, sturdy concrete building—one that looked safe and secure. In the decade preceding Hurricane Katrina, everyone always expected the "Dome" to be opened at the last minute and for the larger storms, and it always was.

Perhaps one of the unfortunate consequences of this "last resort" strategy is that the city never took advantage of the potential to use the building as a staging area for immediate disaster assessment and recovery activities, whether in New Orleans, or across the broader Gulf Coast. With its multi-level design, proximity to the interstate and City Hall, and national recognition as a location for NFL football, it has the potential to be an emergency command center for the city and region. As evidenced during the storm's aftermath, the building largely escaped serious flooding and provided people with high ground—an asset that is rare in a city below sea level. But, at that time, there was no plan in place to bring in Red Cross volunteers, nor to stockpile food, water, or medicine there; no anticipation of people's needs in case the power went out and their own supplies were spoiled, and certainly no expectation of the massive flooding that would besiege the city.

In fact, most of the hurricane preparation work at that time focused on contraflow plans—the reversal of the highways so all lanes leave the city to hasten people's departures in their own vehicles. In response to Hurricane Ivan, which produced gridlock on the interstate when the contraflow stopped at Baton Rouge, the plan in place for Katrina was a vast improvement, and in fact, a success for those who left on their own. However, this singular focus on traffic flow systematically failed to acknowledge and accommodate an essential constituency—the 28% of households who did not own a car[1] and within this population, the subset who were kin outsiders—for without a car, even the best evacuation traffic pattern is of little assistance.

This chapter describes the Louisiana Superdome and the New Orleans Convention Center through the eyes of survivors to analyze their personal, lived experiences.[2] While the Convention Center was never an officially sanctioned shelter of last resort, it became one as thousands of people fled the rising floodwaters that engulfed their homes, seeking help from local, state, and national governments who were slow to respond. To their surprise, in those terrible days following the storm little help came. No food, no water, no hope. Instead, as the stranded waited in the hot sun outside the Convention Center, and others sought to protect themselves and their children while locked inside the Superdome, it took five days for a federal response to begin.[3] Five days of suffering. Five days of Americans dying on the streets. Five days for the rest of the world to watch how little the United States of America values its own citizenry.

The Louisiana Superdome

One of the lingering questions in the years following the storm was: "What really happened in the Superdome?" In the media, there were accounts of murders, violence, rapes, suicides, and other atrocities, at the same time as a simultaneous retraction of these events occurred.[4] There were pictures of thousands of evacuees waiting for help and video footage of snipers shooting at them as they tried to evacuate onto buses and rescue boats. There were images of SWAT teams roaming through devastated neighborhoods seeking those breaking curfew and the law. There were neighborhood watch groups to protect each others' property against gangs of looters who threatened to destroy it. And there were guns—on the National Guardsmen as they arrived, in the hands of police, in the snipers' hands—creating a military response to a humanitarian effort. Amid this media bonanza of images, the truth is difficult to discern.[5] While the following account cannot be comprehensive due to sample size, it begins to peel back the layers of media hype, to reveal the deep traumas that women did confirm during their time stranded within the shelters of last resort.

A Community Center

How families came to choose the Superdome as an evacuation shelter depends on circumstance. At the time, the Superdome seemed a safe place to weather the storm, and reasonably speaking, it was. With its concrete structure and multistory design, it has the solid feel of a medieval fortress, though modern. When you enter the building at the main level, you need to take escalators to get to the corridors surrounding the football field, which are 4-5 stories high. These corridors are completely interior, with no windows directly in them. In better times, their primary purpose is as an extensive concession stand, and they are lined with food stations and bathrooms, as is common in most stadium designs. Moving toward the center of the building, you have the football field, with stadium seating running from the edge of the football field up to about 15 feet from the start of the domed ceiling. So high are those uppermost seats, that even if every single levee in New Orleans broke, one would never drown at that height.

From there, the seats swoop down to the level of the field, with a band of box seats at the mid-level, just above the scoreboards. Those boxes are small suites, with private bathrooms, couches, televisions, and their own separate seating areas, with the suite itself all glassed in with perfect views of the field. They, too, are completely interior. The football field itself is a vast, open expanse—a place where Mardi Gras parade floats enter and wrap around the field as krewes throw the last of their beads to ball attendees who are dressed to excess and clamoring for those long strings of molded plastic, which are magically transformed into symbols of status during the Mardi Gras season.

Moving back outward, on the levels closer to the entry floor exist conference halls—large staging rooms where anxious and happy graduates often gather in anticipation of receiving their diplomas at the numerous convocations held there. From local colleges to high schools, the Superdome not only offers football, but stands as a community center for celebrating the academic accomplishments of students in the New Orleans community. These outer rooms are often large in size— some are over 1000 square feet. They, too, are elevated and are at least two stories high.

On the outside of the building, at the "main" entry level, which is really about three stories tall, there is an extensive patio that surrounds the entire building. Thousands gather there for community events, just as thousands gathered there to wait for help in the storm's aftermath. Below this level lies extensive parking, which wraps around the entire building, forming the outer foundation for the patio. So vast and repetitive is this area that if one forgets their parking zone, it can easily take an hour just to find the car.

Within this behemoth of concrete lies not only a shelter of last resort, but a community center for greater New Orleans: a place for football, as well as graduations, concerts, Mardi Gras balls, and community celebrations. More than a beautiful arch on the city's skyline, the Superdome represented community and a place to be safe from the storm. It is reasonable that one would evacuate to the Superdome, when that place represents pleasure, fun, happiness, and good memories. The Superdome was a part of the city's sense of soul.

A Shelter in the Storm

Of the women who shared their experiences with me, only two—Alika and Barbara Jean—survived the wind storm portion of the hurricane by seeking shelter at the Superdome, out of 21 who had been stranded. A third, who politely declined the interview, was audibly shaken at the mere memory of her experiences.[6] A fourth, Iris, was transferred to the Superdome from a bridge to wait for evacuation buses, spending just a day at the site, and Ruth, a fifth, spent two days waiting with her family. During these women's interviews, the tone of their voices left me feeling absolutely confident that their descriptions of experiences were completely true, to their core. This section is prefaced because these are the accounts that receive the most scrutiny at conferences and during conversations, are most frequently rejected outright, and most deeply force our society to critically question why and how the events that unfolded were permitted to occur. These rejections are a form of power, intended to delegitimize the voices of victims and blame them for structural failures caused by the broader society. As such, I stand by my respondents and argue that the accounts are as true as memory allows. If anything, the accounts minimize the gravity of those days locked in the Superdome as a way to deal with the overwhelming horrors they observed and endured.

One common factor explains the choice to stay at the Superdome during the storm for Alika and Barbara Jean: family. Keeping the family together and close explains the caravan of kin, the choice to stay in the "safest" location, and the choice to evacuate to the Superdome. Families chose to stay together, to take risks together, and to evacuate or stay together. For Alika, the Superdome was a compromise she made with her mother who wanted to leave the city altogether, when she did not. Yet, despite their disagreement, keeping the family together became the deciding factor on where to go. Barbara Jean, whose husband worked for the Levee Board and was required to stay in New Orleans, also chose to keep her family close together, staying in the Superdome. Because family and kin obligation can both encourage and discourage evacuation, we need to acknowledge the power of family unity among low-income populations for future disasters because people refused to separate from their kin, even when it would have been safer to do so. This is commonly understood in the existing literature,[7] but among poor families, it is important to acknowledge that family ties are far more important than wealth in predicting disaster behavior.

Staying at the Superdome for the storm was initially a lot like camping. Residents had to wait in line to enter, submit to a bag search, and bring their own supplies. These supplies included food, water, medicines, blankets, clothes, diapers, formula, and other resources to pass the time, like coloring books for kids, or playing cards for adults. For Alika, this meant bringing food for herself, her mother, and her daughter: "We had a little Vienna sausage, crackers, water—we didn't think we'd be there that long. [...] We had enough to last two days, but that's about it. Chips, pickles, sandwiches."

For those souls sheltered there, the building that seemed so safe at first quickly became dangerous, as Katrina's winds tore past with such ferocity that after several hours the roof began to cave in. Alika described how the Superdome ceiling, and her sense of safety, disintegrated before her eyes:

> When we first got in there, we get in a line, then we had to get in a seat. After we sat down, we were just talking and waiting until the storm pass over. We wait for like an hour or two, Katrina was coming, and she start tearing the roof off the Superdome. She took a panel, then she like peel off the rest, like five or six panels off the roof.
>
> Everyone just started running. It was like a stampede. Then we heard like a loud boom, and maybe like another boom and we heard the boom.

The "boom" was the sound of the centermost part of the ceiling collapsing on the football field below. In that instant, the sense of safety that this community center had exuded, this place for graduations and good times, this reliable shelter from the storm, was replaced with a deep sense of terror that the rest of the roof might also collapse, killing everyone underneath it.

Barbara Jean, too, shared the sense of fear, urgency, and crisis that overtook the Superdome as the ceiling crumbled overhead:

> I get upset every time I talk about it. I'm gonna tell you what I went through. After we got into the Dome, and were there a while, the wind started. We was sitting in the aisle, looking at the hole where the ceiling fell in. Big pieces ripped through, so we all moved up the ramps, into the bleachers. The water started coming up on the floor. We got through that. Then the lights went out.

With the wind peeling off pieces of the roof, these images of the damage inside the Superdome were being broadcast on television, for evacuees elsewhere to see, until broadcast transmissions went out. Yet, within the Superdome itself, information was largely absent and controlled, escalating feelings of fear, uncertainty, and terror. Powerless, with the wind howling and the ceiling collapsing before them, Barbara Jean, Alika, and countless other families were trapped in the dark, desperate to survive.

From Fear to Violence

In the days between the collapse of the Superdome ceiling on Monday and the evacuation of thousands of New Orleanians who stayed in the Superdome or were evacuated to it after their own neighborhoods flooded, the descriptions of the events inside become contested. What is clear is that in addition to the helping behaviors that tend to accompany major disasters, known as the emergence of the therapeutic community,[8] violations of social norms also occurred within the Superdome. These violations were enabled by the spatial entrapment of the stranded, the increasing population as more evacuees arrived, the rising sense of despair and uncertainty caused by the lack of information, and the militarized nature of the rescue efforts.[9]

28-year-old Alika, sheltering the storm with her mother and her daughter, described these norm violations, and how they affected her family's Superdome experience:

> Alika: It was hectic, people's killing themselves, raping little children. I had to hold on to my daughter—I didn't let go of her. They keep telling us we'd be rescued, that people's coming. I knew we gotta get out of New Orleans. After the last day we gave up on it, got up, and got out of New Orleans. I will never go to the Superdome no more in New Orleans. It's cursed.

Jessica: So you kept your daughter close by?

Alika: I keep my daughter stuck to me like glue. "The Guard" or whatever you call them army people,[10] they didn't do nothing, they wasn't trying to do nothing. We survived on our own. No one can tell us we ain't survivors, we survived six days without eating, and there was hardly any water that they gave us.

Jessica: Who came first after the storm, was it the police or the National Guard?

Alika: I never saw the police, not before, not since. We just saw like 100 army men surround the whole Superdome.

Jessica: Were you allowed to leave?

Alika: No. They would not let us leave the Superdome—in fact, they putting more people on the Superdome to get raped and killed. People was coming in the Superdome instead of out the Superdome.

Jessica (gingerly): If you don't mind, could you tell me a bit more about the violence?

Alika: The violence? I'll tell you; it ain't no secret. It was very bad. They had drugs, people selling food to people. All types of stuff. A lot of stuff going on, and the guards weren't doing nothing but looking; they had their guns pointed to keep you in. [...] They attacking, raping, killing, raping the childrens. People jumping off the Superdome, killing themselves; killing the guards. I'm comfortable talking about it.

Effectively imprisoned inside without food for six days, the context for interpretation of the events originates from this reality. Unable to meet their own subsistence needs, residents who evacuated to the Superdome in advance had brought supplies for a day or two as directed, but no more. Assuming Hurricane Katrina would pass over in a couple of hours, allowing them to return home to survey the damage by Tuesday morning, few were prepared with enough supplies to last a week. For those transferred there from flooded homes, they had nothing at all. In response, people began violating social norms to stay alive.

Selling food to others, as opposed to simply sharing it, reflects both the ingrained nature of capitalism, as well as the awareness that after the Superdome, one would need money to survive wherever one lands. In the absence of the state or federal government to provide immediate aid in the form of food, evacuees had to consider the reality that all they had available to get by in another city was whatever they had on their person. Unable to leave or return home, selling food became a form of microentrepreneurship, however distasteful it may have seemed. As for drug sales, the desire to abuse reflects people's need to cope with the disaster and the severity of the damages in a context in which professional trauma care was unavailable. New evacuees arrived, many of whom had watched family members drown, starve, or face other untimely deaths. Drug sale and use also reflects the reality that those with an addiction may have faced withdrawal symptoms in a place where no options for managing withdrawal were available. In terms of understanding the violence, this discussion is reserved for below, as Barbara Jean's detailed account provides a fuller context for interpretation.

Returning to Alika and her kin, these acts of violence threatened her family most directly as she attempted to board an evacuation bus with her daughter and mother after five or six days. When I asked if she had been separated from her family, since families of survivors were often put onto different buses and planes as part of the federal evacuation strategy,[11] she replied:

> We ain't got separated—they would have had to cut my arm off. Some man on top of the roof, he was trying to get through to where the buses were going out, he shooting, and they told us to duck, and so the National Guard shot him in the head. He fell in the water. He was shooting, and he fell down in the water. There was shooting all over the place. We had to get down, 'cause snipers set on trying to shoot us before we got on the bus. Then, they said it was women and children first, but them men didn't care. They was running over the women and children. It was more the men, them men took over. More the men than the women. The men really took over.

Exposed to violence, terror, danger, and desperate uncertainty; amid suicides, rapes, homicides, and sniper-fire; held in captivity at the Superdome for nearly 6 days, with no protection from the "Guard," Alika and her family survived. Once she was finally evacuated, Alika's family was transferred to the Houston Astrodome, where she spent two weeks until she was transferred again to the Reliant Center for another week. From there, Alika finally found a temporary home of her own.

Barbara Jean also confirmed the violence of those following days— the suicides, rapes, and murders, as well as an act of retribution against the rape of a 15-year-old girl. Her quick, minimalist description reflects the severity of the traumatic events:

> There was rapes and killings. A baby was raped, and it was right down from us—the baby was raped, and killed, and then set on a pile of trash. A fifteen-year-old girl was raped, the man was beaten bloody. The man had his throat split, from ear to ear. A man jumped off the balcony, but then he lived. There was one whole family who got killed. There was a six-year-old boy who got raped, and beaten. One of the guards got shot. It was horrible in there. You had to be in there to see it. They had gangs, and homosexuals, and drugs. What you thought went on, it did. It was like animals in there. A lot of people had been sick and were elderly. There was nothing you could do. You couldn't get out. It was hot, and they had the care rations. And water. You know.

So devastating was the trauma for Barbara Jean that her description lacks all sense of time, identifying a string of one horror after another, including the rape and murder of a baby, which she personally observed. Articulating her sense of shock and loss, she openly expressed her inability to comprehend what she witnessed at the Superdome: "You just don't understand. I don't know how people can treat each other like that in a time of need. How can they rape? How can they be killing, beating each other?"

Perhaps the one mercy for Barbara Jean was being there with her family, who shared the responsibility of protecting each other and the children. Like other families who used the caravan of kin to enable evacuation from the city, Barbara Jean's internal evacuation engaged the caravan concept within the Superdome in order to survive. Among her caravan were "my two sisters, my niece, her three children, my son, his wife, his three children, and two more who stay with me," for a total of six adults and eight children. While everyone was "alive" and "came through it," Barbara Jean's experience was simultaneously permeated with fear for her husband, who was working for the Levee Board, and her mother, who was in a local hospital. In the end, both were safe, located by the Red Cross after Barbara Jean and her family were taken to a shelter in Texas.

Examining the violence, there are several dimensions to consider. First, the idea that people would behave violently in a time of need seems to contradict common post-disaster helping behavior, specifically the rescue and inventory actions.[12] According to Drabek, after a disaster impact, people rally to:

> ... help those around them that may require it. They don't wait for officials to get there and tell them to which hospital they should take their injured child. They will go to the nearest hospital or source of

medical assistance they know about, often the one they might have selected in a non-emergency situation.[13]

While this helping behavior was happening in the broader New Orleans community, why was there such violence in the Superdome? And was that violence always malicious?

Among rape victims, the common identifier was that they were children. As the most vulnerable, children were harmed in all the cases of rape reported here. Yet, these rapes did not always happen without consequence to the assailant. As Barbara Jean acknowledged, the rapist who attacked the 15-year-old girl was "beaten bloody. The man had his throat split, from ear to ear." While a horrifying image, the reality is that others within the Superdome took immediate, decisive action to punish this man for his crime, reflecting a grotesque form of social control to stop further violence against children. While murdering another human to punish rape is questionable, it does reflect the upholding of one mainstream social norm, albeit while breaking another, suggesting a maintained commitment to the idea that children are innocents who should be protected. Barbara Jean also identified a family who was killed and a guard who was shot. As Ruth and Iris describe below, sniper fire may be the cause of these deaths, though there is no way to know definitively.

For Ruth and Iris, each arrived at the Superdome with kin after their homes and the city began to flood. While several days had passed since the storm, the danger had not. Both women confirm the violence as they waited for evacuation buses to take them elsewhere. Ruth, at 76-years-old, was also threatened by the sniper-fire. Evacuated from her damaged apartment where she weathered the storm with several family members, she described the disorder at the Dome:

> Ruth: It was a mess. People was standing around like fools. People shooting up in the air, I don't know if it were the police on horseback, but people shooting, people fainting in line, laying on the ground, passed out. I ain't saw no killing or nothing.
>
> Jessica: Did you feel safe there?
>
> Ruth: Not really, uh-uh. The people had no fear, no consideration for senior citizens. They didn't care.
>
> Jessica: How was it for your daughter and grandson at the Dome?

Ruth: They were there in line with me. Without them, I don't know if I would have made it. They have to get me up and carry me some when I was walking in the water.

Jessica: [...] Were you at the Superdome a long time?

Ruth: Yeah, we left that morning and got there to get on the bus around about 7 or 8 o'clock, or something like that.

Jessica: Did they have any food or supplies for you on the bus?

Ruth: They had nothing on there.

Iris, an 82-year-old who spent two days and nights at the Superdome, also describes a dangerous scene were rape and violence made staying there frightful, especially given the suspected perpetrators:

We were cut up so bad in the Superdome. We was so disgusted with how they was fighting, and two little girls got raped. Some men caught the dudes and beat them half to death. The authorities raped them girls, and we wanted to get out of there. We went outside where the buses was transporting people to other states. We missed the bus. It was two hours for the next.

The fear generated by authority figures committing rape against "little girls" layered yet another dimension of complexity to the situation. Initially, the accusation may seem baseless; however, the malicious, condescending, dehumanizing treatment of survivors[14] suggests its absolute possibility, as will be discussed at the chapter's end.

While thousands of residents were appropriately behaved and focused on getting out of the city to safety, the few who violated social norms—and the media reaction to those events—set the narrative frame used to justify the militarization of the space and the city as federal assistance finally arrived.[15] The consequences of this media frame included the extreme incivility of first responders toward the victims they were sent to rescue. In many cases, such incivility made the behavior of the rescuers more dangerous and harmful than that of other survivors or the storm itself had been.

The New Orleans Convention Center

The New Orleans Convention Center was the second major evacuation site established as floodwaters overtook vast sections of the city.

Located adjacent to the Mississippi River in downtown New Orleans, it is a long building, extending about four blocks between the Riverwalk shopping area and the Crescent City Connection bridge. It is surrounded by hotels, intermittent eateries, and sculptural artwork. Like the Superdome, in typical times, the Convention Center is a place for celebrations such as Mardi Gras balls, and retained that function after the storm, hosting Bacchus and other balls in January of 2006. During the remainder of the year, the center serves as an intellectual and commercial rendezvous destination for numerous professional associations and conferences, the attendees of which often embrace the location as a chance to visit the city for both work and pleasure.

From Tuesday, August 30, 2005 until the middle of the next week, the Convention Center assumed a new role as residents sought its high ground to protect them from the floodwaters that had consumed their homes and threatened their lives: it became a gathering ground for residents awaiting help. Yet, unlike the Superdome with its security forces and policemen preventing departure from the building, the Convention Center was more fluid in its borders, allowing residents the ability to move around to seek food and other goods in the surrounding neighborhood. As thousands congregated beginning on Tuesday, they waited until Friday before the first National Guard troops entered the city, and another full day before food and water followed. Five days—it was five days before food and water finally arrived.

Waiting

As hundreds, then thousands gathered at the Convention Center, the humanitarian need for displaced residents became undeniable. Without food, water, clean clothing, medicines, or much else, residents did the best they could to pass the time, waiting for help to arrive. Flooded out of their homes, with no money, identification, or spare clothing, days passed before any help arrived at all. With temperatures in the high 80s, families baked in the hot sun, waiting.[16] As the media descended upon the city, most Americans were stunned by the level of desperation they viewed endlessly on their television sets—masses of people waiting, crying out, asking for food, water, and help, begging and pleading to be evacuated. Dead bodies were laid out on the street, babies cried from hunger, elderly people laid down on the ground, sickly. For Vanessa, Jada, Lillian, and Ann, the images barely did their lived experiences justice.

For Vanessa, who arrived there with her kin and neighbors after the traumatic, rapid flooding of their homes, the Convention Center was far from the safe shelter she expected:

> Yes, we went to the Convention Center on Wednesday morning. We had no food, no water. They had so many people out there, maybe a thousand, two, three thousand. Some was laying down in the Convention Center, 'cause it was hot. And it was the most horrible smell you'd ever smell, and elderly was dying, folks having hallucinations, children gone missing.

As more and more people gathered at the Convention Center, the severity of the conditions intensified and families began to run out of resources.

Just to get to the Convention Center, 31-year-old Jada and her children—two sons of six and eleven years old, and two daughters aged three and fourteen at the time of our interview—had to walk miles across the city, over several bridges, and through floodwaters. Once they arrived, the building was already in a state of disrepair:

> First, when we got there inside, it was crazy. Then the lights went out, the air conditioning went out. The bathrooms was smelling, and it was crazy, crazy wild. We had to move outside. One part was the air. At least everything was open on the outside. Only one side of the Convention Center had that smell. The smell was in certain areas, and then there was the heat.

The "smell" Jada refers to is the pungent combination of urine, feces, sweat, and the decomposing bodies of those who died awaiting help or who were victims of violence.

From Tuesday to Saturday, Jada and her children waited there until finally being taken to the airport and sent onward to Arkansas. In this horrific environment for days on end, the strain affected Jada emotionally:

> I think I was at my breaking point. I made myself walk, but I was so drained. I made myself walk even though I was ready to lay down. I could have been dehydrated. There was so much heat and no water, and it was real hectic. You could see it in the kids, one night they sleeping in a bed, then the next night they sleeping on the street. It was a hurting thing also, because they wasn't used to that.

Stopping By

Without rigid entry points, the spatial layout of the Convention Center allowed people the freedom to "stop by" to gather information or check if help arrived without restricting them to the area. Given the deplorable conditions, both Lillian and Ann used a stopping by approach as they awaited evacuation from the city. For Lillian, an elderly woman who arrived with her daughter, grandchildren, and son, waiting at the Convention Center for help was too chaotic and dangerous. After a day, Lillian and her kin continued to her brother's apartment, where they stayed as unwelcomed guests until their evacuation nearly a week later, engaging the strength of even the weakest kin network tie.[17]

Utilizing a similar scouting tactic, Ann, a middle aged-woman living in the nearby River Garden community, used her undamaged home as a base from which she ventured out to seek food, water, information, and to check on the homes of other family members who evacuated, such as her mother. Describing the Convention Center, she said: "It's something you can hear about, but to experience it.... I left and came back home, I came back home."

Without power, Ann and her grandson ate what food they could, sharing it with the neighbors before it spoiled, again reflecting how patterns of network-based assistance in the low-income community[18] translate into the post-disaster helping ethic.[19] Yet, after a few days, Ann had run out of water, and went with a friend to find some so her grandson would remain hydrated:

> I met a guy that I knew, we rolled around and tried to find something that may have been open. There was a grocery store, we call it 2000 Magazine, but they didn't have the door open. You went up and they got you something, and they wouldn't charge you.

In the absence of formal assistance, this local business shared the resources they had, working to preserve the community in a small, yet significant way. Rather than mark their store with a notice that "looters will be shot," they shared their goods free of charge as an act of caring, kindness, and survival, engaging in the helping behaviors that are known to be common following disasters.[20]

From there, Ann and her friend continued toward the Convention Center to look for her daughter, stopping along the way:

> We went into a bar, and that's where we got the juices, and milks and orange juice. Then I rolled out by the Convention Center looking for my daughter. And the little babies, they had no water, no milk, so we

was just giving it to them, wasn't selling it or anything. I had to do something for the babies, they was newborn babies, and I felt bad for the elderly. [...] I had a shopping cart I took to the Convention Center, and you can't imagine the stench of it. They had the doors cracked open, then the second time we went by they was fighting in the dark. You could hear them in the dark, but can't see them. It was very frightening.

While a small act, even Ann felt compelled to share upon seeing the need of those waiting. By seeking the resources needed to care for her grandson and help others care for their own kin, Ann was enacting her agency as a survivor, and behaving in a pro-social way to help those in her own community.[21] While technically this behavior could be considered looting, if a white woman was helping babies by giving them milk and juice, would the actions be viewed in a similar way?

How looting was portrayed largely reflects pre-existing social biases, particularly against African Americans in general, and Black men in particular. As Tierney, Bevc, and Kuligowski explain:

... reports characterized post-Katrina looting as very widespread, wanton, irrational, and accompanied by violence—in short, as resembling media characterizations of riot behavior. Moreover, the media confined their reporting to the putative lawless behavior of certain categories and types of people—specifically young Black males—to the exclusion of other behaviors in which these disaster victims may have engaged during the disaster, producing a profile of looters and looting groups that overlooked whatever prosocial, altruistic behaviors such groups may have undertaken.[22]

By casting looting as riot behavior, rather than as disaster survivors in such desperate need of food and clothing that they were forced to steal because their government failed to provide them food and water for five full days, the media redefined Katrina's aftermath from a humanitarian crisis to a militaristic one by shifting the need for protection away from people and onto private property. As citizens were trying to do what they could to keep family members alive and even help others along the way, these efforts challenge unidimensional interpretations of the looting as riot behavior. Most importantly, such a focus on looting as lawlessness deflects responsibility away from the government failure to respond.

Waves of Panic

As survivors of the flood continued to arrive at the Convention Center, the trauma of the hurricane and its aftermath took a toll on the stranded. In just a moment's time, complete confusion would take over as rumors of approaching waters sent nervous survivors into a wave of panic. Lillian, who was bound to a wheelchair, described how rapidly the feeling of panic spread: "It was pure chaos. Someone came in yelling that the water was rising, and people panicked." In an instant, hundreds went running, causing a stampede that knocked Lillian to the ground.

Vanessa also experienced a similar stampede. After four days without food for herself or her kin, feelings of desperation and fear permeated the Convention Center. The fear of rapid, massive flooding had everyone on edge:

> I had a wheelchair and I fell out of the chair, because they stampeded, and everybody was running, and they knocked me out of the chair. I had a bruise on my leg for a month or so. [...] Someone said something about the water, that it was coming and everybody panicked, and was running, but we didn't know what we was running from. [...] My son broke his toe. There were little babies out there that didn't have no water, and it was hot, and we were hungry until the army came and gave out rations. And there was a lot of looting and stuff. They went to a local hotel, to get blankets and pillows. It was so horrible in there, we slept under the bridge. There was no place to use the bathroom.
>
> Jessica: How long were you there?
>
> Vanessa: Wednesday morning to Saturday evening.

While Vanessa described looting, the intent of the actions was to provide pillows and blankets to survivors to keep them comfortable as they waited for help. This is hardly equivalent to the media representation of looting as the riot behavior described above.

Yet, in the face of helping behavior, there was also violence. Adding to the sense of crisis, Lillian mentioned that someone was shot at the Convention Center during her time there. Expanding on this account, Vanessa provided further detail:

> One guy, he was killed by the cops, and the body just laid there until somebody put a blanket over him. You had kids getting raped—it was just chaos until the army came and put some structure in the thing. They gave us food, but you had to walk so far to get the food. It was really, really horrible. [...] The food, well, the food was at the

beginning of the Convention Center. We was by section H, so we had to walk down to get the food. You'd pass the dead bodies. This one guy laid in the middle of the street, and nobody picked him up. Somebody was in the median, with a yellow blanket on them. There was maggots and flies all over the bodies, and people on the side of the Convention Center, they were dead. [...] Oh Lord, have mercy—it was scary. They say they had rapes, and there was bodies all over. It was heartless, and so stinky. We had no food, no water.

Death, rape, shooting, desperation—here we see a more complex view of what being stranded at a shelter of last resort meant. Still, only one murder is identified, and the perpetrators were the police—those who were supposed to help, not harm. As others perished from heat stroke, exhaustion, dehydration, and starvation, the biggest threat from other survivors seemed to be the rape of children. Rape is a crime of power, with children being the most vulnerable to this crime among those stranded and waiting for help.

As residents tried to survive the moment, the singular purpose these women shared was to get out of the city with their kin—alive. For Gloria, an evacuee whose friend was at the Convention Center during the wait for help, coping with what happened was a challenge:

It was mentally distressing. To see the mood, seeing the Superdome and thinking of my friends and family in the Dome. My friend was shot in the Convention Center while he was looking for his wife. He got shot in the head. I'm kinda, I'm kinda trying to get it together. This guy was like my brother. We was like babies coming up together.

Undoubtedly, this experience of facing the violence, fear, loss, panic, and danger was incredibly devastating for Gloria, Jada, Vanessa, Lillian, Ann, and anyone with loved ones stranded there. As Jada explains, getting by was a matter of keeping herself moving, in large part for her children's sake; "We were there four days and four nights before we got food and water. You had to live on your own. There were no police. You had to get food and stuff where you could."

Dehumanizing Survivors

For five days, survivors of the flooding waited for "help" to arrive. Survivors were in need of water, food, medicine, and shelter. It was shocking to watch the media images of civilians being treated as if they were hostages in a war zone when first responders finally entered New Orleans. While the assistance was needed, it came at a significant price—being treated badly, as if the victims of the storm had caused its destruction:

> Jada: Then the policemen came. The National Guard came and treated us like we was bad, bad people, pointing at us with guns. After that, they gave us food, and we spent one last night and got on the bus.

Why would survivors at the Convention Center be held at gunpoint? Why would people who just watched their family members drown, who barely escaped themselves, who have been living on minimal food and water be treated like criminals rather than as American citizens in need? Why would they be seen as dangerous, so much so as to warrant guns pointed directly at them? They were not the snipers on the rooftops.

The unacceptable treatment Jada describes was consistent for women whether they were stranded at the Superdome, Convention Center, or in other staging areas. In fact, it mirrors the poor treatment refugees receive when they are forced into refugee camps internationally,[23] yet with one major difference—this was Louisiana and these were American citizens experiencing a disaster on American soil. They have citizenship rights. They were victims, not enemy combatants. And yet the treatment of the displaced, whose homes and lives were flooded before their eyes, echoed a military exercise where the victim traumatized by immense, painful loss was cast as the enemy to be controlled,[24] not the citizen to be rescued from catastrophe.

Perhaps the National Guardsmen and other first responders were reacting to media images of the lawlessness of the city,[25] or to real, tangible acts of violence such as sniper fire at the Superdome and the downtown hospitals. For many women though, the militarized nature of the rescue efforts created new sources of trauma, rather than relieving it.

> Ann: After we went home, soldiers were riding around in Jeeps and things; they had guns pointed at you, it was just ridiculous. It was more frightening than anything. The police was rolling around all day and all night. Walmart had the doors open, but when I got there, there was no food at all. There was no water, no canned goods on the shelf.

In need of basic necessities, residents who attempted to locate food or water to care for themselves were seen with scrutiny, as thieves, rather than what they were—traumatized survivors. Amplified by the threat of violence from first responders, for those who were not flooded out of their homes, the time spent waiting for evacuation buses to leave was the most traumatic of all.

Objectified Suffering

Contributing to the fear and trauma was the refusal of those in charge, whether police, building security, the National Guard, or others, to provide basic information to residents about what was happening. For Barbara Jean, this information control began while Hurricane Katrina was passing overhead as she waited within the Superdome, where the guards were censoring information:

> At the Superdome, you couldn't go out for a couple of days. They wouldn't let you out. We were all on the TVs, but they wasn't letting you see anything on TV. They weren't telling us anything. Even when we were in Houston, they wouldn't say what was going on.

Alika, too, described the way she felt dehumanized and incarcerated, as if she and other citizens were animals to be controlled. Remember, Alika was a citizen seeking shelter within the Superdome's solid concrete walls. She was not a criminal, not a thief, not a looter. She was a mother, caring for her daughter and her own mother. So, why was she threatened with guns and confined to the Superdome? Why was she left starving for five days without food or water? Alika explains how devastating such treatment was, stating:

> I felt like dirt when I was in the Superdome, I was treated just like everybody else was treated, like animals, like we was caged and couldn't go nowhere. Everybody feel like dirt—those folks from other states, they came to rescue us. But Bush wasn't trying to do nothing. We need to do something with him. He's no good. I put him in the Lord's hands, the Lord take care of him now.

After surviving the trauma of viewing suicides, rapes, the Superdome's collapsing roof, and sniper fire, the earliest National Guard units failed to provide food and water as they entered the city, establishing a military presence first. In this context of terror, fear, and danger, Alika, Barbara Jean, and numerous other survivors faced dehumanization by those same individuals sent to rescue them. Evacuees at the Superdome, Convention Center, and throughout the City were rounded up, remained nameless, and kept on the premises in much the same ways as refugees are,[26] stripping them of their civil and human rights.

The presence of the militarized assistance was perpetual once it arrived in the city, but was barely reassuring. As Ann explains, "there were all these helicopters at night, and the police would come by"— never to check on her or her grandson, but rather to show their presence as a deterrent to civil disobedience. In fact, this militarized response continued right up until their evacuation:

> Ann: A third time we left, not knowing where we was going. [...] The polices and National Guard were very nasty, very, very nasty.
>
> Jessica: What were some things the National Guard and police did?
>
> Ann: Well one time we went to the Convention Center around this time of the evening, the police stopped us on Tchoupitoulas, before we can go to the Convention Center, they was searching our bags. They were looking for guns, and I have a gun but I left it back at home. They said "You know you're not going to need all these things." But I don't know if I was going back home, and I did not know if I could buy clothes, and I knew we had to evacuate so I started packing my bag and Lamar's bag.

For Ann, the storm experience itself was intense and traumatic. Protecting herself and her grandson by staying away from the Convention Center until as late as possible, she minimized her exposure to the desperation and despair. Then, even when her chance for evacuation did occur, she and her grandson were *strip-searched* at the airport before they could board a plane.[27] Throughout the experience, it was interactions with first responders such as this one that were humiliating, leaving Ann and many others feeling less than human.

The final insult of the "rescue" story was the failure of first responders to provide information to evacuees about where they were headed once they boarded buses and planes. For example, while Vanessa and her family were relieved to leave the city, they had no knowledge of where the buses were to take them, disabling their ability to draw on kin networks for support in displacement locations. So severe was the desire to leave the city and be anywhere but New Orleans, that one woman explained the situation thusly: "They just stuck us on a plane. There could have been a plane ride to Hell and we would have gone."

Conclusion

The experience in the shelters of last resort was violent, dangerous, and desperate, especially when weighed against the expectation of no violence and that assistance such as food and water would arrive more quickly than it did after the storm. As Alika stated succinctly, "It was like a hell hole ma'am, excuse me, but it was Hell." Yet, by focusing on the violence as a collective—i.e., rapes, murders, assaults—what real issues are subverted from view?

To critically consider the events in the shelters of last resort, the task becomes to carefully separate out those that were initiated by ill-meaning survivors such as rapists, and those that were not. Another challenge is to isolate the nuances of the circumstances that enabled such behavior in different types of spaces. Looking more closely at the lived experiences reported here, the shelters of last resort teach us about the circumstances in which post-disaster helping behaviors dissolve and are maintained, even if in morally ambiguous ways. For example, when comparing three spaces in the city where people were stranded—in their flooded homes and rooftops, in the Superdome, and in the Convention Center, the worst violence was happening at the Superdome, where citizens were treated like prisoners and forced to stay in the building and on the premises. Yet, even then, when children were raped, citizens took matters into their own hands to protect other children from the same assault. While addressing violence with violence is problematic, it also reflects a contorted form of social norm maintenance, and ultimately a commitment to helping behaviors. In spaces where people had the freedom to leave and return, as the Convention Center and personal homes offered, there was a far greater reported ethic of sharing food and beverages, and fewer reports of murder and rape, though those atrocities still occurred.

This difference in violence can be attributed to the capacity for self-sufficiency each space afforded. During circumstances where people know they have to be self-sufficient and care for themselves, they were doing so in creative ways. For example, residents who were free to leave their home or the Convention Center could use their pre-existing social capital and kin ties to stop by a family member's or a friend's house to get more supplies, without looting to do so. They could also seek out businesses that were helping others to meet their survival needs of water and food, as Ann did. By contrast, in spaces where people were herded, imprisoned, denied access to information, and promised vague offers of rescue and federal assistance that failed to come for days on end, more violence broke out. Disconnected from their social networks outside the Superdome, the entrapped were forced into dependency and desperation, even if family members in non-flooded areas could have taken them out of the city to safety.

While the ability, or lack thereof, to access social networks can explain looting for food, theft, and perhaps some fighting, what explains more severe forms of violence such as rape and murder? While these crimes somehow seem especially unacceptable in the content of disaster, the reality is that their prevalence simply reflects the ways in which patriarchy permeates our society, empowering men to enact violence against women with little, if any, consequence.[28] In the context of disaster, where women and children are typecast as the vulnerable who need to be saved and men are hyper-masculinized in their roles as protectors and first responders, women and children are further disempowered.[29] Layering on the reality that survivors in the Superdome and Convention Center were almost exclusively Black, as the marginalization patterns from everyday life were transplanted into these spaces,[30] it is somewhat unsurprising that rape and other forms of violence would occur, exacerbated by the militarization and masculinization of the experience. In this way, gender and racial inequality were maintained during the disaster, and exacerbated once the humanitarian recovery was transformed into a militaristic one.

As we move forward, we must acknowledge that in the future the levees will break. Hurricane Katrina was merely a Category 3 storm as it passed New Orleans. With enough time, a stronger storm will pass through with stronger winds, breaking the levees again. Or perhaps a very wet Category 2 storm will stall atop the city, flooding it from the bottom up, as rain falls faster than the pumping system can dispel it. In the end, it doesn't matter how the storm itself behaves—its wind speed or rain; the true potential of a disaster lies in what choices we make in our preparation and response.

As this chapter closes, consider briefly the critical questions that remain unanswered by this dataset: Why weren't the shelters of last resort established as rescue support centers, with food, water, generators, blankets, clothing, medicines, and first responders on standby so they could have canvassed the city and provided assistance as soon as the danger passed? Why weren't MREs and water depots positioned around the city in elevated spaces, to service residents without automobile access to evacuate, the sick, the elderly, or those too disabled to leave? More importantly, why didn't FEMA prepare convoys of water and food goods in locations outside the strike zone in the days when the storm was a Category 5 and still approaching? Did the Federal Emergency Management Agency not recognize the risk of a Category 5 hurricane? Collectively, these small changes could prevent a social disaster in the future. With preparation, and an absence of media hype and prejudice, thousands of lives could be saved from man-made trauma during the next disaster.

[1] Census 2000.

[2] Seven women stayed at the Superdome or the Convention Center during the storm or its aftermath; another declined the interview because she did not want to talk about her time at the Superdome.

[3] The one notable except to this statement is the U.S. Coast Guard. Rather than wait for bureaucrats to figure out who had authority to control the National Guard and the relief effort (the Governor of Louisiana vs. the President), they simply brought helicopters from surrounding areas and began rescuing people from their roofs.

[4] Tierney, Bevc, and Kuligowski 2006.

[5] Tierney, Bevc, and Kuligowski 2006.

[6] She is not part of the sample for this study.

[7] Dynes 2005; Drabek and Boggs 1968.

[8] Freudenberg 1997: Erikson 1976, 1994; Fritz 1961; Kreps 1984: 311; Couch 1996.

[9] Idakula 2007/2011.

[10] The National Guard.

[11] Idakula 2007/2011.

[12] Drabek 1986; Couch 1996; Tierney, Bevc, and Kuligowski 2006.

[13] Drabek 1986: 139.

[14] Idakula 2007/2011.

[15] Tierney, Bevc, and Kuligowski 2006.

[16] Weatherunderground website 12/22/11.

[17] Granovetter 1978.

[18] Stack 1974; Edin and Lein 1997; Domínguez and Watkins 2003; Henly, Danziger, and Offer 2005; Oliker 1995; Anderson 1989, 1990, 1999.

[19] Dynes 2005; Drabek 1986; Tierney, Bevc, and Kuligowski 2006: 58; Rodríguez, Trainor, and Quarantelli 2006.

[20] Drabek 1986; Tierney, Bevc, and Kuligowski 2006: 58.

[21] Drabek 1986; Tierney, Bevc, and Kuligowski 2006.

[22] Tierney, Bevc, and Kuligowski 2006: 66.

[23] Callamard 1999; Harrell-Bond 1999.

[24] Tierney, Bevc, and Kuligowski 2006.

[25] Tierney, Bevc, and Kuligowski 2006.

[26] Harrell-Bond 1999.

[27] Ann did not indicate a reason for why she was strip-searched, and was still outraged at the violation of her personal privacy and bodily integrity at the time we spoke.

[28] Enarson 2012: 71-85.

[29] Fothergill 1996; Stockard, Stockard Jr., and Tucker 2007/2011.

[30] Idakula 2007/2011; Collins 1998; hooks 1984; Drabek 1986.

PART 3

RECOVERY

Homelessness was one of the most immediate consequences of Hurricane Katrina. Throughout the Gulf Coast, over one million people were forced to find places to stay not just for a weekend, but for an indefinite amount of time. From cars to emergency shelters to hotels to family members' homes, and eventually to FEMA trailers and houses under construction, people found shelter where they could. Yet, the process of recovery, of reuniting with family, creating housing stability, finding work, and enrolling children in school, was excessively challenging within this broader context of uncertainty. How long would you be where you were? No one knew. As public conversations asked openly whether New Orleans should even be rebuilt at all, making decisions about the future for evacuees was tenuous at best.

Amid this uncertainty, evacuees were forced to assess their entire lives and futures based on partial, constantly changing information. From Tuesday, August 29, 2005 onward, as flood images flashed endlessly on televisions, questions like the following arose: Is my family alive? Are they safe? Are my friends alive? My neighbors? What about the people at work? Did Joe evacuate after all? What about Ann, or Sue, or Adam? With cell phone towers out of service, calling people wasn't an option. If service was available, only calls originating from phones with the affected area codes were processed; incoming calls from non-affected area codes were blocked to allow people to call for search and rescue. As the busy signals mounted, fear set in: Is the tower down or is the phone sitting somewhere under 10 feet of water with my friend? Is anyone else I know dead? With the number of deaths on television alone—actual deaths, not made-for-entertainment loss—it became inevitable that someone you know may have died. All one can do is hope for the best.

Once the wave of panic over death passes, evacuees faced another set of questions about the practical losses accrued during the storm: Is my home still standing? If it is, is it livable? If it is not, do I return to New Orleans or move away permanently? Will insurance pay to fix my house? Will they pay for a place to live until it is fixed? If they don't pay to fix it, can we afford to fix our home? For renters, the questions are equally challenging: Do I have to pay rent while I'm away? Will I be evicted if I don't? Will my rent be raised? What happens to my things if my landlord tries to repair the house before I'm allowed back into the city? If I find an apartment where I'm staying, do I sign a one-year lease? What if I can return in four months?

From the basic need of shelter, the worry shifts to other survival needs such as food, clothing, and the mechanism for providing those things: work. One asks: Will I have a job to pay the mortgage with? If I move away, can I find a new job? If I return, will my old job be waiting? If not, can I find a new job? How can I prove my qualifications if my records are lost? Will people even know I was employed if my workplace was completely flooded and all the records destroyed? How can I get references, if I don't even know where people are or if they are dead?

From here, you worry about the needs of others: Where is my father/sister/cousin staying? Are they taken care of? Will my children have schools to go to if we return? Do I enroll my children in school here if we're leaving soon? Does Auntie have her medicine? How do I see a doctor? Where do I go for help? What help is available to me? How long will it take? Where do I go when I run out of money to pay for this hotel? Without work, how will I be able to take care of myself and my family?

The list of uncertainties created by the catastrophe of the levee failures was endless and cyclical. For example, the questions of "Is this person alive?" are repeated for every person you know until you finally find an answer. And for some people, the answers remain elusive. I myself still cannot say if Miss Helen made it through the storm okay. I worked with her for four years, and knew her for nine, but never knew how she fared during the storm. The same goes for former students of mine from New Orleans—could my own former students be dead? I know several who lived in the same flooded public housing described here. So, yes, in fact, they could be dead.

The power of uncertainty is that it leaves you living in liminality, an ambiguous space between your old life and your new one. According to Smith and Belgrave, after Hurricane Andrew, survivors went between two worlds—navigating a normal work life with undamaged buildings, followed by returning to the destruction of their community and home, where the damage of Andrew's wrath was a constant reminder of their losses.[1] When survivors live between two worlds, they are experiencing the process of recovery. In this section, I examine the period of time beginning immediately *before* residents were living between two worlds and their transition into recovery—a time when search and rescue teams were still pulling people from flooded homes and rooftops, while buses and planes were relocating families across the country, and when the only thing anyone knew for certain was that they couldn't come home. From staying in shelters to staying with family, the transition from liminality to the unknown future was a challenge for all residents affected by the storm.

Next, Chapters 8 and 9 analyze the experiences of women who stayed away from the city and those who returned, respectively. Since data collection ended in December 2006, it is beyond the scope of this book to know how many women engaged permanent displacement as a survival and recovery strategy. Rather the strength of this analysis lies in understanding the intermediate experience of extended displacement—to live away from New Orleans in excess of six months—to better understand how low-income Black women navigated their new living environments and considered their options for rebuilding their lives. With recovery for the city estimated to take between 8-11 years,[2] it is important to recognize that these women's opportunities for recovery, along with that of so many other New Orleanians, is bound up in the city's broader recovery and the structural opportunities gained and lost in that process.

---

[1] Smith and Belgrave 1995.
[2] Kates, Colten, Laska, and Leatherman 2006.

7

Seeking Shelter

Keebra was a "lucky" New Orleanian. Living in the newly built River Garden community near downtown New Orleans, her HOPE VI subsidized apartment was completely undamaged during the storm. With her three children—ages sixteen, eleven, and three—Keebra, in her early thirties, was among the housing elite—those living in the twenty percent of buildings without any flood damage. A full-time home health aid, Keebra was gainfully employed and "not at all worried" before the storm. And while her car broke down the Friday before landfall, with her family's help she left in a small caravan of kin. Together with her mother, sister, and children, Keebra's experience represents how graciously uneventful hurricane and evacuation experiences can be: no mass flooding, no threat of gun violence at evacuation rally points, and no risk of death like thousands of stranded families who waited for water, food, medical care, and buses. Keebra was protected from the worst of the trauma Katrina had to offer, and experienced her biggest personal challenges only after she returned to New Orleans to live.[1]

Keebra is also very representative of the evacuee experience in those early months of displacement, which included living in multiple residences. Shelters, hotels, and family members' homes were all sources of housing for her kin caravan. Her initial evacuation took her to a community shelter in Louisiana, a hotel for Hurricane Rita, followed by a series of other accommodations:

> Keebra: Well we left, trying to make it to Texas. I was going with my mother 'cause my car was totaled that Friday, so I had to leave with my mother and my sister. We stayed in the middle of Louisiana. We stayed in a shelter—a multipurpose building gave us shelter. We stayed a week; then went to Houston. Then, we split up, and I went to Houston, got a hotel, and my mom went to my brother's. So my mom, she staying out there. This apartment is new, and I had no damages and I didn't lose anything. So, I just came home. I tried, but I couldn't

find an apartment in Houston. I was just so disgusted and I was ready to come home, so I came home.

Keebra's case illustrates how women used different forms of sheltering such as community shelters, family, hotels rooms, and more permanent solutions to maneuver through their displacements. By piecing different types of housing opportunities together, women created housing stability even when a particular housing source was itself unstable. This emergent survival strategy of "patchworking" was the mechanism women engaged as they navigated the uncertainty of their displacement.

Patchworking—the pattern of alternating between one shelter source and the next to create overarching stability when no single location is stable, permanent, or desirable—became a common sheltering strategy among women. Across the sample, women and their families stayed on average at three or four different places prior to our interviews.[2] Women who spent less than six months outside of New Orleans lived in two or three different places on average, while women who spent more than six months living outside New Orleans, in an "extended displacement," averaged between four and five different residences by the time we spoke—a statistically significant difference. For many women, this meant that the longer they were displaced from the city, the less stable their family's housing experience was, as just over half the sample faced the predicament of extended displacement. Thus, for the majority of women, housing stability was an elusive experience, with unexpected challenges disrupting seemingly stable arrangements.

In this chapter, I consider women's early housing experiences to illustrate how formal shelters, family, and federal housing assistance formed the foundations upon which women rebuilt housing security for themselves and their families. Just as survival under poverty conditions engaged family and formal assistance, so did women rely on those strategies in the early days following Hurricane Katrina. However, unlike before the storm, at this early phase, work was not available as women could not apply for a job without a residence to list on an application. In this way, being evacuated created a temporary experience within which women began to make sense of the storm and its meaning in their lives, while testing the effectiveness of old survival strategies in new contexts.

From their initial departures out of New Orleans, just over two-fifths (43.1%) of women stayed in a shelter, and about one-fifth of the entire sample was fortunate enough to secure a hotel. Just over one-third stayed with a family member or friend, and two women spent their first night away from New Orleans homeless—living in a car and outdoors.

Whether through temporary shelter, family, or formal assistance, creating housing stability was an essential and necessary prerequisite for disaster recovery. For without a home, the disaster continued.

Liminal Spaces for Survival

In the two weeks following Hurricane Katrina, hundreds of thousands of evacuees were displaced to cities throughout the country, and especially in the Gulf Coast Region. Ultimately, evacuees landed in almost every state, as hundreds of temporary shelters were opened in civic centers, arenas, auditoriums, and churches.[3] Offering basic services such as food, clothing, and medical care, many shelters became bureaucratic systems that funneled evacuees through a flow of checkpoints and sign-ups for assistance.[4] For Sharon, the shelter was a refuge after her experience being held at gunpoint with her family while waiting for evacuation buses from the city's Westbank neighborhood.[5] Compared to the drama of the evacuation, Sharon described her shelter life with gratitude:

> We were in Dallas, and they had food—hot food—and tables set up, and bracelets[6] set up. They served us food, and it was real nice. They don't have beds, but they was telling us they hope to get some, and they had portable showers. Everyone was really nice.

From portable showers to other basics like clothing and beds, the shelters were the first chance many evacuees had to wash off the physical remnants of Katrina's trauma: the dirt, sweat, tears, and floodwater that permeated their clothing, hair, and skin.

With clean, dry clothes to change into, shelters were the first semblance of regular life for women and their children or grandchildren. At Sharon's shelter, the preparations were organized and expanded to meet evacuee needs:

> I don't know what time it was, I lost track, but they bring in blow-up beds, and shoes, socks, and new clothes. I had a few clothes, but not that much. I was cold, and my legs were real sore. Then they brought in more clothes from everywhere, and beds. They told everybody to get blankets and stuff like that, and the next day they had places for medication. They had places for help with housing, public housing—Section 8 vouchers to place you in housing. When they brought us to the housing authority, the people worked Monday through Sunday, nonstop, around the clock. They was trying to find you housing if you wanted it.

Sharon was fortunate to arrive at a shelter that had streamlined its services into an assembly line and was prepared for the evacuees. Sharon received assistance quickly and generously, and unlike her evacuation experience with the organized relief effort, in the shelter she was safe and treated with respect.

For many evacuees though, the level of preparation and the temperament within the shelters varied, which translated into different recovery opportunities. One factor that affects the shelter's atmosphere is the culture of the receiving community, and specifically the attitudes of the individuals who donate their time.[7] For Sharon, part of what made her recovery more positive was a shelter worker named Meredith who took a personal interest in helping her and her daughter get settled in the local community:

> My daughter, she didn't want to go to the shelter or the convention center in Houston. So Meredith brought her to another town, in Texas. She stopped at a doctor's office, then had her ID taken, and then we went to a church in another town. We all have to be searched, then we could go in.
>
> When we got in, they had everything we needed. They had hot food, and it was one or two in the morning. They had a shower and rooms upstairs. It was better 'cause we was separated. They put families in the room upstairs. Then in the middle of the room, it was maybe like two people together, with their beds in the middle. It was much better. We stayed there about three weeks.

Through Meredith's personal actions, Sharon was relocated from the public shelter full of bused-in evacuees like herself to a small church where the services were more personalized and families were able to stay together in semi-private spaces. This individualized interest in Sharon and her adult daughter shown by Meredith helped put them on a pathway to receive extra assistance to locate stable housing and donations from the local community:

> Meredith started to get us help, and found my daughter a place on Maple Street. Then she found me a place across the street, and I live on Oak Street. Then they gave us a sponsor, so then I got a bed, a table, and a television first, then a washer and a dryer. I had other people who helped too. One lady at the shelter, she had seen me, and said she had a computer. She didn't want to bring it to the shelter, so when I got a place, she brought it to me. I had tables, pillows, and other materials. You know, stuff for your house.

One of the benefits of this individualized approach is that it reinforces the idea that total strangers can demonstrate compassion in times of need. In fact, it was through these acts of caring and kindness that Sharon made the transition from evacuation toward recovery. With access to family—her daughter next door, stable shelter, and the material goods that form the foundation of daily life, like toothpaste, clothing, and furniture, Sharon's recovery process began as she settled into a small apartment centrally located near a bus stop. Through a generous receiving community, Sharon's pathway to recovery was optimistic.

Ann also had a similar shelter experience in Texas, were the generosity of strangers was a relief after the humiliation of being strip-searched at the airport before her evacuation. As the local community came together to provide for displaced evacuees, they gathered needed goods like clothing and toiletries. Yet, Ann's experience also illuminates an emergent challenge in the shelters as traumatized survivors turned to alcohol to cope with the loss Katrina created:

> In Texas, everything was beautiful, the people was beautiful. We all had our own mattresses, with bedspreads that Walmart donated. It was a religious little town; there was no alcohol at all. People was looking for alcohol, but there was none. It was very nice.

As time passed and the reality of Hurricane Katrina's trauma began to take effect, many women reported a shift in the nature of the evacuation shelters where they stayed.

As liminal spaces that were always destined to close, the emergence of social problems like drinking, drug use, theft, and sexual violence transformed these spaces of helping into spaces of fear. For Linda, these problems were caused by the arrival of a new wave of evacuees. She stated: "We didn't start having problems until later on. They shut down one shelter, then people come over to our shelter, and they starting in, stealing the clothes we had."

This disintegration of shelter culture from safe and supportive to traumatic, desperate, and disrespectful was mirrored at Angela's shelter as well, as she recounted what she saw:

> When we was the first to arrive, we was alright. Then when the second and third crew came, it wasn't too good. I mean, they took good care of us, it was just the people that was in there—they made it worse.... They was rude, ignorant, sloppy, trashing the shelter. They was thinking about themselves, and wasn't watching their children. The

women were tending to the men, not the children, with the place looking raggedy.

Among those second and third waves of evacuees were heavily traumatized survivors who had previously been stranded in the city during Hurricane Katrina. Since psychological trauma can result in depression, anger, anxiety, and a myriad of other anti-social behavioral forms, it is possible that these behaviors are the manifestations of the trauma of being stranded.[8] In fact, not a single woman in this sample mentioned accessing a counselor for herself after the storm, nor did any mention such services being provided in a shelter where they stayed. Only children, who accessed counseling through their new schools, were described as having received any counseling at that time.

Additionally, for mothers to leave their children unattended while over-investing in attending to men's needs, there is a partial rejection of the role expectations connected to motherhood, while simultaneously overemphasizing the role expectations of womanhood, such that men's needs usurped children's. In this way, gender roles are maintained post-disaster[9] while simultaneously reifying pre-existing power relations between men and women at large.

Continuing the interview, when I asked Angela if there were problems of theft or violence at her shelter, she stated "no," but then recounted an incident of domestic violence and rowdiness:

> I was looking, like, how this young dude would beat up his girlfriends? How the womens were disrespectful with cursing and hooting and hollering? They would voice opinions, but I'd stay quiet most of the time. I'd get up in the morning, tend to my business, get a bus pass, and don't come back until late.... You know, you had all that loudness, and kids making noise, since they parents not minding them. I was trying to mind the children, 'cause they trying to cope the best way they could. They trying to deal with it.

As a mechanism to manage the newcomers without becoming overwhelmed by their trauma, Angela responded by either leaving the shelter or engaging in the care work of helping others by providing small forms of childcare.[10] By keeping tabs on the smaller children whose mothers, she felt, were too distracted to do it themselves, she created a productive way to act out against her frustration by caring for the most vulnerable of evacuees: the children. In taking these actions, Angela was also maintaining her own gender-role expectations of mothering behavior,[11] and community mothering norms emerging from her racial identity and membership in the African American community.[12]

This distraction and indifference toward children was among many expressions of trauma that emerged at the shelters. Sexual violence was another. For 47-year-old Gloria, who evacuated with six family members to a hotel for Hurricane Katrina, it was Hurricane Rita, which hit during her displacement from New Orleans, which forced her to stay at a public shelter in central Louisiana for three weeks. Already populated with Katrina evacuees, the shelter was dangerous and both mentally and physically traumatic as acts of rape, assault, and theft occurred before Gloria's eyes:

> That's where I broke down at, right there. Children was getting raped. I couldn't sleep at all. People was stealing; throwing water bottles at you while you sleep. Girl, it was horrifying. You could see people's spirits hovering, and they was bad. My friend went to stay at her uncle's, she had stayed in the shelter. An 11-year-old boy got raped. A 6-year-old got raped. People got picked up by strangers. I called the Red Cross, everybody—"please get me out of here!" It was horrifying. I started losing weights, stopped eating. I was scared I was gonna be raped. It was horrifying. A mom left her kids by themselves. They come to you crying, everybody crying. People did the best they could do for us. When Rita hit, it was so horrifying. Those winds were so hard, the thunder was so hard I thought the wind would take down the shelter.

The shift in shelter safety reflects a breakdown of some of the helping behaviors among survivors common to disasters, though as Angela previously demonstrated, that absence was not universal. Not only were members of the receiving communities helping, but evacuees did help each other, despite everything they experienced.

Yet, what explains this shift in shelter environments far safer than the Superdome had been? While the Superdome and Convention Center violence was shaped by the absence of resources like water, food, clothing, medicine, the ability—or lack thereof—to leave and access network-based assistance, and the militarization of a humanitarian crisis, the shelter environments outside of New Orleans were quite different. First, survivors did not have the power to draw on kin networks initially, since involuntary evacuation destinations were determined by the government response effort, not the evacuee. This meant that thousands were sent to cities where they had no kin, and no sense of how to start rebuilding until they located loved ones. For example, how does a woman decide where to live if she is the caregiver to her mother, but that mother was evacuated by helicopter to a hospital, and there's no way to locate her, much less learn if she is alive or dead?

Second, evacuees had only the resources they possessed on their persons. For those who knew they lost their homes, the awareness was acute. For those who self-evacuated, the loss was ambiguous, as they had not yet returned to their homes to assess the damages. This range of awareness regarding the loss meant that different evacuees where coping with the disaster in different ways, as shaped by their experiences and knowledge base. So, while basic needs of food, shelter, clothing, and medicine were met, a sense of desperation may have guided some to break social norms and steal, especially if they knew what they had in the shelter was all they owned. In this way, having extra clothes to wear or a watch to sell at a pawn shop might make the difference between having money for food or not in the face of an uncertain future.

Finally, from a structural perspective, the differences may have emerged due to the increased size, density, and heterogeneity of survivors, a la Wirth.[13] Like in a city, the increased diversity of people in high densities makes for more impersonal environments, reducing the sense of shared community. As the shock of the experience abated, and reality sunk in, a sense of despair may fuel this disconnection. With as many as thousands of evacuees warehoused in a single shelter, if even just 1% of the shelter population began perpetrating crimes such as rapes or thefts with impunity, it would be enough to make the entire shelter feel unsafe in the broader context of uncertainty during this liminal time, especially since the victims had already been victimized by the storm, and in some cases first responders, before walking in the door.

For women empowered to seek housing opportunities elsewhere, the shift in the shelter experience was a motivator to seek new accommodations and safer living situations. For others, they had no choice but to stay where they were as they worked to find permanent housing. In either case, women next attempted to rely on kin and government-provided assistance to address their housing needs, to varying degrees of success. As was the case with shelter housing, both alternatives lacked permanent stability, as women were forced to rely on the will of others to continue providing that support. Still, despite these challenges, no woman reported sleeping on the streets during this time, meaning their patchwork approach to securing housing was a universally viable strategy across their new displacement locations.

Crowding In with Family

Staying with family was a complicated housing strategy. On the one hand, family can provide safe shelter and other resources such as food, clothing, childcare, laundry, and moral support. On the other hand, that assistance comes with a loss of privacy and independence as well as complicated expectations and emotional attachments that can drain energy and resources. Yet, after the shelter, staying with family was the next most popular mechanism women used to create housing stability following their evacuations, with nearly one-third evacuating to a family member's home. In the case of Katrina, the complicating factor was that the failure of the levees transformed small sheltering favors into significant, indefinite housing obligations.

For some women, the indefinite housing obligation became a burden that weakened kin relationships and forced them to seek housing through formal assistance. For others, the news of the levees encouraged families to combine resources together through "doubling up"—a kin-based survival strategy in which two or more families live in one home to reduce costs, making housing and other expenses more affordable.[14] In the immediate aftermath of Katrina, just over one-quarter of women chose to double up with family and friends. Over time, nearly one-third of women spent the majority of their displacement doing the same.

For families evacuating in advance of the storm, doubling up was often an extension of the evacuation caravan that women used until receiving FEMA[15] money or housing assistance to move into separate apartments. In this way, "the household" expanded to include multiple families until enough time passed and individual families could branch off to establish new households of their own. For women who began in shelters, hotels, or even private rentals, doubling up was often the bridge they needed to prevent living on the streets when they changed housing programs, waited for their own assistance to be approved or transferred, or as they moved from one city to another to expedite their family's chances for recovery, often through reunification with other kin.

Louisa, a 61-year-old woman who lived alone before the storm, demonstrates how family became essential as a source of sheltering during both the storm and her displacement. Accepting her son's offer to ride out Katrina at a large downtown high-rise hotel where he worked, Louisa's "vertical evacuation" kept her safe from the strong winds. On Tuesday, she returned to her home where she stayed until her second son called to insist she evacuate because the levees had broken and the city's flooding was rapidly expanding:

My son said "you gotta come over here," and that water is coming up bad. And we did. My son came, and we got in my baby's truck. I took just a few things and he came, got me, got some more people, and brought us all to his house across the river. Then he went back, got some more people and took them to his house. He got a big pot, and made rice and beans to feed people.

From this launching point, the group of family, friends, and neighbors evacuated as a caravan and pooled resources for a hotel for the first few days. Quickly, this arrangement became untenable as finances ran low. With the help of the hotel's desk clerk, the group was directed to a local church for assistance. Louisa explained the challenges they faced:

> We got a room at the hotel. They only had two rooms, so the men were in one and the women in the other. We paid $60 a night, and the woman told us we had to go to the First Baptist Church. The Pastor was very nice, told us to go talk with the secretary, and gave us cots to sleep on. I'm a little heavy, so I couldn't sleep on a cot, so I slept on the pool table. We was there and then they had these mattresses, you know, with the air—and we slept there. We stayed there, and they fed us three meals a day. Then we took over the kitchen one day and we cooked a meal for 100 people.

Here, the generosity of the local ministry enabled Louisa's kin caravan to access free shelter, preserving their limited financial resources for other needs. In gratitude, Louisa and her kin prepared dinner for everyone visiting the shelter for meals at that time. For Louisa and her family, this assistance was priceless especially given their sizable kin caravan:

> Louisa: At the hotel, we had like 15-20 people in those two rooms, with the men and women separate. There were two beds and a sofa, with two or three people in each bed.
>
> Jessica: How many people were your relatives?
>
> Louisa: [...] My relatives? It was my.... Grandson, daughter, my son and his wife, so seven relatives. All the rest of the people, my son just took people with him.

As seen previously, in the face of devastation Louisa's son gathered as many people as he could to evacuate, demonstrating the helping ethic among many stranded survivors[16]—even those with the fewest economic resources.

In the long-term, hotels and shelters were not sustainable solutions to displacement. For Louisa, the church shelter was the transitional space necessary to meet her caravan's needs until she made arrangements to stay with her sister in Southern Louisiana:

> I went to my sister's house, my son went to his house in Gretna, and my daughter stayed behind. I was in my granddaughter's bed in my sister's house—so, we had a choice of people we could live with. Everything was fine. She had an extra bedroom, and I stayed there, then I came by my daughter's house because my brother got out of the hospital, so he stayed there, and I stayed by my daughter.

During this time, Louisa was waiting to hear if she could return to New Orleans, reflecting the common uncertainty shaping recovery decision making at this time. In this way, her patchwork housing strategy was consistent, but not stable. She managed her housing instability by shifting spaces and doubling up, avoiding homelessness in the process. Through patchworking, Louisa combined formal shelter usage with kin accommodations to keep sheltered throughout her displacement, successfully creating housing continuity while never actually having a home of her own.

While family can support housing continuity, the pressure of providing indefinite assistance can also become a source of instability by putting hosts at odds with the kin they are trying to help. For Faith, the mother of four who was fired from her job as a 911 operator for taking her children out of harm's way, the offer of housing from her favorite cousin ultimately became very complicated. Initially evacuating to Baton Rouge, where thousands of evacuees flooded following the storm, Faith started her housing pathway at a local shelter:

> People were very friendly, I must say. In the shelter in Baton Rouge, they made sure the kids and elderly and sick got first priority in everything. We had enough food, clean linens, and no one slept on the floor. It was comfortable.

Immediately after the storm, Faith's cousin contacted her, insisting she bring her children to stay. Given the option for greater privacy and living with family, Faith decided to leave the shelter. Very close to her cousin prior to the storm, Faith received a warm welcome and lots of help learning the Baton Rouge area, enrolling her children in school, and finding other important places. Within a month's time, however, the crowded living conditions and unexpectedly long displacement began to strain their previously strong relationship. The home that was once "welcoming" had become "horrible":

> My experience was horrible. Me and my cousin, before the storm we talked, we joked. We even talked two or three times a week. We had to use her kitchen at a certain time; we couldn't cook after six o'clock. It was so bad, my kids wanted to sleep in a tent. We were in a three-bedroom trailer. There was no A/C, and she took the screens off—it was so bad we was about to go to the shelter, 'cause we was treated better at the shelter.

When I asked Faith why her cousins' behavior had changed, she became defensive:

> I don't know if it was just the time length; we was only there for a month and a half, or two months, and nobody expected to be there that long. We only had clothes for two days. I don't know if it was her trying to cope with us being there. So, we headed to Texas. If there's ever a next time, when it comes to a family member, I will not go to them.

Later in the interview, Faith further explained the experience of living in her cousin's home. Over time, Faith's cousin began to take passive-aggressive actions to encourage them to leave, never explicitly asking them to go. As the burden of helping grew heavier, the supportive aspects of using family as a housing strategy disappeared:

> A month, two, three weeks later, everybody was fighting. It was like an attitude that just progressed. My cousin would wake up, get her coffee, then go to her room and lock the bedroom door. She disconnected the water in the ice maker in the fridge. Then she don't want us cooking anything after six o'clock, and she'd lock up her clean linens. It was like giving us signs to get out. We was looking for apartments there, but with everybody evacuating to Baton Rouge, it was hard to find one. I found something in Alexandria, then Mom and Dad got in the queue to come home, so we all packed up and came back to New Orleans. We had three families in a two-bedroom house in Baton Rouge.

Overcrowding was a primary characteristic of Faith's temporary living arrangement. Among her evacuation caravan were herself, her four children, and her parents. Additionally, her cousin had also invited other kin to live at the home, including Faith's brother, his wife, and their two children. Faith's eldest brother, who was handicapped, and required special care, also stayed in the trailer. Collectively, her cousin and her son were hosting *eleven* people in a three-bedroom trailer for nearly two months. This burden exceeded the strength of the family ties, breaking their bonds. In response, Faith was embittered, stating, "I'm telling you she called everyone, then we got there and it was like Hell."

Overall, using family as a source of housing worked best for providing short-term shelter, where women would stay for a month or less, then move on quickly to a new location. Doubling up over an extended period of time tended to favor the evacuee, while it drained resources from the provider, without replenishment. As a result, several women identified brewing tensions and massive overcrowding in their kin accommodations as the reason they left for the next temporary shelter. Another issue was just being surrounded by constant reminders of the storm:

> Twila: It was okay at my cousin's house. [...] We was crowded in there and it caused problems in the end when people just started fussing. They getting frustrated, and her and my sister's daughter was fussing.

> Vivienne: My niece, she say "you could stay here." It was all of us in the house. Thank God, it was a big, beautiful house. The house is very big, but you know, I had to make a move. Basically, the depressing part was being cluttered; it just bothered me living in somebody's house. Everywhere I went, everywhere I went, just a gas station, it was just people, everyday just needing—not wanting—just needing. If you went to the office to get help, it was people that needed something. It was too much, for me. I need to try to get away from so close to where disaster did happen. The more people I was in contact with, they didn't want to branch out too, too far. I had to get out of Louisiana.

> Joanna: My mom didn't want to stay by other people. It was like living on eggs, on eggshells. It wasn't the lady, it was her mom. We bought our own food, cleaned the bathroom, the kitchen, and any food we cooked. The lady was evicted, but she come home to the house being clean, clothes was washed. Like my mom said, we used to living on our own. We had twenty people in one place, waiting to use the bathroom. We had to wash towels for days, it was real hard.... Once it was two weeks over, everybody gradually moved into apartments and stuff like that.

Callista elaborates:

> Callista: We had no electricity, no water. And the heat.... It was a bunch of people, and attitudes changing, personalities changed. [...]

> You couldn't stay in the house, it was overheated. So we were ate up by mosquitoes.
>
> Jessica: Did you have power?
>
> Callista: No, no, no! That's why we left.... There was a lot of cursing, and talking about hitting one another. And the condition in the house—inside, it was a four-bedroom and three-bathroom home. The bathrooms were a mess, with that many people. The children, from my sister-in-law, they can't find the bathroom. So there was feces and urine on the floor. It was disgusting. The whole house, it was like a toilet. It was terrible, the conditions and so forth. The house was enclosed, with people, all like that.

For women who had been living independently, albeit with housing subsidies, the loss of freedom that doubling, tripling, and quadrupling up entailed encouraged them to seek their own apartments, especially as FEMA rental assistance and HUD disaster vouchers became universally available.

Unlike doubling up in normal times, where the strategy benefits both families by reducing overall costs, post-disaster doubling up threatens the financial stability of the host family, as expenses like food, water, and electricity increase, creating the potential for a parasitic relationship to develop. While Joanna described keeping the house clean and other efforts to contribute, neither Vivienne, Twila, Faith, or Callista describe their contributions. In this way, doubling up becomes untenable in the long-term as a survival strategy if the displaced are not able to contribute back to the household economy, or the host family cannot unilaterally support them until such a time when they can. Because of the economic limitations of host families, in the end, relying on the government for housing proved the most stable arrangement, since FEMA rental assistance was pledged for twelve months, while the HUD-based disaster voucher programs were guaranteed for eighteen months.[17] Since many women planned to return to New Orleans, these programs provided the duration of assistance necessary to wait out the initial inventory and remediation stages[18] in the city's broader path to recovery.

Formal Federal Assistance

Moving away from family and into one's own home was a significant transition for evacuees because it represented increased independence from kin and tangible steps toward recovery from the storm. To have your own home, even in another state, provides the foundation for rebuilding your life and making decisions about the uncertain future. Following the storm, evacuees had access to three housing programs to help with this transition: FEMA's IHP program, the KDHAP program, and HUD's DVP program. The primary difference between the programs is that FEMA assistance was a cash payment granted for one year, while the KDHAP and DVP were housing vouchers provided for eighteen months.[19] As public shelters closed and kin networks were strained, most women shifted into one of these programs to establish more stable housing.

Initially, all housing assistance was administered through FEMA, the Federal Emergency Management Agency. Their first program, the Individuals and Households Program (IHP) provided rental assistance and trailers, as well as money for other basic needs and expenses, a standard FEMA post-disaster assistance package.[20] Assistance was assured for 1 year. To participate, applicants would receive approval from FEMA; then locate a private rental. FEMA would pay the landlord directly on their behalf, with no required contribution for residents.[21] This program was the standard assistance for housing after the storm.

Recognizing that low-income families have special needs and greater challenges to recovery following a disaster, the (Katrina) Disaster Housing Assistance Program was created to provide housing assistance for public housing residents and homeless families.[22] Known as the KDHAP or DHAP program, it provided a special housing voucher structured similar to that of Section 8. The DHAP voucher had no required rental payment, though its value was limited to HUD's fair market rent standards and families paid any amount beyond the voucher's value.[23] Several months into the program, DHAP was replaced with the DVP or disaster voucher program. Disaster vouchers were identical to DHAP vouchers, with an assistance period of 18 months. Eligibility for DVP was limited to prior public housing residents, excluding the homeless who were part of the DHAP legislation.[24]

Illustrating this transition from temporary to permanent housing, I return to Jada, the mother of four in her early thirties who was stranded at the Convention Center for six days with her children. In her life before the storm, Jada was a stable resident in a major public housing complex in New Orleans, where she lived in the same unit for eleven years. After her family's evacuation to a military base in Arkansas, Jada quickly made arrangements to relocate her family to Virginia where she stayed with her brother and his wife from September to February. While her experience there had been positive and supportive, she decided to move to Texas near her grandmother to help her 6-year-old son Terrance adjust to the changes of life after Katrina:

> Well, my 6-year-old.... They had problems with him at school, but it was with the circumstances. I think it's 'cause we was so far from my grandmother and he used to being around her. Now he calmed down, because he close to her and family that they know.

With financial help from the Catholic Church in Virginia, Jada was able to make the move to Texas to reunite her children with their great-grandmother and recreate the stable kin relationships they shared in New Orleans.

Arriving in Texas in mid-February 2006, Jada's family stayed with her grandmother for about six weeks until Jada could get established in a separate apartment. This move was the children's fourth move in the seven months since their evacuation. With each relocation, Jada had to reestablish her housing, her children's schooling, her food stamps, and any other benefits she was receiving. At the time we spoke, she was not employed, nor had she been prior to the storm. Participating in the disaster voucher program in Texas, Jada was finally able to achieve housing stability. Like many evacuees, Jada's experience demonstrates that the transition from shelters or the homes of kin to establish independent housing was not a direct pathway. Instead, women engaged a patchwork approach that achieved overarching housing stability through a succession of unstable arrangements, even after federal housing resources were secured.

Many women in this study engaged the patchwork approach to secure viable housing for their family time and time again. Yet, housing vouchers and FEMA aid were not a panacea of stability for all women. For 45-year-old Linda, who evacuated with a boyfriend with whom she later broke up, then joined up with a kin caravan before she moved in with her adult son, the frustration of being without steady housing was mounting as she had stayed at *nine* different places by May of 2006. This persistent instability was triggered by the rescission of her FEMA rental aid:

> ... when they set up an apartment, the apartment was supposed to be for a year, I signed a lease for a year, and was living there for five months. That put the most stress on you, 'cause you have to find a place to live. Before, I was feeling like "I'm on a lease for a year, that give me a chance to pull it together," just feeling like 70% better, even though everybody was separated [...] but only five months lasted and we had to find somewhere else to go.... FEMA stopped paying for

it.... They stopped paying for it because the rent was so high. They told me I have to find somewhere else to go, and I've been going from house to house ever since then.

Linda's housing struggle began because competition between displaced families for rental apartments and homes drove rents higher in areas flooded with evacuees. Since she was located in an "evacuee flood zone," her ability to find affordable housing was reduced, especially in states like Texas and Georgia where she stayed. In response, Linda stayed with family members wherever she could:

> We go from house to house, sometimes we go from state to state trying to find a place to go. First we go to Georgia, but the kids, they are bad—they can't sleep, can't rest, so we had to find somewhere else to go.

The displacement continued as Linda received a KDHAP voucher, only to find "now a lot of places is not accepting it no more, some take it, but some not accepting it. There's a waiting list." Again, like FEMA, the HUD-based voucher did not materialize into the physical housing source Linda needed to begin her recovery from the storm. Instead, housing instability dominated Linda's family life, the frustrations of which she expressed by saying "There's always something, something, something. We need help, Miss. There's always something."

Like Linda, nearly one-third of the overall sample stayed at five or more places by the time of their interview: Trinity, Lillian, Gloria, Perla, Regina, Louisa, Linda, Vivienne, Callista, Aliyah, Vanessa, Iris, Jada, Keisha, Mary, and Amaya,[25] with three places being the mode. Among those with high housing instability, 90% were living in extended displacement, being displaced from their home community in New Orleans in excess of 6 months.[26] In their need to survive, women repeatedly moved between formal shelters, kin housing, and voucher-subsidized independent residences, combining and dissolving households as circumstances required. However, the transition between housing types was not fluid; instead, it was an inconsistent alternation between periods of calm stability and unexpected rapid change. A single HUD or FEMA notification could force another move and erase much of the progress toward recovery a woman and her family had made, whether that was finding a job, enrolling children in school, or buying furniture for the current home.

Exacerbating the tumultuous nature of women's displacements were the short durations of those stable times. On average, women and their families spent 139 days living in a single residence, or about four and one-half months. Those lucky enough to return to the city within six months tended to spend about three months (102 days) in a single place, disabling work as a recovery survival strategy in the process, as just three women located a job while in the early phase of their displacement. For those living an extended displacement, their most stable housing situations averaged 199 days—or about six and one-half months.[27] This equates to moving homes roughly twice per year. Furthermore, the challenge for these families was that the longer they were away from New Orleans, the more they moved around, meaning they never really settled anywhere, even though they were able to stay in a single place for longer periods of time. In this way, women who returned to New Orleans had less housing instability and a better chance to begin recovery than those living in extended displacement. By contrast, extended displacement led to more frequent housing moves, with longer average durations in any single residence, but a recovery process that could never really begin.

For many women, the experience of finding stable housing was a perpetual challenge that had not been resolved at the time of our interviews. In fact, every woman who received a voucher was left in uncertainty as to what would transpire when the assistance ended. Based on the findings here, the kin network would likely accommodate them to prevent homelessness, but in the long run, their housing stability remained uncertain at the time we spoke. What is known, though, is that housing was not the only survival challenge women faced while they were displaced from New Orleans. In fact, for many, housing was the easy part; paying the rest of the bills was another matter.

Conclusion

Housing matters. Housing is the foundation for our citizenship. Where we live determines more than just our neighbors and taxes—it determines our rights and privileges, especially to public goods like education, healthcare, and social services. While social assistance programs like unemployment, social security, Medicare and Medicaid, food stamps, public housing assistance, and TANF originate as federal programs, their implementations are localized, which translates to different levels of assistance in different locations despite being part of the same program. So, while FEMA aid is given directly to individuals, all the other programs that displaced evacuees used to begin their recoveries where fragmented across state, county, and even city lines.

Housing matters most of all because as women faced high instability during the first year and a half following the storm, their ability to meet their other needs, like clothing, food, education, and healthcare were also at constant risk each time they moved. And while it seems simple enough to say "Don't move, then!," the reality is that at the point of evacuation from New Orleans, many families were forced to separate, just as Regina and her pregnant daughter were when the baby decided it was ready to be born in the middle of a hurricane and flood. In other cases, families were separated by age or gender before being put onto buses and planes, and shipped off to other states. Thus, by evacuating families as individuals instead of groups, and refusing to let them choose their destinations, fragmented families were forced to spend their limited FEMA resources to reunite with each other as an important step toward their disaster recovery.

One unintended consequence of this forced family fragmentation was that each time members changed locations across a program's jurisdictional lines to reunite, their assistances would be terminated. So when Jada moved her entire family to help Terrance recover by bringing him closer to Grandma, all the help she received stopped and could not be taken with her. Once established in Texas, Jada had to begin again with new applications to secure whatever assistance was available, which might include food stamps, social security, housing vouchers for public housing residents, and Medicaid or Medicare. With all programs except FEMA aid tied to states rather than individuals, women had to choose in some cases between the stability that was created by being a resident of a particular location versus the stability created by having supportive family or friends nearby. As a result, housing is so much more than a physical shelter for a family—it becomes a structural predictor of the potential a family has to recover.

---

[1] See Chapter 9: Returning Home.

[2] The full sample mean number of places stayed at the time of interview was 3.74, with a standard deviation of 1.79. Displaced respondents (less than 6 months outside New Orleans) resided at an average of 2.42 places, while respondents who experienced extended displacement (greater than 6 months outside of New Orleans) averaged 4.31 distinct housing locations. The highest number of residences in the sample equaled 9. This difference is statistically significant at alpha = .05.

[3] See the Weber and Peek (2012) for a detailed discussion of displacement patterns.

[4] For a detailed discussion of these "one-stop shopping" bureaucracies, see Haney 2007/2011 and Pardee 2007/2011.

[5] See Chapter 5: Stranded.

[6] The shelter required identification bracelets, like at a hospital.
[7] Miller 2012.
[8] Erikson 1976, 1994; Freudenberg 1997; Picou, Marshall, and Gill 2004.
[9] Fothergill 1999; Enarson 2012; Enarson and Scanlon 1999.
[10] Fothergill 1999; Enarson 2012.
[11] Fothergill 1999; Enarson 2012.
[12] Collins 1995; hooks 1984.
[13] Wirth 1938.
[14] Edin and Lein 1997.
[15] Federal Emergency Management Agency.
[16] Drabek 1986; Tierney, Bevc, and Kuligowski 2006.
[17] For a detailed discussion of these women's experiences seeking housing assistance, see Pardee 2012.
[18] Couch 1996: 69.
[19] See Pardee 2012; FEMA 10/1/03; HUD 2005; HUD 1/23/06.
[20] Pardee 2012; FEMA 10/1/03.
[21] FEMA 10/1/03.
[22] Pardee 2012; HUD 2005; HUD 1/23/06.
[23] Pardee 2012; HUD 2005; HUD 1/23/06.
[24] For a detailed analysis of the effectiveness of federal housing assistance for this sample, see Pardee 2012.
[25] 16 women stayed at five or more places by the time of their interview.
[26] Extended displacement is defined as maintaining residence outside of one's home community for a period of six or more months following a disaster for the purposes of this project.
[27] Comparing the group means for those who were displaced less than six months and those displaced longer than six months, there is a statistically significant difference in longest one-time housing duration.

8

Living Displacement

For anyone who has ever moved homes, especially to a place where one has no social connections, there is likely an appreciation for the amount of work it takes to build a new life. From the basics of finding a home and job, to turning on the power, water, gas, and telephone, starting anew is never easy. With a family, a move involves everything from enrolling children in schools, to finding doctors, pharmacies, and dentists, to locating grocery stores and shopping areas, to plotting out your commute, accessing public transit, and learning traffic patterns. In the best of circumstances, moving is a hectic, intense, and challenging experience.

Now, imagine moving without notice, as residents of New Orleans did—Thursday they were living in their own home with friends and family near, and life's amenities at their disposal. By Tuesday—less than a week later—they were facing the reality of living in a new place, indefinitely. Imagine doing so without money in a savings account, while being given no choice about one's destination. For many, their cars were flooded along with their homes, creating a need to rely on public transportation or taxi cabs, if they even existed in one's new town. For those affected by Hurricane Katrina, many experienced precisely this reality in their struggle to recover. Their displacement was swift, unexpected, and fundamental in changing the pathways of their lives.

So, how does one build an entire life from scratch? Can one recreate the relationships and resources needed to get by everyday in a new location? Will poverty survival strategies learned in New Orleans work elsewhere? Reflecting on the prior chapters, low-income Black women's survival strategies did work to weather the storm and provide housing in the early weeks during their displacements. From riding out the storm at the safest location, to sharing food while waiting for evacuation buses, to caravanning with kin to leave altogether, or staying with family or in a formal shelter outside of the city, survival strategies prevailed. Yet, the nature of these survival strategies was fundamentally place-bound. Access to work and social services were linked to geography through residency, and even the caravans of kin originated from families living across the metropolitan New Orleans area. Which begs the question: are survival strategies transferrable over time and across geographies?

According to Theodore Downing's international work on development-induced displacement, the answer is "no" because the skills are developed in response to the local environments in which the displaced normally live, and therefore they are spatially embedded components of culture that are disabled outside their environment of origin.[1] Specifically, the cultural transition resultant from displacement and resettlement can devalue the survival skills individuals engage because those skills are a response to *local* environmental factors, which are altered by displacement. Yet, Kathryn Edin and Laura Lein's work suggests poverty survival strategies *are* transferrable given their presence in multiple case study sites in the United States. In response, this chapter examines if and when women were able to engage previous poverty survival strategies successfully in their new post-Katrina homes. By examining the details of day-to-day survival among low-income women during their displacements, this chapter will determine how location affects recovery. As will become evident, for many women such as Mary, Joanna, and Thelma, displacement meant facing deepening levels of poverty as they were challenged to pay new bills, often while receiving lower wages and less formal assistance than before Katrina. Sadly, in the effort to regain their independence and establish stability for their families, many women's survival strategies simply fell short of the task, leaving them to move forward in uncertainty for their future well-being.

Starting Over After the Storm

> Jada: My whole life has changed since the storm. In New Orleans, I had it easy. Now, I have it hard.... I didn't have as much bills. I had money. I could take the kids out to eat, to do things. I had money. Now, all my money is spent on bills. I had a car but only paid for insurance, and low light bills. Now I have a light bill, a car note, and insurance. I can't win for losing. I'm not going to let that get me down. I will fight until I don't have anything else in me. Out here, you need a car. You trying to catch the bus, and it's in triple digits, the temperature out here. You need a car. I would never make it because I have kids.

Jada's experience was commonplace for women rebuilding after Hurricane Katrina, as new locations presented new challenges in the form of unexpected expenses for everyday needs. With the massive flooding, most women who had cars lost them to the water, along with all their furniture, clothing, appliances, linens, photographs, and other resources that they needed for daily living. For so many women in this study, Hurricane Katrina destroyed every possession and material resource they had. The only tools left with which to rebuild were their poverty survival strategies: income from jobs, help from kin, and whatever federal disaster aid they received.

So pernicious was the financial effect of the storm, that when asked, nearly three-quarters[2] of the women stated that they felt less financially secure, another fifth felt about the same, and just five women felt they were in a better financial position when we interviewed. While some news media reports proclaimed the displacement might offer new opportunities to evacuees by relocating them to better labor markets, the reality is that for over three-quarters of the women in this study, more expensive bills were a significant source of stress in their new lives. In fact, most women who spoke with me stated they were worse off after being displaced. Considering the deep poverty of these women to begin, with most making less than $20,000 per year, the reality of being less financially secure suggests they were at exceptional risk of falling into dire conditions, including extreme poverty[3] or homelessness.

The most destabilizing factors to overcome were increases in rent, utilities, and food—necessities that cannot be eliminated. Unlike women's experiences in the New Orleans pre-Katrina housing market, rent after the storm more than doubled from an average of $262 prior to the storm to $567 after, for women living both inside the city and out. Specifically, the mean difference of rental costs before and after Katrina was an increase of $305 per month, which equates to an additional $3,660 per annum. Since the majority of women earned less than $20,000 in annual income, the new rental "burden" consumes 18.3% of that maximum salary range. The rental increase burden is even higher for those earning less, such that a woman earning just $15,000 per year now had 24% more of her salary dedicated to rent. Since not every woman in this sample was receiving housing assistance anymore, this increase is a devastating impediment for women to overcome on the road toward recovery. Likewise, the high standard deviation, $398 dollars, reflects an extreme range of rents, from as low as $25 in New Orleans traditional public housing to a high of $1600 per month in a private rental. By contrast, the rent range before the storm was between $25 and $650. Such extreme rent increases stifle recovery by reducing or eliminating money for other basic expenses, such as food, medicine, or clothing.

Beyond rent, once settled into new homes, electricity and other utilities became the bill that was most challenging for women to pay, as nearly a third identified this as their "biggest bill" after the storm. Illustrating the gravity of this challenge is Mary, a 44-year-old grandmother who had hit a new level of economic desperation in the face of having her lights turned off for the first time in her life:

> The way I'm living now, I've never lived like this. I never lived like this. I'm not able to pay my bills. When I was in the projects I didn't have a light bill. But even when I was in New Orleans in a house, I never had my lights off.... Every month my lights is turned off. I'm under a lot of stress. I worry. How we gonna eat, when we got no lights today? It's a mess. My life is in shambles, it is. [...] I have a $222 dollar water bill. I can't pay it, Miss.... I don't ask for money. I'm not getting nothing for me, for my grandkids.... I need to get some income. It's hard for me, it's rough.

Deeply committed to the care of her grandchildren, ages twelve and thirteen when we spoke, Mary was displaced in Houston and unable to afford the transition from the subsidized housing and included utilities she relied on for daily survival in New Orleans to paying many of these bills herself in Texas, especially as she attempted to do so with fewer resources than ever.

So desperate were the challenges of covering all the bills that Mary actually began to reverse the little progress toward recovery she had made by selling off the few things she bought with her FEMA assistance following the storm. Mary describes her new life after Katrina:

> It just messed up everything. Everything. Nothing is going right for me. My family, they all apart. My son is in Florida, my daughter, they got their house together. They got a little money from FEMA. I had to spend it all on life, clothes, to start all over. Then what I did buy, I had to pawn it all. Just to pay bills! Miss, I had a deep freezer, I had to pawn that too. $50 for a deep freezer! I lost everything in the pawn shop. I hope I can make it home, and get that freezer back. Then I got grandkids, and they want a snack, they want this and that. They cut the food stamps off. It's been two months. It's been the hardest two months. I can't even buy anything 'cause nobody's got room to put food in their icebox.

Living most of her life in poverty, and six years in public housing before the storm, Mary demonstrates the immediacy of needs as she described the prior two months as the "hardest." Learning to manage within the limited benefits of Louisiana's assistance programs, Mary developed a survival skill of buying food in bulk at the month's start when food stamp monies are distributed all at once. Using a deep freezer to store the food is a common tactic among the poor, but this strategy of maximizing her food stamp assistance was dismantled when her displacement to Texas resulted in lower benefit amounts. Mary's food stamp reduction was almost a hundred dollars per month following Katrina. Furthermore, she was not transferred to Texas' permanent food stamp pool despite her inability to return to New Orleans in the foreseeable future, resulting in the elimination of this valuable resource altogether. Forced to pawn her deep freezer and skip payment on her power bill to purchase food, this combination of lost formal assistance (food stamps) and regular losses of power effectively doubled Mary's food costs. Since she cannot store food purchased in larger quantities, she must pay more for less. Additionally, any perishable food may be wasted when the power is turned off for non-payment. Mary now raises her grandchildren without the security of food and power, knowing every day that the next level of poverty from here is homelessness.

Layering on her survival challenges, it is not merely the loss of food stamps that inhibit Mary's recovery, but the concurrent increase in housing costs and a decreased income that left Mary desperate as she attempted to care for her kin. This interaction of her social class, her disaster status, her gendered familial obligations, and her geographical location in an evacuee-swamped labor market directly hindered her recovery:

> Before Katrina, I was paying $35 per month for rent, then $75. I was paying for the phone. Now, I ain't getting no income. I can't get a job here. They cut me off, but my children have to eat too. I have to suffer and my grandkids have to suffer. And we lost our food stamps.

With the dismantling of assistance-based and work-based poverty survival strategies,[4] Mary's recovery at the time of our interview was just as devastating as being stranded in the days following the storm, except this trauma was extended over time. Without money, returning to New Orleans was not an option, while getting by in Houston was not working either. In this way, Mary could not return to life as it was before the storm ("recovery"), which translates into the possibility she may never truly recover from Katrina, experiencing the storm instead as a never-ending trauma.

In short, recovery was unavailable to Mary at the time of her interview, as she faced an alternative pathway in which the disaster caused deepened levels of poverty, with the threat of homelessness knocking on her door. So, while the community around her was intact (Houston, Texas), her extended displacement to a new environment dismantled her work and assistance-based survival strategies. As the caregiver for her grandchildren, her role suggests she is the reliable family to which others turn for help, reflected by her inability to engage a family-based survival strategy to meet the gap in her bills. Finally, in the absence of aid-based assistance as determined by her geography, her race may also be a factor preventing employment as well, to be discussed at length below.

The experience of increased poverty and financial instability was commonplace. In fact, over four-fifths of women were worried about not being able to pay their bills when we spoke. Like Mary, many women struggled to engage their survival strategies successfully in new contexts; contexts largely characterized by more expensive housing markets and utility costs, more sprawling spatial arrangements that made cars necessary for survival, and limited or non-existent kin networks to help with bills, food, and shelter. Whether relying on work, kin, or federal aid programs to help them recover, the transferability of using these strategies in new contexts was uncertain at best.

Strategy Dismantled: Jobless in New Labor Markets

With national news reports suggesting New Orleans would need years to recover, one of the most common ways women began their recovery work in new locations was to search for a job. For the previously employed (41.2%), a new job represented security, independence, and some protection from the risks of unemployment, such as homelessness. It was also a mechanism for starting over and saving the money to get back home to New Orleans.

Before Katrina, the New Orleans job market was heavily focused on three primary sectors: tourism, higher education,[5] and the medical industry. Reflecting this pattern, many women who spoke with me worked in the medical profession or with government institutions, holding positions such as a certified nursing assistant, home help aid, retirement community staff member, 911 operator, and public school teacher. Just two women held service jobs, including a position in food services and one in a retail shop.

Devastatingly, job loss was a major consequence of the storm. Only nine women were able to find and keep work at the time we spoke. One of the major impediments was discrimination in hiring, which disabled work as a survival strategy. In fact, seven women reported discrimination against evacuees as a reason they could not secure work: Regina, Joanna, Jada, Mary, Sharon, Julia, and Amaya. The basis of the discrimination was a combination of women's intersectional statuses as racial, economic, and geographical minorities. While race- and class-based discrimination are typical and well-documented in labor markets throughout the U.S.,[6] geographical discrimination occurred when employers refused to hire people from New Orleans in communities where an evacuee stigma had formed.

This stigma was founded upon media-driven hype that evacuees were refugees and dangerous looters who shot at the same relief workers who tried to help them, frequently defrauded FEMA to cheat the system, and brought increased crime and violence to cities like Houston where they relocated.[7] Yet, according to Tierney, Bevc, and Kuligowski, looting during Hurricane Katrina was reported as "very widespread, wanton, irrational, and accompanied by violence" even though no actual empirical data documenting the extent, instigators, or motivation behind the acts was available.[8] For the low-income Black women of this study, the lived experience was that they faced terrible scrutiny and discrimination on the job market resulting from a combination of pre-existing racism and sexism, further complicated by the stigma placed on all Black New Orleanians as a result of the media-representation of looting as riot behavior. Yet in reality, these women were attempting to rebuild their lives in honest and modest ways through hard work.

The loss of work not only affected income but also reduced other resources women could rely upon to reestablish their independence, including health insurance. First, work had been a consistent experience for previously employed women, who had a mean working time of just over six years and averaged 37.5 hours per week. As a collective, these women had been stably employed, reliable workers. Additionally, since almost all were full-time employees, several had benefits such as sick leave (53.3%), health insurance (40%), and retirement contributions (26.7%) through their employers. Work enabled these women to move toward self-sufficiency, while Katrina forced them back into reliance on the government.

Leaving New Orleans to survive the storm meant leaving access to their employer and employment opportunities. To document how effective this survival strategy remained in new contexts, women were asked about their employment status at three points in time—before Katrina, while evacuated from New Orleans, and at the time of the interview. When asked whether they worked during their evacuation, just one woman reported having the same job, while fifteen working women reported being let go, and only three women received employer assistance. Yet, the loss of employment did not result in many women securing new jobs. Instead, just three women secured a new job during their evacuation, representing a meager 6% of the total sample. At the time of interview, just four women had found work. Among these women, all reported the job being better or just as good as before. Still, with the vast majority of working women unemployed during their evacuation and displacement periods, 92% of the full sample either chose not to work (especially those caring for aging parents or younger children), were retired, had a disability, or had not been able to locate a job at the time we spoke.

Among previously working women, there were two common explanations for their extensive unemployment. The first was the presence of a split labor market, especially in communities such as Houston with a large Latino worker base.[9] In these cases, the New Orleans women anticipated higher wages based on their experience in New Orleans than were available. They were not prepared to face competition for those jobs in a market with so many immigrant workers able to accept minimum wage or below. This wage differential is the result of the global poverty survival strategy of sending home remittances, where the strength of the U.S. dollar in an immigrant worker's sending country transforms a non-livable minimum wage in the U.S. into a livable wage in the globalized labor market. As a result, many evacuee women could not demand a livable wage when they were hired, if they secured the position at all. Regina and Mary each described this situation in detail:

> Regina: It's hard out here. It's hard once they see you from New Orleans…. I'm looking, every day. They prefer the Mexican workers. They still making five dollars out here. They don't want to give you what you paid before. Here they pay like five dollars, or five thirty-five.

In this instance, the split labor market divided the workforce, pricing Regina out of the position altogether in favor of an immigrant worker who will accept minimum wage pay.

For Mary, she understood that low educational levels might disqualify her as an applicant, but ultimately identified the split labor market to explain her unemployment as well:

> It's hard to get a job with no high school diploma. If you want a good job, that's what you need. I took a temp job. I was working every week. I made $260 per week, and it was some help, and every two weeks I was getting paid. One week, I even made $407 in one week. I'd take NoDoz, but I can't get to the job. I have no transport. I tried to call a ride line. They say if you can't get a ride, then they would get you there. But it was too far out. I was working for a mail packing company. I was the stamper.

Here, Mary identified her unemployment as a result of her lack of transportation.

Certainly, transportation barriers are a common difficulty facing the poor, independent of the disaster.[10] However, as the interview progressed, Mary edited her reasoning to address the issue of ethnic preference by employers:

> A lot of people had good jobs, now they give them to Mexicans. Cousins, aunties, they don't want them for their job because Mexicans take less money. They have to be deported and so they can't get their jobs. They give it to somebody else working for lesser pay. We behind all them here, you know? And they gotta start all over. They was set up to retire, you know?

This statement demonstrates building resentment toward Mexicans, and the lower cost labor they represent. At the same time, Mary's comments also reflect the sadness she felt over the losses to her and her family caused by Katrina. Without the ability to find new work, she and her extended family, some of whom were financially stable and approaching retirement, have to start over to create financial security in job markets where they are not considered the most desirable hires.

Yet, it is unclear if the real issue in hiring is about race and ethnicity, or a broader discrimination based on geography. Toward the end of the interview, Mary replaces the split labor market explanation with a more generalized one about discrimination against evacuees from New Orleans:

> Jessica: Why do you think you can't find a job?
>
> Mary: They don't want to hire you when they find out you from New Orleans. I even got a Texas ID. I went to Burger King the other day, just to give her an application and she said she'll call. I know what that means. She's not gonna call. And she ain't called me yet.

For low-income women with limited job skills, the split labor market in places like Texas presents a tangible barrier to gainful employment. However, the evacuee stigma that encouraged discrimination was much more insidious, since it was often dismissed as playing the victim.[11] For Jada, she too faced the New Orleans stigma in her job search in Texas:

> I just want to go home. I don't see how I can make it out here. I can't get a job, and there's nothing but Mexicans here, and I guess since we looking like we come from New Orleans, there's not a lot of people who are hiring us. I'm still trying, I'm not going to give up, but it gets frustrating sometimes. [...] When I came here, I applied for a correctional officer position, I applied at Office Depot, I applied at a gas station, and I still didn't get a job. I passed the test, interviewed at the sheriff's office, finished the physical, passed the drug test, and did everything. It's a matter of them calling me. Today I got a call from a security job—they called me to fill out an application. I guess they want to hire me, because they called twice. Hopefully, that will pan out. But I'm looking.

It is not a lack of effort on Jada's part that has kept her unemployed. While she still is somewhat reluctant to identify her experience as one of discrimination, other respondents, such as Sharon, were not. Stated bluntly:

> The ones from Louisiana, they definitely didn't get hired. I had one lady tell me from the outreach center that she thinks Louisiana people have been there long enough to get jobs. I reminded her. I agree most people should have gotten jobs. But I have a grandson, a daughter, a granddaughter.... They get 4 hours a week, then they not on the schedule. They can't live off of the jobs they get, you know? I mean, before you talk, you do some research! I'd like to get something I can do. I just need a car. I'll be okay.

In small ways, discrimination can unfold—being hired, but "fired" in a de facto manner through the reduction of hours is one mechanism. More classic forms include saying a position is filled, when it is not. While each of these accounts could be argued as a biased report from the victim, implicit prejudice theory is consistent with these women's claims of discrimination.[12] Based on media coverage of Katrina "refugees" as dangerous looters who were shooting the same relief workers who were trying to help them,[13] it is reasonable to argue that employers, service workers, and others in receiving communities were primed to assume the worst of all evacuees, and thus became resistant to hiring them. Layering on society's well-known bias against low-income individuals and ethnic minorities,[14] it is logical the low-income, African American women of this study, more than others, would face discrimination in hiring, based on geography as well as race and class.

So challenging was the act of finding a job in Texas, Julia, a 46-year-old mother of an infant ultimately returned to her undamaged HOPE VI apartment in New Orleans just so she could find work, even though doing so compromised possibilities for her emotional recovery in the process.

> Julia: Well, I didn't like where I was at in Texas. When I called River Garden, they said it was okay, I could come home. If I wouldn't have came back, I'd probably be homeless myself.
>
> Jessica: Why do you think you'd be homeless?
>
> Julia: 'Cause FEMA ain't paying no money. It's hard to find a job out there. I knew the jobs was here. I had to get back to find a job; where I was, they didn't have none.
>
> Jessica: What made it hard to find a job in Texas?
>
> Julia: Well, I really can't say why I couldn't find a job. When I went to apply, they didn't have no openings. We "New Orleans evacuees." I hate to be labeled, but that's the way it was, so I had to get home to take care of my grandchild and daughter.
>
> In Louisiana, you not gonna get anything. I appreciate them for letting us come, and I don't fault them for anything, but they should have took care of us better than they did. Not everyone was fortunate enough to get a house and pay for itself. Not everyone is a millionaire. I'm a working person, I just want to live, work, and be peaceful. That's all I ask for. It's like a suicidal thing here. You don't know which way to go, so you go with it. I just keep praying. A lot of my friends, family members, they at the edge. They can't come to they family's apartment because we can't have them here. I don't try to bicker with nobody. I work every morning at five in the morning. I make my home be a home. That's all we can do.

While most women did not work during their evacuation and extended displacement, it was not because they preferred to receive family and government assistance—they were simply not hired, despite being qualified.

Scattered Kin, Dismantled Strategy

The role of kin in everyday poverty survival is essential—while they may not have money to lend to cover bills, they can offer in-kind assistances, such as childcare, free meals, emotional support, transportation, and small basics like offering an egg or providing diapers for a child.[15] During the evacuation, kin were also essential in providing immediate access to transportation from the city, non-flooded housing within the city, or temporary housing at hotels and residences in the evacuation zone. As time moved forward though, the ability of extended kin to care for low-income displaced families languished and was dismantled, because "it's hard to ask for help, to ask a family member. They have family, too."

Rarely did women explicitly discuss the negative effects of displacement on family support systems, such as the loss of the everyday material help they received. Rather, time after time, women engaged in a language of loss that hinted at the new isolation they faced without their family and friends nearby. In the absence of family and community, Linda's explanation of the saddest thing about Hurricane Katrina reflects these feelings of isolation and loss:

> I was sad—when the families, everybody being separated. I didn't know where nobody was. That part hurt you most, living in a city where they didn't care about you. That was sad. It was more.... The saddest part for me is like family—being separated from your families. Stories that you heard, some of the things that they went through.

Sharon, too, explained how family and kin were lost due to Katrina:

> The saddest thing was just being separated from everybody, and so many lives being lost. Not knowing right now, today, not knowing if someone I knew died. I had friends from the 9th ward, I'm wondering about them, friends from work. I have no way to find out. So many was dying, just from the stress. I lost so many friends, right after the storm. They sick, and then the storm bring on death faster. I lost a lot of friends. They just died. That's one of the things. Then, when I first got here, I was in a "Star Wars" state of mind. I was thinking: "Will I ever see my friends again?" I felt like I was in a world all by myself.

For Abigail, who evacuated with family and ultimately found a rental in a rural town in Louisiana using FEMA assistance, Katrina was a trigger for repetitive loss due to displacement and death. "Most of my people, friends I've had for 35, 40 years, they scattered across the United States. Since my daughter passed, I've talked to a lot of people.... I know a few people that passed who had heart attacks. And one of my co-workers drown." Just a week before we spoke, Abigail's daughter had passed away from cancer, and her other daughter had returned to New Orleans, taking Abigail's grandchildren with her. As was the experience for many women, displacement from New Orleans meant more than just displacement from their homes; it meant separation from an elaborate circle of friends based in their residential neighborhoods, workplaces, and churches. Even among the poor, Katrina caused a loss of communality—the sense of community and shared state of mind[16]—reflecting the importance held by networks of friendship and support beyond those of the extended family. As Sharon lamented, the loss was about "being able to go to a neighbor's and sit out and talk. Everybody's so far apart."

So important were kin networks that some evacuees willingly gave up the initial security they had created through various social service programs in new locations in order to reunite with specific family members elsewhere. Recall Jada, whose positive experience in Virginia staying with her cousin and his wife was not sufficient to keep her there. Because living displacement meant more than just securing housing and other forms of stability, it also meant dealing with the emotional trauma of the hurricane and its aftermath, Jada gave up her aid-based security to reconnect with kin-based support as her children struggled to understand their experiences at the Convention Center in New Orleans:

> Well, the children were traumatized for a while. They have counseling at the pool in Virginia. They in counseling. My youngest, he say, "Mom, I don't want to go back. New Orleans stinks." All he could remember is the smell. He keep asking "what is that, Mamma?" and I'd say "That's the smell." Plus, my eleven year old, he made eleven at the Convention Center cause we didn't leave 'til that Saturday.

With her youngest son acting out at school, Jada moved again to be closer to her son's grandmother in the hopes that proximity to the kin network and its support system would help her son recover emotionally.

While this new arrangement benefitted her son's emotional recovery, Jada's ability to find work after her move to Texas was dismantled due to discrimination and the split labor market there. Sacrificing the family's financial recovery for the sake of her youngest son, her effort to recreate the kin support system dismantled other survival strategies in return. In many ways, Jada's entire experience centered around the care of her four children, and making their safety and needs a priority, even if it meant a more difficult experience for her in terms of finding a job or accessing social services to cover the bills. This commitment to motherhood was reflected by her response when asked what the saddest part of the Katrina experience was for her: "Just seeing my kids and the expressions on their face, leaving their home, and sleeping on the ground of someplace they've never been."

Uncertain Survival: Aid-based Strategies

In the absence of work-based survival strategies and the ability of family to make up the difference, low-income women turned to FEMA and other forms of social assistance to aid in the transition to a new, post-Katrina life. As a household of one, I personally received two payments from FEMA after the storm. The first was for a total of $2,000 and the second for $2,358. These payments occurred once, and it was unclear how long they were meant to last. It is my understanding that these payments were the same for larger households, meaning there was less money to go around. During the interviews, only one woman identified receiving the $10,000 FEMA payment reported on television in the early weeks in Houston, Texas. Instead, most families received very modest sums of money, barely enough to cover food and new clothing; nevermind the more pressing needs of shelter and healthcare.

Compared to before the storm, assistance following Katrina was less sustaining even when its dollar value was greater, due to the high cost of living in new locations and the variable assistance rates by state for programs such as welfare, food stamps, Medicaid, Social Security, and public housing.[17] As a result, where an evacuee resided had as much of an effect on their potential for recovery as their determination to survive—in short, evacuees in states with more generous social services had better chances to recover than those in states with smaller safety nets. The two programs where these differences were most apparent for low-income women were food stamps and Medicare.

Despite devastating increases in rent and utilities, women did receive increased food stamp allocations following Katrina. Comparing food stamps before and after the storm, there was a net increase of $19.33 per month, and participation in the program increased from 67.7% of the full sample prior to the hurricane to 78.4% after the storm. Unfortunately, this increase in amount and participation is deceptive, since most families received immediate, post-disaster relief, which was terminated shortly thereafter, or reduced significantly as federal budget cuts to the long-term food stamp program decreased regular assistance levels overall[18]—and by as much as $248 for one case in this study. As many families combined households across generations out of necessity when they evacuated to locations without enough of a housing supply, the household size increased by .18 persons on average, which increased food stamp allocations by as much as $151. This household recombination in conjunction with the presence of short-term relief and program restructuring explains, in part, the changes in food stamp allocations.

Perhaps the more important determinant affecting food stamp allocations was the displacement location, since non-disaster food stamp allocations are distributed through local jurisdictions, which can apply local level criteria for program participants.[19] This pattern is illustrated by Ingrid, a 52-year-old married woman who lived in public housing with her husband before the storm:

> Well, my husband and I, we went to Texas. [...] He applied for food stamps, and they gave him food stamps for him; then when we went to Virginia, the food stamps stopped. Then he applied in December, and they gave him $10, which was a big step down from $150. That's to feed two people! I was getting $198 before the storm in New Orleans.

Here, changing locations resulted in a loss of assistance as the family transitioned from the disaster food stamp allocation of $150 to the local allocation of $10 in Virginia, both of which pale in comparison to the $198 the family was accustomed to receiving prior to the storm in Louisiana.

Yet even Althea, a 70-year-old woman who returned to New Orleans faced food stamp reductions from approximately one hundred dollars a month before Katrina, down to a mere a $48 after the storm. This reflects a devastating loss of nearly half her assistance amount, despite returning to New Orleans to live. Stifling her process of recovery even further, Althea explained that FEMA was now trying to make her repay the $4,358 they provided, because she failed to keep receipts for the clothing she purchased during her displacement:[20]

> I'm stressed out with the FEMA mess—they need receipts. I had to buy everything. I don't have no receipts. I got receipts for the ice box, the deep freezer, but not clothes. It's just messed up. All this borrowed money.[21]

In the effort to start her recovery, it was sadly the exact assistance program meant to aid in that process that was putting the most strain on Althea. From FEMA to food stamps, one of the important lessons of the storm is exactly how incapable our social safety net actually is when we need it the most.

Rounding out the challenges women faced while engaging their assistance-based survival strategies in new locations was the variability of services offered under Medicare in different states and locations. Unlike so many places, New Orleans had an extensive charitable hospital system, allowing low-income individuals to access medical care at reduced, if any, cost. This was not the case in new evacuation locations, where access to medical care and prescriptions became an emergent survival challenge for displaced women and their families. As Joanna explained,

> When we came down here, I was used to going to Charity Hospital. My medicine got wet, and I have 10 types of pills. This woman asked if I was working, then she said "I'm sorry, you can't be seen."

For Joanna, to be denied access to healthcare because she was not employed was surprising based on her expectations of free access to medical care.

This surprise grew when Joanna learned she was no longer eligible for Medicaid either, because her FEMA assistance money counted as "income." These unexpected changes to her medical access challenged her physical recovery following the disaster, as she became unable to meet her medical needs:

> On February 6, I got so sick, I passed out. I didn't want to tell my mom. I thought it was a heart attack. I had to call the ambulance. I thought it was my appendix. Then the doorbell rang. It was my mom's nurse. I had passed out 'cause my gallstones ruptured. After that I went to social services, and tried for a Medicaid card. I was turned down because of the $2000 I got from FEMA. I reapplied, but then I had a problem because of my income tax. There's just all kinds of situations, they keep you going to the bottom of the ditch. I need to go to Dallas. There's a hospital where they do it for free, and I'm trying to see about the procedure. My last ultrasound, they said I needed surgery to have my gallbladder removed. I'm still trying to get a Medicaid card.

In short, by engaging the aid-based survival strategy of accepting $2000 in FEMA disaster aid to meet immediate housing, food, and clothing needs, Joanna's income became too high to maintain her eligibility for Medicaid. Given her need for surgery, Medicaid was by far more important than FEMA assistance for her long-term recovery. Sadly, at the time we spoke, Joanna's future was uncertain in the face of declining health and a genuine risk of death.

As women attempted to transition into longer term survival by using aid-based assistance, it became clear that doing so successfully required a degree of finesse and applied knowledge to be able to layer the help correctly, so as to prevent one form of aid from disqualifying an evacuee from another. Unfortunately, since programs such as food stamps and Medicaid are administered at the state-level, the rules for eligibility vary by state, meaning knowledge from Louisiana's assistance system is not directly transferrable to Texas, Alabama, or any other state in the nation. This non-transferability supports Downing's argument that survival skills are not universal across contexts.[22] While the broad survival typologies (kin-, aid-, and work-based) do transfer,[23] the specifics of program knowledge do not. For Thelma, a 71-year-old stable Section 8 resident for ten years before the storm, her experience in a new context was exceptionally challenging. In fact, things were not going well at the time of our interview because Thelma's reduction in Medicare benefits was preventing her from being able to meet her bills in other areas. Thelma summarized her place-based assistance inequality quite well:

> For me, it's like my medical needs—in New Orleans, the doctors I had been seeing were the same for years. They would give me samples of medicine. It's so expensive now. I'm on about 14 medications, and it runs out quicker on me than it do for someone on one or two medications. They gave me a medical card, but here they only give you three medications. And it's only for four or five months.

While Thelma had some medical security after the storm from her Louisiana Medicare assistance, her benefits were rescinded when she applied for Medicare in Texas (as required by law), where she had found temporary housing during her displacement. She told me:

> My biggest problem now is I have no coverage, seeing Louisiana was paying my Medicare premium, so my FEMA doctor is sending me all my bills. I had to apply with Texas. But when I applied for Texas, Medicare in Louisiana dropped me. I got a letter saying Louisiana is taking my premiums from my FEMA money, but I have a letter saying Texas will pay the premiums.... Texas is paying my Medicare payments. Social Security tells me it takes a while to get it straight, but it's been four months. They're only sending $500 and something a month now. The medicine cost is almost that. I offered to fax them my letter, but they told me it must come directly from the state of Texas.

Her family was staying in a town barely across the Louisiana state line, only because it was the first town with available motel rooms when they evacuated before the storm.

By mere circumstance, Thelma's entire disaster recovery was directly affected by the nation's fragmented system of social assistance, leaving her in worse poverty than ever before and in genuine risk of declining health and homelessness:

> With housing you get a voucher for 18 months; then what you going to do? Food is so high, but now I'm on the same income. If people are working, that's different. But you on a fixed income and medicine costs keep going up. What you going to do? I have $1000 in medical bills; I don't have the money to pay for anything. I have a Walmart credit card to buy food. I have to pay that. The only thing I have is a bed to sleep in, that's it.

Thelma's ability to recover was questionable as she addressed her food and medical costs, barely making it work. On a fixed income, she was forced to rely on her voucher to cover her housing costs, but also recognized this assistance would end after 18 months. While she was housed, fed, and getting necessary medications at the time of our interview, she knew her patchwork of survival resources would inevitably shred in the future when her voucher payments stopped, undermining her recovery in the process.

In this way, Thelma's pre-Katrina aid-based survival strategy of using Louisiana's Medicare program combined with free samples from doctors dissolved into a pile of bills and delays until the Texas system would add her to their program, and social security incorporated the transition into their system. In the meantime, Louisiana was garnering Thelma's FEMA payments to cover her medical expenses, which should have been covered by her Texas Medicare. Thelma was also faced with the decision of which three out of fourteen medications were most important for her to take, while trying to afford the rest in addition to her other bills, despite the fact her medicine costs were equivalent to her entire monthly social security benefit. Thelma was not recovering from the storm.

Conclusion

When women could, they worked. When work was unavailable, they relied on kin-based and aid-based assistance to compensate for the inability to locate a job in areas that had both a pre-existing split labor market, as well as active discrimination caused by the evacuee stigma. Women actively attempted to translate their work-based survival strategies to new locations only to find them ineffective in the face of employment discrimination. As much as possible, women used the same aid-based survival strategies in new locations, but with no guarantee that doing so would actually help them make ends meet.

On the whole, it is apparent women were housed and fed in the short term, but struggled to pay increased utilities or meet other needs like clothing, medical, and school supplies. Furthermore, the new contexts of how social services were implemented in displacement locations inhibited a return to their pre-Katrina level of very finite financial stability. With work dismantled as a displacement survival strategy due to rampant and unexpected discrimination, women were increasingly forced to rely on kin- or aid-assistance when they could. As a source of short-term housing and emotional support, kin-based networks were helpful, but when composed of other displaced New Orleanians who were also struggling to rebuild their lives from scratch, they simply could not function in the ways they once did.

When the kin networks could not support the women, as was frequently the case in a network where everyone was strained, women were forced to do without—including electricity and medicine—or to sell their limited possessions for cash to pay bills, reversing their efforts toward recovery. Finding that many survival strategies were non-transferrable across contexts and locations, women who were able to return to New Orleans did, where the primary limitation to getting hired was actually finding a job to which to apply.

---

[1] Downing 1996; Lein et al. 2012.
[2] 69.4%, n=49; 2 women skipped the question.
[3] Extreme poverty is defined by the Census Bureau as having an income at 50% of the federal poverty line or less.
[4] Edin and Lein 1997.
[5] Tulane University was the City of New Orleans' largest employer.
[6] Wilson 1987, 1996, 2010; Holzer 1987; Tomaskovic-Devey and Stainback 2007; Bonacich 1972.
[7] Tierney, Bevc, and Kuligowski 2006.
[8] Tierney, Bevc, and Kuligowski 2006: 65-66.
[9] Bonacich 1972; Davis 2000.
[10] Seccombe 2007.
[11] Quillian 2006.
[12] Quillian 2006; Gladwell 2005.
[13] Tierney, Bevc, and Kuligowski 2006.
[14] Fothergill 2003.
[15] Stack 1974; Edin and Lein 1997.
[16] Erikson 1976.
[17] Lein 2012.
[18] Dreier 2006.

[19] As constructed, the indicator does not specify between food stamps received immediately after the storm, versus those at the time of interview.

[20] A request that was never made by FEMA of myself, a white, college-educated renter from New Orleans.

[21] Interestingly, Althea's evacuation was basically the same as mine—she left in advance, stayed with family and friends to keep her costs down to a minimum, and returned to the city to live after a couple months. Yet, FEMA has not asked me for my receipts nor to repay the money. Instead, I was offered a trailer after a FEMA representative saw my undamaged and completely livable New Orleans apartment. This differential treatment reflects the power of race and perceived class in shaping how a person is treated by institutions and creates variations in the ability to recover.

[22] Downing 1996.

[23] Edin and Lein 1997.

9
Returning Home

Returning to the city after living in displacement was a jarring experience. On every street, and among virtually every house, there were signs of the damage and destruction, which became daily reminders of the storm. In the worst damaged residential neighborhoods, piles of wood boards, furniture, and the everyday artifacts of normal life where strewn across yards and streets, or bulldozed into massive piles filling the spaces that were once homes themselves, as well as neighborhood parks and neutral grounds.

In other neighborhoods, among those homes that were still standing, dirty brown bands about a foot thick marked the height where the floodwaters had settled. Driving around to see Katrina's effects, one was often devastated by the reality that the brown flood line two feet below a door jam was still several feet above people's heads on a home already perched on pillars to raise it three feet off the ground, as most bungalow and shotgun homes in the city were. Entire neighborhoods were marked by these flood lines, all across the city. Home after home, flood line after flood line, each house represented the potential for death—someone not making it through the storm. Each home with a flood line was a place where someone may have drown. On the houses that still stood, spray paint hash marks symbolized the death counts as each home was entered, often forcibly, to search for bodies. Seeing the debris, the flood lines, and hash marks, it was undeniable how completely Katrina's waters transformed the comforts of home into painful piles of trash symbolizing all that was lost, including life itself. Returning to New Orleans to live was a trauma unto itself.

In late September and early October 2005, as the first neighborhoods reopened to residents after their streets were initially cleared, the city bore the marks of the storm everywhere. Downtown, on the famous Bourbon Street, bars and tee shirt shops reopened almost immediately, bringing with them a hint of life. Adjacent to them, strip clubs reopened to service the countless male relief workers who were paid to remove the debris from around the city, magnifying sexism and racism in the absence of the traditional community membership and its norms. In those early weeks, cat calls and stares assaulted women when walking down the streets, as overtly racist comments permeated the bars and locales.[1] The loss, devastation, and destruction were often blamed on the very victims who were stranded, desperate to stay alive as they waited days for help to arrive. In a decade of living in the city, the period between October 2005 and January 2006 revealed the most overt racism I had ever observed in New Orleans.[2]

Slowly, day by day and week by week, more people returned. As more restaurants and corner stores reopened, the city began to reclaim some of its identity. Blue tarps faded away, music returned to the streets of the French Quarter, and universities, with their masses of educated employees and eager students, reopened to both populate and energize a devastated community. Depression was abundant, entrenched, and omnipresent—it was the normal in those early months of recovery.[3] Loss—from the deaths of people you knew, to those who decided not to return, to friends who came back only to collect their things and leave again—threatened every day in that first year after Katrina. Some losses were large like a family member dying from the stress of the storm; some were smaller but very significant such as learning the insurance would not cover your damages; others were trivial, like learning your favorite store or restaurant went out of business. Yet, whatever it was that happened, loss was ever abundant during that time.[4]

Within that first year, the city of New Orleans struggled to both maintain its rich identity as well as recreate itself into something new after the storm. Like a cancer survivor moving into remission, no matter how good the recovery, the memory of the struggle will always be there, as will be the fear of a recurrence. In that first year, Katrina was part of the daily conversation; it was simply inevitable. So pervasive was its wrath, only when one left the city and faced its complete absence in the dialogue did one realize how deeply the storm permeated social life in New Orleans.

Amid this context, women living their displacements had to make the crucial choice as to whether or not they would return to New Orleans. New Orleans was a dangerous place, with the experience of being stranded challenging the idea of home as safe. In response, there was a common ambivalence about the feasibility of going home. What if another storm came? Where would the kids go to school? Are the hospitals open? Grocery stores? Are the buses running yet? Women based their decisions on factors ranging from whether others in their kin networks had returned, accounts from neighbors and friends about the conditions of their homes and the city, the lack of affordable housing, the loss of jobs, and the limited access to medical services. Together these considerations determined whether women would build their lives anew in displacement communities or return home to New Orleans, a place with distinct challenges of its own to overcome.

This chapter examines the ambivalence women held when making their decisions to return to the city or stay away indefinitely. For many, children, grandchildren, and connections to extended family and social kin were among the most important reasons to stay away, as well as return. Next, the chapter examines what happened to women who came back to live in the community at large, and how their ability to engage survival strategies in the post-disaster context was altered. Finally, the chapter examines the experiences of women returning to live in the River Garden neighborhood, a HOPE VI mixed-income public housing community that had no structural damage or flooding. Of any group in this sample, these women had the best potential for a full recovery.

Through these comparisons, it will become clear that returning to the city meant no guarantee of a recovery for any group of women. Instead, the new geography of post-Katrina New Orleans had just as many challenges in daily life as living in extended displacement during this time. As a result, recovery—defined as a restoration to one's status prior to the event—simply was not available for any of the women in this study.[5] Instead, women and their families lived in uncertainty, struggling to piece together new systems of survival in a post-Katrina world—to limited success.

Is It Safe to Go Home?

After the trauma of being stranded, hostile evacuations, and watching events unfold on television, most women developed a sense of ambivalence toward returning to live in New Orleans. By the completion of interviews in December 2006, the combination of hurricane damage and social disaster shattered women's sense of security and trust in the government and levees. In fact, only their faith in God remained unaltered, as many women expressed an unwavering sense of faith despite everything.[6] In contrast, the return of high levels of violent crime; the loss of family, neighbors, and community; and the lacking healthcare, employment, and housing markets left women feeling reluctant to return to the city. At that time, just under half of the women in the sample were already living in the city, though another third stated they were willing to come home. When I asked each woman if she would ever return, Linda and Sarah expressed their sense of fear about that decision:

> Linda: Um, once it gets built up better than what it was. Right now, they still acting crazy down there. The least thing you do, they take you to jail. No, not now. The levees not fixed. I will go back, but the city will have to get a whole lot better before I return there.

> Sarah: I'm missing New Orleans. The New Orleans there is not the New Orleans I left. As of now, I can't say. Maybe by then I'd really be content here. The longer I'm away and in another place and get established I'm not going to want to go back—you become satisfied where you are.

These feelings were reasonably commonplace after the storm. As global warming increases both the frequency and intensity of hurricanes and with the federal government's commitment to rebuild the levee system to the same level of protection as before Katrina, a mere Category 3 storm means the risk of another flood remains imminent. Layer on the experiences of violence, racism, and trauma during the storm, evacuation, and in the shelters, and it becomes even more difficult to make the decision whether to return to the city. Finally, as women consulted with kin who returned early, those reports factored into the decision whether to return, just as they had during evacuation decision making.

One additional way women made their decisions was to visit New Orleans and see the damages for themselves, as Regina's experience demonstrates. While each woman had general ideas about the recovery and the city's livability, for Regina, the deciding factor to stay away from the city was a vicious run-in with the New Orleans police during Mardi Gras in 2006. Regina's altercation forced her to withstand direct harassment and racism:

> Like at the parades, I went to Endymion and Bacchus. At Endymion, they would overlook the Black kids. We were between St. Andrew and Josephine. There was nothing for the kids. I used to love Endymion, it was always a favorite but.... Everybody said they didn't want to come back no more. They should have not even had Mardi Gras. They stopped Zulu at 6 o'clock. We went to Orleans and Claiborne and the police was cursing at us. They told us to "go the fuck back where you came from." How did they know we not even from town? [...] They don't gotta worry about me no more!

Previously ambivalent, Regina's visit to the city solidified her decision to remain in Texas and rebuild a new life there, abandoning New Orleans as her home.

Among her Texas-based social circle, this sentiment was dominant: "Other families I know here, they not coming back either." It also sparked anger toward political figures such as the mayor, who she felt had "sold out," as he visited Texas churches—including hers—to pander for electoral votes:

> They didn't care about us in New Orleans. Don't come out here to sit in church! Nagin—nobody want him. He sold out on the Blacks 'cause he didn't know what he was doing in the first place.... He sold out not knowing what he was getting himself into—he's getting a free ride. He has a house out here all paid for, so if it doesn't work out.... He sold out, too, to get federal money.

Themes of government mismanagement and mistrust, combined with the loss of pre-Katrina community, permeate this expression of anger, as well as guide the decision to resettle elsewhere, transforming extended displacement into a new form of recovery.

For Regina to recover from Katrina's trauma and the city's continued racism, she chose to stay away completely, rejecting the city as her future home. Regina continued:

> There's NOPD police here in jail. They might as well close New Orleans down. There's hotels closing, filing for bankruptcy. I know like six women, they work for hotels, they back in town and they got laid off. People need money for a living. Even welfare—you gotta go to Houston, you go to Atlanta just to get a little help.

Regina's comments identify very serious, persistent issues that continue into the present. First, the City of New Orleans did not court low-income families to return despite their low-wage labor being an asset in the recovery of the city's tourism and health services economies. In fact, since Hurricane Katrina, the public housing authority has demolished thousands of homes, preventing return for those who previously used an assistance-based survival strategy to meet their shelter needs.[7] Next, Regina notes the economic shifts that affected her friends who had returned, mainly that without tourists, there was no tourism industry and no need for numerous workers in a post-Katrina economy, reflecting the dismantling of the work-based survival strategy. This economic trend especially destabilized low-income families whose skill sets limited them to low-wage work.

Finally, in making comparisons across locations about the welfare system and assistance variability, Regina illustrated the manner in which some locations and states were more conducive to recovery by offering superior services and assistance opportunities than others did, particularly Louisiana.[8] With reliance upon aid-based survival strategies as the last stop before homelessness, access to a more comprehensive safety net was a key component of working toward recovery. For example, offers of free housing and services made Colorado an attractive state to which to relocate, as evacuees "heard through the 'evacuee grapevine' that Denver was a good place to be: there were far fewer evacuees and thus there was less perceived competition for jobs and other resources."[9] This last factor, the inconsistent implementation of federal programs and social services,[10] became a key pull or push factor for evacuees faced with the decision of where to stage their recoveries. In states with more generous assistance, evacuees were pulled to move there, while hostile environments with low levels of services pushed residents to return to New Orleans.

Yet, to the surprise of many evacuees, this same pattern of push-pull relations existed within New Orleans itself following the storm. For Regina, despite being in Texas where many other respondents reported tensions, discrimination, and hostility, her experience in New Orleans was so very racist, hostile, and assertive that it determined her future residency would be outside the city, despite her kin connections there. Like Regina, other women returning to the city to live also faced hostility from the police, as well as neighbors, landlords, and even the public housing authority—all of whom saw little place for low-income families in the "new" New Orleans. Through these contentious social relations, the city itself became a place of displacement, with new social boundaries that hindered recovery for those low-income families who were fortunate enough to afford to return.

Surviving in the "New" New Orleans

While recovery implies returning to your community and working to rebuild it,[11] returning to New Orleans did not guarantee a woman would heal from her trauma and material destitution. Rather, Hurricane Katrina transformed New Orleans into a place in which old survival strategies were dismantled. As Olivia, Simone, and Faith's accounts demonstrate, there were both structural and personal reasons why women remained in extended displacement rather than returning home. In particular, the physical loss of housing, the loss of community, crime and violence, a lack of services, and the increased costs of food and rent were major barriers to beginning the recovery process within New Orleans. As women quickly learned, coming home was not a guarantee of a return to normal life even when one's housing was completely undamaged. In fact, for many women coming home meant a harder life than ever.

Evacuating nearby to a small town in Cajun country, Olivia was the first woman in the study able to return to New Orleans, just a month following the storm. When she arrived, she found "my door busted wide open; rats in the house; leaves and everything up in here." After cleaning up her home, it became the primary residence for six of her kin—a sharp contrast to her lifestyle of single living prior to the storm. In fact, while many women relied upon family to help them survive outside the city, for women who returned to live in New Orleans, the roles were frequently reversed. In New Orleans, women with livable housing became the foundation of survival for other members of their kin networks. As a result, the reciprocal nature of kin-based survival strategies meant they had the potential to hurt the provider while helping the recipient by draining off the resources needed for the provider to initiate recovery.[12] Specifically, one way in which resources were drained off was if households that used to be considered separate were merged into one large household in the eyes of social service programs, such as food stamps or FEMA assistance. As a result, doubling up to address housing needs could result in lessened assistance overall due to bundling, as many programs offered fewer dollars per capita as family sizes increased.

Beyond the material losses of the storm, for many women the loss of community was a notable change as they worked toward recovery. While low-income neighborhoods are often recognized for their crime, violence, and other social ills,[13] they are also communities in which women can have successful and supportive social networks, family relationships, and even romantic lives as well.[14] In New Orleans, where sitting on the porch or stoop and talking to your neighbors as they walked past was commonplace, the absence of those experiences was notable, as Olivia explained:

> It's not the same, but it's been okay. [...] The people, the people different. I don't feel like I felt before…. I don't—I don't know, I just feel that way. It just feels like something different. I can't explain that.

Like Sharon who wondered about her friends while living in displacement, Olivia's experience in the disaster-ravaged city presents this same sense of loss and longing for friends and community. Exacerbating her disillusionment with post-disaster New Orleans, Olivia later told me how the crime was affecting her: "now it's bad with the murders here. You can't walk outside your door now." Like many women who had returned, Olivia's story highlights two of the primary themes that dominated the decision making process over returning home: crime and the loss of community.

Women's ambivalence toward returning to a city without fully operational social services and medical care, and with ongoing tensions between police and low-income residents, was so pervasive that some women were considering moving away from New Orleans after their post-Katrina return. Simone, a New Orleans native and life-long resident was frustrated with the non-responsiveness of the police to the increasing crime in her community:

> Well, for one thing, they don't have enough cooperation from the police department, it's too.... Things just not like they was before. Then here, I'm by myself. I'd like to be closer to family. I'm getting older in age, I'll be 69 next month, and I'd like to be closer to family so if I get sick, they can look after me. My two sons are here, and they stop in, but they not like ladies. My five daughters are all in Indiana. [...] That, and it's not the city it used to be—I don't like it no more. I mean I like it because I was born here. I like Indiana, and other places I've seen too. The crime rate is so bad in the city. It's worse than it was—now they shoot back at the police. They lost all respect, now they shoot at the police. I'm near the French Quarter and they don't care about this place. There's more crime.

While displaced, Simone was able to reunite with her daughters, some of whom lived in Indiana prior to the storm. Though she had returned to her public housing unit where she'd lived for 6 years, the benefits of having a network of "ladies" while displaced made the return home bittersweet, as their gendered care work made life easier for Simone. While she retained network ties with her sons, these were not supportive enough to outweigh the uncertainty she felt about the crime and about the police, who were non-responsive in her community.

During her displacement, Simone was able to utilize situational social capital in the form of support and care from her daughters. In the absence of police protection in New Orleans, and limited support from her sons, Simone was beginning to seriously consider a permanent relocation by exchanging the aid-based support of her housing voucher for the kin-based support of her daughters' attentiveness. Just as it had been for evacuation, the decision to stay or leave again for recovery was shaped by social network resources, not just the basics of access to housing and aid-based assistance.

The non-responsiveness of the police was a source of great personal strife for many residents, including Faith, who returned to New Orleans only to face the murder of her son. After losing her job as a 911 operator before the evacuation, and her complicated stay with her cousin and kin in an overcrowded trailer, she had planned to move her children to Alexandria, Louisiana, where she had found an apartment. This decision was partially based on the fact that her son did not want to return to the city. However, the plan fell apart when her aging parents decided to return to New Orleans. Out of a commitment to her parents and their health, Faith felt she must oversee their medical care because, "My dad is a heart patient. And my mom's got emphysema. Neither of them drives, so I came back." For Faith, the return home was meant to usher in a quiet period of recovery. Not long into her return, her life was altered in a devastating way:

> My son was at a friend's house, out in Central City. He's at a friend's, and they were out on the porch, playing Monopoly. Then they took the dice, and were playing dice. It wasn't for money. It wasn't like they was gambling.
>
> I've heard three different stories. One is that they were playing dice, and another boy got mad, he left, and later on came back with three guys, they pulled guns and started shooting. Another story, my son was mistaken for someone else. He was with four other guys. No one will say nothing. They all playing dice, but nobody saw who started shooting.
>
> He died before my insurance policy took effect. I had to raise money to bury him. I didn't have anything when I got back. FEMA didn't do anything until months later—not until after my son's funeral. I had to bury him with a closed casket 'cause 90% of his face was gone. The mortician tried to reconstruct it, but you couldn't recognize him. It's still an open case—no suspects, no leads.

For Faith, this ill-fated loss was an affront against her decision to return to care for her parents. Torn between the responsibility of care work for her parents and the guilt of causing her son's death by relocating him to the city, Faith's potential for recovery from the storm itself was effectively obliterated by this loss, one she connects with the disaster.

As the loss rippled through her family, both she and her remaining children attempted to cope through mutual care work as her children cared for her, while she attempted to "keep it together" for them in return:

> I tend to them, I tend to them, and they tell me to just go to bed. They is trying to help me deal with everything. If I break down, they break down, and I can't afford it. They can't afford it. I ask God to help me through it.

Faith's response to the trauma is tempered by her need to care for her other children. Rather than dwell in the moment, she was insistent and focused on providing housing, and doing what she could to cover her bills—the mundane, albeit still significant, recovery challenges every woman faced.

In the "new" New Orleans, housing costs and basics like food and utilities were much more expensive, layering material difficulty on top of emotional for Faith. When asked if there was any positive outcome from the storm, Faith had little to say, returning to the death of her son and its devastating effects:

> Positive? No, not really. My job, the only good thing is leniency. With the police department, you couldn't leave if your child is sick and you need to get them from school. Here, I can leave and come as I want. I'm my own boss. Nothing other than that. I have to pay $540 more for rent, the light bill is extremely high—now it's $400 per month—and I'm struggling with my son even after. Then, I'm still dealing with him, and anger management, and how to cope with different things. People tell me I need to seek counseling. But, if I can't work, I can't provide for them. They struggling and hurting. I gotta be strong for them.

From Katrina's wrath to her own family's struggles, Faith and her children have never had enough stability to begin their recovery. With the murder of her son, it seemed unlikely to occur soon, if ever. At the point in time of the interview, many of Faith's questions remained hauntingly unanswered:

> I bury my son with "ifs, ands, and buts." The police can't even say why he was shot—I can't close the case. I can't say they did a good job. This detective on my son's case is on 50, 60, or more cases. How can he find a killer? I try not to let my kids see me break down. If they see me crying, then they crying all over and they go through the same trauma. I can't say some nights I'm not in my bed crying. I can't let them see it. I have two girls and a boy. If they see you crying, they depressed for the rest of the day.

From start to finish, Katrina was cruel to Faith as she was fired on the spot for wanting to evacuate her children only to return to New

Orleans to work through the storm, to her experience living in an overcrowded trailer with a lock on the fridge, and her return to the city out of duty to her parents, only to bear the trauma of the murder of her son. Faith's story shows the intricate and complicated experience of lived poverty in the face of disaster, and the unexpected forces that encompass it in a devastated, impoverished, urban environment. It also demonstrates how kin networks, which are often a form of support for low-income women, can simultaneously become the catalyst for new trauma where recovery ought to exist. Like women both displaced from and living in New Orleans after the storm, the challenges of life in poverty prevent the traditional healing and return to normal life experienced by most affluent members of society. Like many women whose post-Katrina lives were more difficult than ever before, for Faith, there had been survival, but no recovery.

Market Tensions at the River Garden

For many women, living in displacement became a way to recover and rebuild following the storm. But when they could, women returned to New Orleans to live. In the case of women residing in the River Garden HOPE VI community (formerly St. Thomas public housing),[15] each had to return to prevent eviction from their apartments, the tossing of their property to the curb, and the loss of their New Orleans public housing subsidy. Yet, returning home was not a guarantee of a warm welcome. In fact, five women reported direct harassment from the management at River Garden, including Ann, Keebra, Callista, Faith, and Julia. Additionally, four women felt discouraged by HANO[16] when they inquired about returning home.

Amaya, a 36-year-old mother of two, described the ruthlessness of the eviction process by the housing authority and the management company toward other tenants in her complex:

Jessica: Have many residents returned to the River Garden?

Amaya: Some of them are back, and some are trying to come back. Some can't afford to come back and try, but it wasn't right to just have thrown their stuff out. They shoulda showed some kind of sympathy until they could get back. Some people couldn't afford to come back.

They said if we didn't come back and pay rent, we'd be put out. There was no consideration. All they worrying about is rent being paid, lights being paid. That's all they worried about. They wasn't letting people's family staying. They told us we had to put them out after a certain while. That ain't right. They showing us they don't give a damn about us. You have to tell your family they have to move, or you will lose your house. And they have to go.

With minimal wind damage and no flooding, the newly constructed apartments became a profit magnet in the tight and limited housing market that emerged after the storm. The effect on subsidized renters, however, was harassment by management and active efforts to force them out in exchange for higher-rent occupants. This contentious relationship emerged due to a loophole in the HOPE VI legislation that stipulated that if a management company could not locate qualified, subsidized families, they could fill subsidized units with market-rate renters. In New Orleans, this created a not-so-subtle campaign to remove low-income families from undamaged HOPE VI units. The most devastating effect of this campaign of displacement was to prevent the potential for a pathway to recovery among the women in this sample most able to achieve it—women returning to the city with no damage to their homes.

One of the primary ways the private management company pressured women to move out was through vigorous enforcement of the tenancy rules. Upon return, women began receiving violation notices at unequal rates to their market-rent neighbors, reflecting discrimination against subsidized families within the housing complex. One specific issue was doubling up, as relatives stayed with women temporarily to repair their homes or seek new ones in an extremely competitive rental market. As women supported others in their kin networks through sharing their housing, they jeopardized their own recovery by running the risk of breaking the lease and being evicted for having undeclared occupants staying in their homes. Faith described the inequities regarding the management's response to doubling up, framing it as an issue of Section 8 regulations. When asked whether she and other subsidized families would be living in the new housing in five years' time, Faith replied:

They have some people from the old St. Thomas now, and some want to come back, but they can't come back. High paying people come in and pay rent, and the management company let the people come. But they don't want fixed income people 'cause it's $250 versus $1400. [...] People that used to stay here didn't have any problems coming back, but they getting kicked out because they have family members staying with them, but they like parents and have nowhere to go. They stuck with the Section 8 rules.

When I asked if the market-rate tenants were getting the same treatment, such as being evicted for having family living with them without being on the lease, Faith was quick and firm to reply, "Nope. Nope. Not at all. I see it with my own eyes. Not at all."

With competition for rental housing at unprecedented heights due to the damage of 80% of the city's housing stock, the subsidized residents the project was built to house became secondary to private renters who generated greater revenue. Therefore, it was in the interest of the management company to chase out and discourage public housing residents from returning or applying for the subsidized units at all, so as to garner greater profits from the tight rental market.

While enforcing occupancy rules is a legitimate management practice, the techniques used by the management company at River Garden were infuriating to families attempting to rebuild. For Keebra, a 31-year-old mother of three, this constant harassment made her want to move, even though financially she could not. As she explained,

> Well basically, it practically—you know this the River Garden? [...] So nothing—it's a mixed community. It's a great neighborhood, but I don't know it, it's.... I don't.... I'd really like to buy my own. [...] It's the management, all the rules and regulations. They always harassing me. I get picked on here. I still with public housing—it disgusts me to stay here. I can't afford to move, but I have to stay and make the best of it. It's a real headache out here.

I asked Keebra if she would describe her harassment:

> Okay, I was.... By me being with HOPE VI—like two doors down my neighbors, they allowed to have BBQs or other functions, have company over. If I had something, I'd get a letter saying they observed I was outside. Like they say I was outside of the unit using profanity, which is a lie. Or the garbage, they pass only once out of a weekend. You get a can, but sometimes you have more garbage than a can. Then, you get a letter. The people with HOPE VI.... Everything is just on us. I understand they pay more than we pay, but they don't get stupid letters, or 90-day probation.

Keebra's explanation continued, identifying the issue as one of race, class, and money:

> If I had a job I'd have to constantly take off to go to the River Garden office. Everything you do is a problem, you get a note. Nobody else gets no notes. We the only ones being harassed. [...] It like this every day, for everybody. They begged us to live here. We moved back and

they just bugging us out. I think it's different at Desire. [...] Ain't no white people going to live in Desire, and the crime rate is higher. But this "the Garden District," so we facing police harassment. [...] Like the tenants' children, what they can't do. They aware, they knew we had kids. It's rough. I don't want to come back here. It's stressful, it's too stressful.

Here Keebra demonstrates how returning home has prevented her recovery from the disaster, leaving her to live in uncertainty and fear that after enough notices, she will be evicted from her home and lose her housing subsidy in the process. Her basic tenant rights are denied, as she cannot use her own yard space, have company to visit, or put trash outside, while these same activities are tolerated by management among the market-rate renters. This form of discrimination is so aggravating that Keebra wants to leave, despite having nowhere else to go.

So persistent was the harassment that a community lawyer was preparing a class-action lawsuit on behalf of the subsidized residents against the management company for their actions in River Garden at the time of these interviews. For Ann, her troubles with management began while she was still displaced from the city, because her daughter was staying at her New Orleans apartment during the nights. In response, Ann was put on an eviction list, forcing her to move back to the city in early November of 2005 or lose her unit and subsidy:

River Garden put up a notice to evict, stating that they noticed that someone has been living in my apartment, and I am not at home and will be evicted if I don't return as soon as possible. I couldn't get assistance to return, thinking I'm on a housing authority lease. [...] The rules! Where I'm at now—the rules—it's bearish!

Through fierce enforcement of occupancy rules, the management company systematically threatened to dismantle women's efforts to maintain their aid-based survival strategy of subsidized housing. For women sheltering other family members, it was the process of fortifying their kin-based survival networks by providing temporary housing to family and friends that put them into lease violation and risk of eviction. As a result, in the post-disaster context, it was possible for pre-disaster survival strategies to contradict one another's effectiveness.

Once Ann returned home, the harassment continued with a new focus on more trivial violations. Like other women in the complex, Ann's violations demonstrate the pressure low-income renters faced to be perfect tenants, even when the standards were different for market-rate families:

> The management agency, they just put a flyer out telling me my Christmas decorations have to come down. Or the wind chimes. [...] They said I had to take the wind chimes down, 'cause they was by the light fixture. When I moved here I wanted to put a flagpole up, but "No"—they say you can't have nothing tacked to the building. For the 4th of July, I wanted to put a big flag up.... Or outside—My grandson can't play ball outside. [...] On the block where I live at, Miss June, you have to go through her to go through anybody. She just moved on the block a year ago. She stopped the kids from playing.

Ann is still living in uncertainty, even though she should have the best opportunity to recover of any of the women in this study. By returning to her own home from before the storm, her life was altered, but not in the devastating way in which many low-income families lost everything they ever owned. Yet, with the harassment from the management and select neighbors, Ann was facing strains on her health and emotional well-being:

> I plan on staying here another year. They just pick things. I got that letter, now I'm just trying to stay here. When they put in flyers, you don't know who. They run up, ring the bell, leave a flyer and then run away. They got garbage men putting out flyers. [...] Eviction notices—they put them on people's doors without facing them. [...] I got a notice for my Christmas decorations, and because I had a shopping cart I use for Walmart back by the A/C. They said it was a violation. It's nit, nil, nit-picking things. They get you aggravated, so you can move. The people from St. Thomas all moving. They help with putting you out.

On a personal level, Ann has also had problems with Miss June and other community members who serve as "watchdogs" for the management company. In May of 2006, a neighbor confronted Ann's mother who asked the neighbor to move her car from in front of Ann's driveway. They argued, and the neighbor called the police. Two days later, Miss June called the police again to have Ann falsely arrested on drug possession charges after a visitor of hers was seen smoking marijuana while parked in her driveway after he left her house. Ann was evicted, but refused to move. Instead, she chose to fight the drug charge and the eviction with the help of a community lawyer, and won:

> I didn't have drugs, we don't do drugs. You see when they send the eviction notice, I had to move in 10 days. I didn't go anywhere. I got me a lawyer, and Miss June, she tried to throw out things that I said to the judge. And I told the judge I said those things, but I wasn't under the impression they had no drugs. I thought they had gone.

Ann does not believe her actions have violated her lease, or were extreme enough to merit the constant barrage of notices she received. Without hesitation, Ann identified the real issues—profit and social class discrimination:

> What it really is, is 'cause I'm listed with the housing authority. I only pay $65, while some folks pay $1800, and they trying to get rid of our asses, pardon my language. [...] Sydney Bartholemy, a bunch of polices, firemens, they all live here. They want our asses out! They want to rent it for more money, that's the bottom line.

Sadly, management was prevailing. At the time we spoke, Ann was trying to get her name on a list to return to traditional public housing, or at least another development without the pressure of management constantly forcing her out. Through the persistent threat of eviction, Ann's potential for recovery was stifled by the politics of profit, as her family's housing stability lingered in perpetual uncertainty.

While profit was a motive for Ann's eviction, the actions of her neighbors also reflect ongoing discrimination against the poor throughout the city, which was amplified after the hurricane. In fact, it was not uncommon for locals to question why I chose this study for my dissertation work in the years following the storm. On numerous occasions, it was made clear to me that Hurricane Katrina was seen as a solution to New Orleans' poverty problem. With the poor displaced and lacking the resources or homes to enable a return, Katrina was often lauded as the solution to crime and poverty that blemished the city.

In this social context, Ann's struggles represent those among the underclass of society, who were assumed to devalue by their presence an otherwise new, beautiful, upscale community in the Garden District, or so the argument went. Despite the fact that HOPE VI was designed to provide high-quality housing for the poor and restricted occupancy to the most stable low-income tenants,[17] the post-Katrina context provided thousands of unsubsidized renters who make more "desirable" and profitable neighbors. Precisely because market-rate residents in River Garden have a parallel interest with management to force out low-income families, their actions as described above are reminiscent of the ways white families would force out Black families entering their residential communities through acts of intimidation during desegregation.[18] The major difference is that the target has shifted beyond race alone and centers now on intersectional identities of race, class, and gender simultaneously.

The result of this harassment and intimidation for Ann has actually been a reversal of her recovery trajectory. While living in displacement, Ann had some stability. Since returning home, she described her life thusly:

> I've been so stressed, I don't eat—can't eat. I gotta get back to mental health. I'm waking up in the middle of the night. I'm very stressed out—trying to be evicted from them. They were saying the drugs was from my apartment, but my apartment was not searched. It should have been searched. They could have gotten a warrant if they were suspicious. I don't have any drugs here. I had company to see me, but I'm not with the two other guys. Like I said, the house is nice, everyone wants a brand new place. I always lived on the old side, I never had nothing brand new. I thought I will raise my grandson in a different atmosphere. I was totally wrong.

Harassment was prevalent in the River Garden community, from preventing children from playing games in the street, to attempting to evict a resident for an unsubstantiated drug charge. Clearly, there was directed animosity towards low-income tenants within this mixed-income community. Yet, Ann and others recognize that these actions were motivated by money.

While the HOPE VI promise is supposed to provide a better life for the privileged among the poor, in River Garden it has been manipulated as yet another way to remove low-income residents from the rosters of public housing. By devolving responsibility for public housing away from the public sector and into the private sector through the use of independent management, low-income families are faced with the same competition for housing within the subsidized market as they face in the private housing market, one that persistently fails to provide affordable housing.[19] In this national context, Hurricane Katrina was merely a catalyst that brought these tensions to the surface—tensions that are really about our waning commitment to help disabled, elderly, and low-income families have safe, reliable shelter at all.

Collectively, the experiences of women like Keebra, Faith, Ann, and others encompass the difficulty public housing residents are facing across the city as they attempt to recover from the storm. Whether using a voucher, or living in a subsidized unit with a lease, these women had no entitlement to their homes and often faced evictions, ultimatums, and short deadlines by which to return. This rigidity of requirements reinforces the sentiment that these women were not wanted as members of the "new" New Orleans community. So intensive was the message that even public housing residents stranded outside the city took notice. As Miss Thelma stated:

> Thelma: If something could be done about the housing authority to make it easier for the people out of state, even if they could do it over the phone or something. Now you have to go to New Orleans to get a voucher, the voucher is only good for 30 days, and you have no place to live. If you have no hotel or money, and you can't go there to search, how will you find a place if you are living out of state?
>
> Jessica: Do you think the city wants public housing residents back?
>
> Thelma: It seems that they don't. It's good and bad in all parts of the city. I lived in public housing all those years. I never had a problem. It was crime around me, I raised my children there, but I had no problem. They always put it on the project. It's not the project, it's the people. Half the people come into the project and do things. Where I was staying, in Lafitte, it was mostly elderly, and we looked out for each other. The younger people respect us, and I only lived there not because I wanted to live there—it was because I couldn't do no better.

Through poor organization during the city's recovery, harassing management practices, and direct public comments, residents from public housing understood they were not to be part of the "new" New Orleans. New Orleans after Hurricane Katrina was for the affluent, not the poor. The demolition of multiple public housing complexes made this desire loud and clear.[20]

Instead, to stake a claim to their prior lives and rights, River Garden residents required legal counsel to fight against the same housing authority that was created to help ensure access to secure, sanitary, reliable housing. In these ways, competition and profit combined to solidify the barriers to stable housing, such that returning home to New Orleans did not open up a pathway to recovery, but instead was another direct barrier to it. As low-income, Black women, living in public housing, their intersectional status marginalized them from the recovery conversation; in fact, that conversation transformed their displacement into a solution for the city, not a problem to be redressed.

Moving beyond housing stability, women in this study also struggled to balance the demands of kin-based networks that often relied upon them for temporary housing, against the requirements of aid-based programs such as public housing vouchers, food stamps, social security, and other benefit sets. While working to rebuild their survival systems, new expenses, such as grossly over-estimated power bills, increased food costs, and the lack of formerly free medical services altered the way their survival mechanisms could operate after the storm. As Amaya from the River Garden community explained, living in New Orleans was a challenge in and of itself:

> I'm just saying that, "Is they gonna give us any kind of help, financial-wise?" I can't afford to buy my children nothing for Christmas. With every check there's some kind of bill you got to pay. I never enjoyed a check since I got it. Not to treat myself to anything. It is all bills, bills, bills, bills, bills, bills. They supposed to help for the utilities. Now they said, "If I'm eligible." It's on the man to say, "You eligible" now. So, I don't know.

Working within weeks of returning home, Amaya was deeply concerned about her children as she struggled financially in the face of harassment at her housing complex and the potential homelessness it represented. Like all the women in this study, Amaya openly expressed the ever-present challenge of stifled recovery through her following questions to me: "I'm worrying about 'how you gonna feed the kids the next day?' and 'how you was going to live?,' you know?"

Conclusion

Despite the fact that many women returning home had undamaged housing, their system of pre-Katrina poverty survival strategies was no longer adequate within the post-Katrina context. First, work-based survival strategies were dismantled as service jobs contingent upon tourism and healthcare vanished during the initial recovery period. For many women the inability to work made extended displacement a preferable recovery strategy to returning home, as Lydia explained previously. For those living in New Orleans when we spoke, it was rarely jobs that pulled them back—instead what did draw women back to the city were family and the threat of eviction.

As Faith's experience painfully demonstrated, women's deep commitments to kin networks were a deciding factor in the decision to return home, even when moving back to New Orleans threatened to destabilize the recovery progress low-income women had made during displacement. In the post-disaster New Orleans context, kin networks that were generally positive before the storm took on more complexity as the demands required for their maintenance increased in their burden after the storm. As was the case in River Garden, women who returned to the city were reciprocally obligated to provide housing to other displaced network kin. However, doing so jeopardized their own housing stability as it violated provisions in their lease, placing them at risk of eviction. In this way, even low-income women with the best chance for a recovery were stifled in their efforts to rebuild, as kin-network survival systems became less effective to promote daily survival than they had been before.

Finally, aid-based survival strategies were also tenuous at the time of these interviews, especially due to the temporary nature of assistance. Faced with the inevitability that FEMA aid would terminate, the closing of Charity Hospital as a source of affordable healthcare, and new threats of eviction within public housing units due to family members doubling up and property management enforcing tenancy rules with exceptional vigor, returning home did not represent a return to normal life, by any means. Rather, returning to New Orleans made women a target for harassment, in the hopes they would voluntarily relocate, opening up their undamaged apartments to renters with more money to spend. In this way, low-income, Black women were made vulnerable not only by the storm and its aftermath, by also by the profit agenda of actors working to rebuild the city as a whole. Not only were public housing residents discouraged from returning to their own homes, the city and public housing authority took aggressive action to demolish thousands of units in subsidized complexes across the city as well.[21] In this way, the "new" New Orleans was gentrified not only by new housing, but by the systematic removal of its poorest residents—many of whom are represented by the women in this study.

---

[1] Pardee 2007/2011.
[2] See Pardee 2007/2011 for a description of these changes.
[3] Rose 2005.
[4] See Chris Rose's *One Dead in Attic* (2005) for a deeper examination of the texture of that sense of continuous loss.
[5] Couch 1996: 68.
[6] Pardee and Barry n.d..
[7] Arena 2012; Pardee 2012.
[8] Weber and Peek 2012; Peek 2012; Lein 2012; Miller 2012.
[9] Peek 2012.
[10] Pardee 2012.
[11] Couch 1996: 68.
[12] Domínguez and Watkins 2003; Anderson 1989, 1990, 1999.
[13] Wilson 1987, 1996, 2010; Massey and Denton 1993; Murray 1984, 1994; Dreier, Mollenkopf, and Swanstrom 2001; Rainwater and Yancey 1967.
[14] Wilson 2010; Stack 1974; Anderson 1989, 1990, 1999.

[15] 26 women in this study lived in the St. Thomas public housing project before the HOPE VI redevelopment. Of these, 22 women had returned to the city to live after the storm.
[16] Housing Authority of New Orleans.
[17] NHLP 2002; Goetz 2000; Finkel, Lennon, and Eisenstadt 2000; Forrest and Williams 2001; National Housing Law Project 2002; Kingsley, Johnson, and Pettit 2003.
[18] Massey and Denton 1993; Gotham 2002.
[19] Pardee and Gotham 2005.
[20] Arena 2012.
[21] Arena 2012.

10
Redefining Recovery

Hurricane Katrina was a technological and social disaster, but it was not a natural one. The technological disaster was the failure of the levee system, which was left to languish in disrepair after Congress repeatedly denied funding requests to fortify and fix it.[1] The social disaster occurred when the federal and state response was delayed for five days, and those first responders reacted to victims by militarizing a humanitarian crisis. Fortunately, we as a society have the power to prevent both technological and social disasters in the future, and remedy the lasting consequences of them in the present. To do this, all that is required is social and political will.

The endemic nature of prejudice and racism in the United States was never more on display than in the days following Hurricane Katrina's landfall. Now, quiet racism shapes public discourses about immigration, access to quality K-12 education, access to jobs, and access to the ability to gain wealth, all often without any acknowledgement of its pervasive power.[2] The policies created within such a framework generate structural inequalities with lasting, negative effects for all Americans. For example, as emergency FEMA and food stamp aid was approved by Congress following the storm, that same legislation reduced funding for regular food stamps for citizens throughout the nation.[3] As low-income women in this study transitioned from disaster food stamps into regular programs during their displacements, their ability to use food stamps to create stability after the storm was dismantled, as Ingrid's experienced demonstrated. In this context, the potential for disaster recovery has as much to do with the larger political landscape as it did with any single woman's effort to rebuild.

In a culture of social inequality, understanding how marginalized populations survive is more important than ever, as working and middle class families are increasingly facing similar fates, whether triggered by

Hurricane Sandy, a mortgage meltdown, or the failure of major banking institutions. Understanding the ability and limitations of survival strategies such as work, kin networks, and formal assistance to provide a pathway toward recovery in post-disaster circumstances is a major contribution that the women of this study provide through sharing their experiences during Hurricane Katrina. The next section will examine each strategy to highlight their efficacy within the broader disaster context. Finally, the chapter will conclude by proposing an alternative conception of disaster recovery among the poor, who by definition live in communities with the same characteristics as those that have failed to recover from previous disasters.

The Transferability of Survival Strategies

The lived experiences of low-income, Black women during Hurricane Katrina provide a window into the capacity of poverty survival strategies to transfer under disaster circumstances. Survival strategies are the techniques used to address and meet one's basic needs, and include work-based, kin-based, and aid-based strategies.[4] Work-based survival strategies include work, whether in the formal or informal sectors. Kin network survival strategies are conceptualized as assistance received from relatives, whether child care, temporary housing, money, or food.[5] Aid-based survival strategies include the use of such formal assistance programs as public housing, food stamps, welfare or social security, or the receipt of goods and services from local non-profit agencies like church groups, food pantries, or soup kitchens.[6] When combined, these three strategies create a triad of resources upon which women draw to meet their family's daily needs.

In the context of Hurricane Katrina, work-based survival strategies were the least effective. During the pre-storm evacuation, work actually kept women in harm's way, as Vanessa, Giselle, and Lydia each demonstrate. Others, like Faith, lost their jobs due to the storm and were unable to find new ones while displaced, or after their return. While 41.2% of women in the sample were working before the storm, just 7.8%, or four women, were working at the time of the interview. Facing competition, discrimination, and an evacuee stigma during displacement outside the city, and mass job loss in New Orleans, work was not a viable survival strategy at that time. As a result, women who were formerly self-sufficient were forced to depend upon kin assistance and aid-based strategies as they worked to rebuild their lives.

Whether during the evacuation, while stranded, or during the first efforts toward recovery, kin networks were the most important mechanism engaged to survive Hurricane Katrina. While network-based survival strategies were often rendered ineffective in particular contexts, they were omnipresent as an essential tool in how poverty and disaster were lived. Starting with evacuation decision making, kin networks provided new perspectives about the storm's risks, often redefining the safety narrative into one of threat. They also offered tangible mechanisms for evacuation through the combined resources of the caravan of kin. In the immediate threat, kin networks emerged to provide access to transportation, shelter, and food that individual family units lacked on their own.

Yet, these networks were not without limits. In some instances, kin networks kept women in the city who would have otherwise evacuated, stranding them in flooded homes or the shelters of last resort. In these instances, the desire to stick together endangered women and their families. Additionally, as the crisis shifted in nature from a short-term threat to a protracted disaster, the ability of kin networks to sustain the caravan and support displaced relatives dwindled. Networked to kin who also had limited means, tensions that arose from overcrowding and the indefinite nature of the displacement became an impetus for women to seek the opportunities aid-based strategies could offer. Over time, without work available and kin resources exhausted, the social services system became the primary source of survival.

Similar to the other survival strategies, aid-based strategies varied in their success dependent upon context. In places with supportive receiving communities, churches, shelters, non-profit agencies, and private individuals worked hard to help in those early weeks following the storm by providing women with shelter, cots, clothing, some limited furniture, and money for personal items, like toothbrushes and undergarments. As time passed and federal funding was approved for disaster assistance, every single woman, except one, received money from FEMA, as well as food stamps, and in many cases housing vouchers from HUD. This assistance combined to create the first sources of stability in these women's lives since the storm.

Just as quickly as need-based assistance could create stability, its absence could trigger homelessness and deeper levels of poverty than ever before, as Linda, Mary, and Jada remind us. With the devolution of aid-based assistance to the states, women's capacity for rebuilding a stable survival system in new locations was hampered by the need to reunite with scattered kin. As mothers, grandmothers, and caregivers, being near family was often the first step toward recreating a normal life in a new place for the women in this study. When reuniting forced them to move across jurisdictional lines, placing family first often ended their access to aid, which was based in one's geographic location. While FEMA money was transportable, other essential survival programs such as housing vouchers, food stamps, Medicaid, and Medicare were not. Given that evacuees stranded in a flooded New Orleans had no choice where buses and planes were sent, this system of fragmented social services reduced the effectiveness of women's efforts to rebuild their lives and the recovery efforts for all evacuees, as their needs were constant, while their access to those services precisely intended to support recovery was not.

Defining Low-Income Disaster Recovery

For the women in this study, traditional disaster recovery was not available. According to Couch, recovery is theorized as a stage during which a community seeks "resolution" toward normality—to return to normal by reconstituting the old social structures, including the return of government agencies, businesses, infrastructural services such as water and electricity, and other collective needs for day-to-day community existence, such as groceries and hospitals.[7] That resolution begins at the community level as residents unite, initiate search and rescue activities, pool resources, and provide mutual support to one another. This increased social cohesion evolves into a "therapeutic community."[8] Within this therapeutic community, recovery is achieved by the rebuilding of the physical environment, as government institutions, schools, services, and businesses reopen and resume. For individuals, the negative effects of natural disasters are expected to be short-term, as social, cultural, psychological, and economic consequences are typically absorbed by the larger (intact) social structure.[9] The goal is to return back to business as usual.

In the context of Hurricane Katrina, the definition of recovery as restitution is extremely problematic when one considers the long-term, irreversible effects of housing stock loss (both public and private),[10] closed social institutions such as schools, hospitals, and workplaces, the elimination or reduction of social services such as Charity Hospital and food stamps, as well as the undeniable narrative of threat which is now connected to living in the city. In general, the negative effects of past massive technological disasters are documented to be chronic, and include physical illness, pessimism about health, a sense of being out of control, fear of one's community or residence as unsafe, social and governmental distrust, and stigma.[11] When these responses fail to terminate or be remedied (i.e., by toxin cleanup or relocation), distrust and anger ensue as the community transforms to become "corrosive."[12]

In short, when a community "fails" to recover, the characteristics of that community come to mirror the everyday experience of life in deeply impoverished communities throughout the United States.[13]

Like the corrosive community, low-income and deeply segregated communities are also viewed by their residents as unsafe and violent, with those residents sharing little trust in government and social services to help, despite their dependency on those assistances. With excessive rates of persistent health problems, lack of resources like healthcare facilities, quality schools, and basic public safety, the corrosive community of failed disaster recovery is, in fact, the lived experience of poverty for low-income women every day, independent of a disaster. This parallelism between failed recovery and everyday poverty requires us to redefine recovery for low-income populations, as one cannot recover to a state of failed recovery. What, then, does recovery for low-income families look like?

While New Orleans as a whole may be able to return to normal, in those first 16 months the women I spoke with were nowhere close to rebuilding the modest stability their lives of poverty provided before the storm. From the scattering of kin-based social networks, to the loss of work through discrimination, closures, and layoffs, to the reductions of aid for recipients of programs such as food stamps,[14] the survival strategies women used to meet their needs were dismantled to varying degrees, made more or less extreme by the specific geographies where women settled. In fact, even for women returning to New Orleans, doing so seemed to create more damage to their lives than staying away might have done. With a lack of social services, no medical care, contentious housing circumstances, and questionable access to employment, New Orleans offered little stable structure within which low-income women could rebuild in those early months after the storm. Instead, returning home meant living in both poverty and uncertainty, with attention focused on meeting basic needs like shelter security rather than returning to one's pre-storm life and the sense of stability it offered. What does it mean then to recover when the entire landscape changes?

Recovery for low-income women was not available. Women were able to survive, to rebuild, but not to recover. What women did achieve was movement toward recreating their kin networks and securing some assistances or limited employment with which to rebuild. No woman was holistically better off because of the storm. Many were on the brink of homelessness. They worked to rebuild and survive despite these circumstances. While this seems like an opportune time to engage the language of resiliency as an analytic tool to explain these behaviors, I will not because doing so dismisses the role of structural inequality in shaping these women's lives. The truth is that these women were poor to begin because they grew up in a city that disinvested in its public school system following desegregation. Many of these women grew up in New Orleans in a time when lynching and violence, blockbusting and segregation, and ongoing racial hatred were commonplace and acceptable. The social structures of their lives forced them into a secondary status despite their citizenry, and because of their class, race, and gender.

The struggles of low-income Black women surviving Hurricane Katrina represent more than just the effects of a catastrophic disaster. They are symbolic of the ways in which our society has neglected African Americans, and especially the poor, by persistently blaming them for the lack of jobs, education, and social services that we as a society fail to create.[15] Under the banner of capitalism and competition, we allow our own citizens to suffer while simultaneously blaming them for their own penury. Under the banner of a "natural disaster," with Katrina we have done the same. We blame the victims, call them unworthy, and deny our own culpability in the process for the technological and social disasters we created.

So, what did recovery mean for low-income women? It meant being able to utilize survival strategies, or create new ones, in response to new environments. It did not mean returning to life as it was before, but instead to find ways to create marginal stability in the areas of housing, work, family relationships, access to food and medicine, and meeting the minimal needs of children and grandchildren. It meant staying just above that line between poverty and homelessness.

For some, extended displacement was the best pathway toward poverty-laden recovery. Moving away or staying away from a city you love and miss may provide better opportunities for your family, as was the case for Lydia. From the safety of small towns, to reconnecting with distant kin, to the opportunity to find work, to simple kindnesses from individuals committed to helping you, "not recovering" through displacement was a pathway to stability, to a low-income version of disaster recovery. In some cases, low-income recovery was a necessary fact of survival, as many lacked the money to return home at all.

For others, returning to New Orleans to face the pain caused by Hurricane Katrina—the loss, the violence, the incivilities, the threats, the blaming of victims, the deaths—was the pathway forward. Yet, amidst the altered social and structural landscapes of New Orleans traditional recovery was no guarantee either. The loss of residents, housing loss, job termination, closed churches, closed medical services, reconfigured schools, and a reduction of the regular aid programs that sustain low-income women, all meant that going home to New Orleans did not ensure that the survival strategies engaged before the storm would still be effective, and for women like Ann, Keebra, and Amaya, they weren't. Ultimately, for all the low-income African American women of this study, rebuilding was a question of available options, many of which were more freely available outside of New Orleans than within it. In this emergent post-disaster landscape, low-income disaster recovery among the poor at that moment came to be defined as staying alive, but living in even deeper, more devastating poverty than ever before.

---

[1] Freudenberg et al. 2009.
[2] Davis 2000; Kozol 2005; Wilson 1987, 1996, 2010; Oliver and Shapio 1995; Yinger 1995.
[3] Dreier 2006.
[4] Edin and Lein 1997.
[5] Stack 1974; Edin and Lein 1997.
[6] Edin and Lein 1997.
[7] Couch 1996: 68.
[8] Tierney, Bevc, and Kuligowski 2006: 58; Rodríguez, Trainor, and Quarantelli 2006; Freudenberg 1997.
[9] Drabek and Boggs 1968; Drabek et al. 1975; Picou, Marshall, and Gill 2004; Marshall, Picou, and Gill 2003; Kreps 1984.
[10] Arena 2012.
[11] Edelstein 2004; Erikson 1994; Picou, Marshall, and Gill 2004; Adams et al. 2002; Couch 1996; Roberts and Toffolon-Weiss 2001.
[12] Freudenberg 1993, 1997; Picou, Marshall, and Gill 2004.
[13] See Erikson 1994; Freudenberg 1997, 1993; Edelstein 2004; Picou, Marshall, and Gill 2004; Adams et al. 2002; Roberts and Toffolon-Weiss 2001; Corresponding poverty research: Wilson 1987, 1996, 2010; Massey and Denton 1993; Murray 1984, 1994; Dreier, Mollenkopf, and Swanstrom 2001; Edin and Lein 1997; Rainwater and Yancey 1967.
[14] Dreier 2006.
[15] Winant 2000; Rank 2011; Wilson 2010; hooks 1984; Collins 1998.

Appendix
Studying Hurricane Katrina as a Scholar-Survivor

I am a Hurricane Katrina survivor.

I evacuated from New Orleans to escape the storm on Saturday, August 27, 2005, around 8 p.m., and did not return to my home for nearly six weeks. Since the moment I saw the storm headed for my city on the television, I have never yet had a single day where I did not think about the storm, its destruction, or this study. It is exhausting. As you read this appendix, written as a research process narrative rather than an abstract analysis of methodology, I hope you can begin to understand that who we are as people is as much a part of our capacity to conduct quality research as our professional training. With that in mind, it is my hope that understanding my own experiences as I approached this work will help you with your own research struggles. I consider myself both a scholar and survivor of Hurricane Katrina.[1]

Studying Katrina as a Scholar-Survivor

In this Appendix, I discuss the project origins, methodology, and my own history living in New Orleans as a resident of 10 years when Katrina arrived. The purpose of this self-declaration is to provide methodological transparency about the foundation of my deep contextualization. The reality of my situation is that I lived in and studied about Hurricane Katrina's effects as both a storm survivor and professionally trained scholar. This alternating positionality between insider and outsider provides me with a unique vantage point from which to discuss the experiences of women who shared their accounts throughout the text. Now, let me discuss how I came to New Orleans and this study, as it was certainly not my original plan.

As a young, white, lower working-class woman, I began my residence in New Orleans in 1995 at the tender age of 18. I moved to the city from my suburban Connecticut hometown to attend Tulane University on a need-based scholarship. Soon after my arrival, I quickly realized that I was the "economic diversity" portion of the undergraduate student body. At my federal work-study job I requested as many hours as I could; I admired others who threw money around as if it grew on trees. Knowing the opportunity my institute could provide, I embraced the value of education as a mechanism to achieve my own social mobility—I wanted to be "rich," as many 18-year-olds often do. Yet, because of my background, I always found myself more comfortable around those members of society without, than those who had plenty. I befriended secretaries, janitors, and campus staff, eventually coming to decide that being able to pay my bills comfortably was plenty enough. Choosing to study sociology helped me with this acceptance, and I began to learn of the city's endemic and persistent poverty soon thereafter.

As I completed my undergraduate degree, I enrolled in graduate school at Tulane mostly out of happenstance. A professor left a note on a term paper asking if I had considered further study, and recruited me to the Ph.D. program. Because of this transition, my doctoral research in New Orleans did not originate as a study of the Hurricane Katrina catastrophe at all—in fact, my intended dissertation topic was public housing reform. The federal HOPE VI public housing program had consumed two of the city's poorest communities, Desire and St. Thomas, replacing them with new mixed-income housing and a promise of a better life for residents—I would study whether that promise was kept for the displaced families who lost their homes.[2] As I evacuated for Katrina with books and articles packed in my car, I fully expected to return back to work by Tuesday afternoon. Yet, just a day after Hurricane Katrina made her landfall, the levees failed, and flooding consumed the city. The Desire community hosted 8 feet of standing water. By contrast, the new St. Thomas housing was completely intact, with no flooding and barely any wind damage. In this moment, with one research location destroyed, another intact, and the city of New Orleans in evacuation mode, I was faced with an impossible decision.

The breaching of the levees meant the validly of my housing study was washed away, costing me three years of preparatory work in the process. As I sat questioning the future, my home institution of Tulane University began a process of intensive restructuring. Closed until January 2006, the administration had eliminated the graduate program in Sociology, with remaining students receiving a set period of time to complete our degrees. With no stipend funding left and academic advisors displaced to three different states, I moved ahead into uncertainty, assessing my options as I started my research anew.

Meeting Katrina: Surely another False Call

On Saturday, August 27, 2005, Hurricane Katrina made aim for New Orleans. A day later, the New Orleans Mayor, Ray Nagin, ordered a mandatory evacuation. I chose to leave on Saturday, taking research articles, working papers, textbooks, my laptop, my cats, and a weird variety of work attire in case the "worst" happened. Sadly, I left behind normal clothing like tops and shorts, having just two pairs of jeans and three or four t-shirts to wear. Like others, I assumed this evacuation would be typical—a false alarm with mandatory mini-vacation.[3] I left because Katrina was a Category 5 hurricane, but I honestly didn't believe the storm would hit New Orleans. I never expected that the levees would overtop and breach, or that the city would flood, killing over 1,300 people. Like so many of the women I interviewed, I also believed that the storm was going to turn east, to be "no big deal."[4] We were wrong.

On Monday, August 29, 2005, Hurricane Katrina made landfall. All day long, newscasters did their best to show images of the storm in progress. Safely evacuated to a friend's home in Houston, Texas, I remember seeing the televised images of the storm in progress: window blinds fluttering violently out of broken panes of glass at New Orleans' downtown Hyatt Hotel; the enormous hole in the Superdome's roof with people huddled together below—calm but seemingly aware that the ceiling might collapse on them at anytime. I also remember that on Monday I saw no televised flooding, heard no talk of levee breaches, nor had any suspicion that Hurricane Katrina would be anything other than a very, very close call. I went to bed relieved, and ready to drive home the next day.

Tuesday morning I turned on the television to see when I could go. I saw instead a stream of water—it was powerful, fast moving, dark, and disgusting. I wanted to vomit. The levee had broken in the 9th Ward. The city was filling up with water. I understood before the storm how and why the levees could break, yet their actual destruction left me in absolute shock. It was incomprehensible.

It is one thing to intellectually pontificate over what might cause a disaster or to even watch a disaster, and quite another to have a disaster happen *to you*. The rest of that Tuesday was spent calling New Orleans friends and family, but the phone lines were constantly busy: everyone else who had evacuated was doing the same. As the day continued, more reports of new levee breaches emerged, blending into a barrage of painful images of helicopter rescues and dead bodies floating in murky waters that still bring a knot to my throat and tears to my eyes when I allow myself to think about it for any amount of time.

At some point that Tuesday or Wednesday, the reality of the flooding for my academic life and research began to creep into my consciousness: My research project was gone. The flooding was in the Desire community. And there were other questions, like was there anything left of my university? Would Tulane cease to exist? Would all my work, records, and transcripts for my Bachelor's and Master's degrees, and my Ph.D. coursework be gone, leaving me with no evidence of any higher education at all?—I hadn't packed my diplomas. Was my house flooded? Did I have anything left of my previous life other than a car and three cats?

In all of this, the only area I could control was the dissertation. I knew the women displaced from public housing surely would not want to talk about their pre-Katrina lives, in newly built homes that now sat under eight feet of water. So, I made a phone call to a colleague who had been my Master's thesis chair. Working in Orlando at the University of Central Florida, I asked: "What are my options? Do I have to start my coursework over from scratch?" We discussed transfer possibilities and made a plan for me to enroll at UCF for the fall semester. At minimum, some existing data on the Orlando Housing Authority's HOPE VI programs could be a start to a similar dissertation. After all, I did evacuate with my books and articles on the topic. Within two hours, I had the survey guides to review.

By Wednesday or Thursday, I had a plan. I was enrolling in UCF for the fall semester, and would use the Orlando data set, finishing my degree within the year. Talking this over with my Tulane advisor at the time, he was very supportive. Yet, it felt wrong. As I looked at the survey, I realized there wasn't enough data for a dissertation-length analysis. And what about the women I had been preparing to study for three years? Where were they? Did they survive? Did they make it out of the city alive?

Before long, the women from my old dissertation began to haunt me. How could I walk away from a project I knew was so important? How could I stand at the precipice of the harder, better, "right" path, and instead run some statistics to rush through my doctorate on a new project that had no soul to it? By the week's end, I was determined to locate the women from my original study—I had New Orleans addresses for them and some old and outdated landline phone numbers. This meant they would be near impossible to find. Yet, so were the 1,500 couples in Nock, Wright, and Sanchez's covenant marriage study that I helped locate as their research assistant while working on my Master's degree.[5] Finding displaced populations, whether by marriage or disaster, was something I knew I could do. It defied all logic, yes. But I just *knew* I could do this. So, I chose the harder path. With no formal training in environmental sociology or in disaster studies, I pushed ahead, refusing to allow any one stumbling block to derail my resolve—not even the displacement of over a million residents from the Gulf Coast region of the United States of America.

Weaving Old into New

The development of my new project occurred largely in a vacuum—I wrote the survey without feedback, submitted it to the UCF IRB, and returned to New Orleans to clean my apartment during the last week of September 2005. In two week's time, I was living in New Orleans again, when I received IRB approval. Through all of this, I never discussed the project, the survey, or the conceptualization with my Tulane faculty—they were each on their own evacuation journeys, sprinkled across the nation. In fact, I had very little contact with anyone at that time. While I had a boyfriend, we continued dating out of necessity—the isolation in post-Katrina New Orleans would have been unbearable otherwise.

In my planned study of HOPE VI,[6] I had focused on the physical displacement of public housing residents through social policy mandates. The new Katrina study and its developing survey initially used some of the same theoretical arguments and research questions that had been woven together for the HOPE VI study. With my existing lists of resident names from the Housing Authority of New Orleans,[7] I began seeking my respondents—low-income women who had been living in the St. Thomas (now River Garden) and Desire (now Abundance Square) public housing complexes immediately prior to their redevelopment. The implementation of HOPE VI had displaced women and their families to an array of private, traditional, and Section 8 public housing dwellings throughout the city. Now, Hurricane Katrina had essentially done the same, but on a national scale.

Knowing how difficult these women's lives had been after losing their public housing, and recognizing the tremendous expenses associated with my own evacuation—my car had just broken down a week before the storm and the repair expenses had left me just $500 for evacuation—I could not imagine how poor women with children and grandchildren could manage. How would they leave employment (41%

had it prior to Katrina), locate transportation out of the city, garner sufficient funds for food and shelter, and secure affordable temporary housing? I felt compelled to study these women: How would they survive during their evacuation? How would they rebuild their lives? What would "recovery" look like for women whose pre-Katrina lives assumed the form of an economic disaster?

The challenge, of course, to studying a displaced population is precisely that they are *displaced*. Locating people who have moved from place to place—as money, shelter, aid-assistance, or family goodwill ran out—is difficult and tedious work. My own evacuation journey took me from a two-week stay in Texas to next spend a month with my sister and brother who were in college in Myrtle Beach, South Carolina. Then, it was home to New Orleans to clean my house and assess the damage, then back to South Carolina to get my cats, then back to New Orleans to live. There were also two other trips in there, one to Washington, D.C. for a wedding, since everyone else's life outside of New Orleans continued as usual, and another to Florida to enroll as a graduate student so I could have student loan money to pay for the rent on my undamaged New Orleans apartment—the only way to ensure my things weren't thrown to the curb like those of thousands of other evacuee renters.[8] After the first two weeks of my displacement, I was barely in one place for more than about 10 days.

When I settled home in early October, the city was a militarized space. Humvees drove down the streets with armed National Guardsmen, weapons out and ready. While the rifles were pointed upward, there was a clear sense that you could be shot at any time. I was 28 years old at the time, and I had never felt so threatened on U.S. soil, not even two days after 9/11 when I travelled to a friend's wedding in the Northeast. Rather, the humvees and the blatant disgust and anger I saw on the faces of Guardsmen reminded me of my travels to Peru, when a military truck drove into the central plaza of a small city, creating immediate awareness that the line between safety and danger was very thin. Nothing about returning home to New Orleans was normal.

Exacerbating the alien nature of the experience was the near complete social isolation I felt following the storm. I watched as neighbors packed up and moved away from my street—ousted by the loss of jobs, or evictions and rising rents. At my university, which was closed for fall, I didn't know of any faculty or graduate students who had returned; most lived in neighborhoods that had not yet reopened. Everyday life was slow to recover as well, as grocery stores were closed and the one Winn-Dixie that had experienced no flooding had hour-long waits at each of the six checkout lanes that were open. Buying food was a full afternoon endeavor and one of the few social events that remained.

Of the handful of restaurants that reopened, most served food on paper plates with plastic utensils. Every day, my boyfriend and I would go to the city's webpage to see the recovery progress reports, which listed trash pickups next to stores and restaurants that were now permitted open for business. In my neighborhood, the Red Cross had a hot meal line, but the food was disgusting. It was some combination of white beans and a red meat sauce that tasted nothing like food—it was inedible. It was also accompanied by pissed-off looking National Guardsmen and their guns, furthering the discomfort of both receiving a pity meal and being in the presence of potential violence at any moment. MREs were available as well,[9] but with power returned quickly to my Algiers Point neighborhood due to the close proximity of the electric company's main control center, cooking at home was a ready option of which I took advantage, despite being without a refrigerator for the first week after my return.[10][11]

These personal complications aside, my reason for returning to New Orleans was because it was my *home*. We were not refugees, but Americans who loved where we lived.[12] I would become angry when people would suggest the city not be rebuilt, or that I should move to Florida or South Carolina to do my work in the company of supportive family, colleagues, and friends. I understood the logic, but I wouldn't go despite genuine and gracious offers of help. I missed my home desperately, mourned her losses, and had to see and live the destruction for myself before I could be ready to leave permanently.

Once back and settled, I tried to locate the women from my original HOPE VI study. Between October 2005 and July 2006, for ten months, I lived in immediate post-disaster New Orleans, using my time to locate women for telephone interviews. In mid-March, I learned of an instructor position at the University of Central Florida through the department chair who was seeking applicants at a conference. I applied and was hired, moving in July 2006 to an Orlando suburb. My data collection continued from my new "home" and was completed in December 2006. In Florida, I was commuting two hours a day, teaching eight courses annually plus summer sessions, preparing five new courses at that time, and collecting data. It was an incredible amount of work, but leaving the city a second time of my own volition was my survival and recovery strategy—living in the "new" New Orleans was just too difficult to bear.[13]

Seeking the Displaced

After returning to New Orleans to live, I searched for the women who had been in my pre-Katrina sample—I had their addresses and landline phone numbers only. I knew the task would be difficult, but I began calling numbers and searching names in online telephone databases, similar to how I had as a research assistant recruiting survey respondents for the study of covenant marriage.[14] After a few months, I realized this would not be enough. By March 2006, I had interviewed just ten women, but had called well over a thousand phone numbers. For each name I entered in an online telephone search engine, four or five numbers would appear. Occasionally, a woman would have her new phone number on record with the phone company and I could follow her path to her present location through the automated recording. In other instances, women didn't answer or declined, but even then the refusals were just a handful of respondents. The challenge was accessing updated phone numbers. With phone lines down across the city and internet databases barely updated, I began to think about other ways to find these women.[15]

About this same time, an assistant professor from Tulane approached me about using his survey with my sampling frame. The benefit would be some money for paying respondents, and presumably, a more interactive experience. Comparing his survey to mine, I decided to blend the two since so many of the questions were exactly the same. With this change came a new infusion of enthusiasm, as I imagined every low- or no-cost method I could to find the women—most involved just hitting the street. I began by posting flyers in the neighborhood surrounding the Desire complex—the complex itself was closed and monitored by military forces (I was "escorted" out when I drove through to look at the damage). I also hung flyers in a package store on Magazine Street by the St. Thomas complex, as well as on telephone poles near a few of the service agencies in the neighborhood. Not long after, I returned to the St. Thomas community, placing quarter-page sized slips of paper into people's mailboxes as a recruitment flyer with my information on it. These garnered calls, though in some instances, I couldn't locate the individual's name on the housing authority list, and had to decline them the interview. I also hung full-page flyers in the Lafitte housing community, since some Desire residents had been relocated there and many families had returned to live, despite the Housing Authority's discouragement.

I also contacted churches and social service providers using email for references, though this was minimally effective. In the end, one service provider graciously assisted me with a list of about forty names. He knew about my HOPE VI work from before the storm and remembered me. His help yielded 13 interviews and reflects the power of social networking. Throughout all of this, I interviewed only women whose names appeared on my sampling list or the list from this one provider, as I knew the information was accurate.[16]

As I moved into April and May, I began a new approach for recruitment: letters. I sent personally signed and hand-addressed recruitment letters[17] to approximately 700 women. Each letter included a summary explanation of the study, two counseling hotline numbers for anyone who needed additional support either because of the trauma of evacuation or from participating in an interview about it, my personal cell phone number, and additional contact information.[18] While over 200 of these letters were returned to me, they were still the most effective recruitment approach, yielding 20 interviews. To date, I do not know how many letters actually made it to potential respondents. In order to increase this sample size, I also sought snowball referrals, where one interviewee recommended another one and provided contact information for that person, but this provided just three or four interviews—my records aren't clear.

I used telephone interviews for my study, primarily because many of my respondents were displaced from New Orleans and I had no research funding for meeting with them in person, let alone any idea where to locate them. Whether using cell phones beforehand, setting up landlines in new FEMA apartments or by using someone else's phone, women found ways to contact me upon receiving my letters. Only one respondent interviewed lacked her own phone and she utilized a neighbor's phone to complete the interview.

Each interview had two parts; the first was a section of closed-ended questions on evacuation, employment, assistance before and after the storm, and demographic characteristics. The second section included open-ended questions, allowing women to describe their evacuation and recovery experiences in detail in their own words. The first section required 5 to 15 minutes to complete while the second section typically took between 30 and 90 minutes. Responses were typed during the interview and edited after; interviews were not tape-recorded to ensure respondent anonymity. To address confidentiality, all names in this work and other published works from the study use a set of pseudonyms. Compensation included a $20 gift card and two hotline numbers for free counseling services.

The study's convenience sample consists of 51 women,[19] all Black and averaging among them nearly six years of residency in their public housing unit prior to the storm, though some had been in the system much longer. As a group, their mean age was just over fifty. Most (55%) were single; 12 percent were married, 16 percent were divorced, and 12 percent were widowed; the remainder, separated or cohabitating.

41% of women had no educational degree, while the majority (47%) had a high school degree or a GED. Just 10% had an Associate's or Bachelor's degree and one respondent, a school teacher, had a graduate degree (Master's). With these low educational levels (88% with a high school education or *less*), these women are representative of the limited educational attainment of the broader population of the city at that time.

In addition to, or perhaps because of, their low educational attainment, 90% (n=46) of women interviewed had earned below $20,000 in 2004, the year prior to Katrina. Finally, 29 women evacuated themselves. Of those 29 women, 22 women left before the storm and 7 women left afterwards. 26 specifically identified family or friends with whom they left in private vehicles, while the remaining 3 left in their own vehicles. 19 reported being "rescued" from their flooded homes out of 21 women who were stranded in the city during the storm; among them were Trinity, Lillian, Regina, Louisa, Ann, Alika, Linda, Zarah, Sheila, Vanessa, Angela, Joanna, Jada, Ebony, Morgan, Lydia, Thea, Keisha, Twila, Mary, and Eurdice. Giselle, working at a convalescent home during the event, was neither stranded nor evacuated, nor did she and her husband leave immediately after the storm. The women in my sample represent a population with limited income and finite resources, but also an ability to transform situational social capital into survival resources for themselves and their family members.

Discussing Disaster

Documenting the experiences throughout the book was difficult, because as a researcher there was little I could do to help. Yet, as I reflected upon the interviews, I had to think first of those I was interviewing, not about my own pain over troubling accounts. Knowing before I had even begun interviews that I lacked the financial and counseling resources for assisting women troubled by our conversations, I set out to create a list of social service providers who could help interviewees who expressed a need for such assistance. With the assistance of graduate student friends who were studying school psychology, I identified national counseling and crisis hotline phone numbers as one small thing that I could do to help those who shared their experiences with me. I was admittedly not qualified in any way to give counseling myself. Just the same, a pre-Katrina trauma of my own—in April 2004, I had been raped—made me painfully aware of the complex needs of those who have gone through life-changing pain and suffering. I knew on a personal level how important and helpful counseling could be in the wake of traumatic circumstances.

Despite this small service, throughout the interviews I felt guilt about the inherent benefits that I would receive from each woman's loss. Was I insensitive for using women's pain as a basis for my dissertation? Or might the story that I would tell impact in some positive ways on these and other low-income women's lives? Could these women teach disaster planners about the diverse needs of those fleeing disasters? Could municipal, state, and federal governments learn from the gendered disaster experiences of poor women? Admittedly, I have never fully resolved these questions for myself: I cannot ignore that the women's experiences presented here benefit me professionally. Yet, through this book I have worked to present their experiences, however difficult they were, to assure that the voices of low-income Katrina survivors be heard.

Living Losses Together

The duration of data collection, sixteen months in all, was made longer than its "real-time" by the stressful aspects of the interview content. Many women had lost family members, been stranded in floodwaters, or trapped in shelters of last resort. As a very early returnee to New Orleans, I could see the painful aftermath of these realities. Dwellings were spray painted with hash-mark symbols indicating that a first-responder had been there searching for survivors, dead human bodies, and animals left behind. Buildings were stained by dark black water lines where the flood had risen and settled, with many far in excess of eight or ten feet. Overturned cars and never-ending piles of debris cut across the New Orleans landscape.

Each time I called a woman for a prospective interview, I feared that I would encounter someone whose loved ones had drowned. It was normal for women to have lost all of their possessions. Additionally, there was uncertainty about homes and whether women would be allowed to return to their public housing units. Often, women looked to me for answers, but I typically had none. To manage the mix of emotions that I felt every day, I collected data in fits and starts, conducting four or five interviews in a week, until I was emotionally and physically exhausted. Then, I would cease interviewing for two or three weeks, using the time to muster the courage to begin again.

Returning to New Orleans in October 2005, the city was devastating, depressing, sexist, and racist. In my own Algiers Point neighborhood located just across the Mississippi River from downtown New Orleans, there was a home with a wall missing. It looked like a giant, life-sized doll house, with the contents of its owner's life on display for all to see. Another house had collapsed on itself, leaving a splintered pile of wooden debris spilling into the street. Most homes had blue tarps on their roofs, and many had shingles and siding missing. But the real devastation was not the state of New Orleans' built environment, but a social culture marked by intolerance. At neighborhood bars, relief workers and locals alike confided in me as a white woman that "the Blacks" had burned down the shopping mall, looted local grocery stores, and "invaded" my Algiers neighborhood.

By contrast, one of my interviewees had told me that the mall had caught fire when people broke in to cook food there, because they had nothing to eat without power in their own homes. My neighbor told me that New Orleans police had given his landlord permission to "shoot the niggers" and "just kick 'em to the curb" after looters had been shooting blindly into the air. Meanwhile, a co-worker from a neighborhood restaurant where I had worked told me that she had to leave after three days because the neighborhood was "too rough" and there were too many shootings happening. In all these accounts was a deep racial tension and hatred, stronger than any I had ever observed in the prior decade I lived in the city.

Race relations weren't the only things changed after the storm; gender mattered then too. Walking home from a coffee shop during the first week that I was back in New Orleans, I was gawked at by relief workers—one so intently that I feared he might follow me home and rape me. There were very few women in the city in October 2005, making the few of us there very visible and potentially vulnerable. Again, I had never felt unsafe in this way on public streets, especially places like Canal Street or Bourbon Street. In Katrina's wake, this all changed.

My beautiful city had become white, masculine, and scary. Police-citizen interactions were laced with racial power. Citizen behavior was scrutinized. One day I was talking with a Black neighbor and a police patrol car stopped beside us. We were grilled about why we were talking to each other. My neighbor said we were making lunch plans. We had actually been talking about her renter rights and whether ACORN[20] could help her fight eviction. In light of all of the tension in New Orleans, I began to stay home more often to avoid uncomfortable interactions with police, other first-responders, and my racist community neighbors. When I learned about the one-year Visiting Instructor position at the University of Central Florida, I decided to apply and moved at the end of June 2006. Amid the corrosive environment in New Orleans, interviewing had become even more heartbreaking and painful. Life was just too difficult in a militarized city with such deep racial hatred and persistent reminders of destruction and death everywhere. I still feel a deep sense of loss over leaving New Orleans, even though it was the best choice for my recovery.

Personal Growth through Silence

While the previous accounts of my time in New Orleans might suggest that I derived little that was positive from the post-Katrina interviews, I often saw great resiliency and strength among women who had faced the worst Hurricane Katrina had to offer. With each interview, I was growing personally from seeing the courage and commitment of the women I interviewed. Just the same, two questions were particularly difficult for me as a researcher and most definitely for interviewees themselves: "Could you tell me about your evacuation experience?" and "What was your saddest disaster experience?" Some women rushed through their answers, others became upset, and a few cried and could not speak. When this happened, we stopped, talked off the record and then each woman decided for herself if she wanted to continue. In those moments, I suggested the counseling telephone numbers. In every case, my bias favored the woman's well-being—I never judged her, but observed the difficult position she was in, no matter what choices she had made. This openness built a rapport that benefitted both of us. When I lost part of an interview because a woman was unable to continue, I knew that her well-being was far more important than gathering data.

Perhaps the strength I most developed throughout this process was learning to listen. I learned the value of waiting for each woman to guide her own narrative—asking only minimal follow-up questions during a natural pause. I used these follow-up moments to clarify things I didn't understand and to inquire further about specific points of interest. I was surprised at the end of an interview when several women expressed relief and appreciation that someone had listened to them. These moments moved me forward emotionally toward recovery even more than they impacted upon the completion of my research.

[1] Some scholar-survivors are having difficulty when their articles are sent for blind review. In essence, the situational knowledge which we possess as residents of the city is being framed as a form of bias in our research, instead of as an asset that allows us to accurately contextualize the events; see Haney and Barber's work (2013) for a detailed discussion. In response, I argue who I am as a person, feminist, survivor, and researcher enabled women to feel comfortable enough to share their experiences with me. Extended interviews are a social interaction shaped by the people in that interaction. Discounting the importance of the "who" and the power relations embedded within that interview is to be blind to a different type of bias—the bias the interviewer inevitably contributes through what data is gathered, how the meaning of that data is constructed and interpreted in the moment of the conversation, what follow-up questions are asked, and most importantly, how those inquiries are worded. If anything, I would argue my "biased" position gave me greater access to more intimate and accurate information than I ever could have achieved if I took a more positivist approach to the interview process. For scholars seeking to engage the insider voice, see Brunsma 2007.

[2] While I was unable to study this issue, Jay Arena's book *Driven from New Orleans* (2012) provides a detailed discussion of this critical topic in Chapters 4 and 5.

[3] Bankston 2007/2011.

[4] Every storm eventually follows the jet stream east. The true gamble for New Orleans is *when* that turn will take place—when a storm is well south of the city in the Gulf of Mexico, or over dry land after passing through the city.

[5] Nock, Sanchez, and Wright 2008.

[6] HOPE VI, also known as the Urban Revitalization Demonstration program, was a federal initiative passed in 1992 to address the unsanitary, dangerous, and severely distressed conditions of urban public housing nationally (Bacon 1998; Popkin et al. 2004). In an effort to undo the unanticipated consequences of high rise, Le Corbusier-style public housing, HOPE VI provides funds to renovate and replace dilapidated housing by creating healthy, self-sustaining communities with social service programs such as job training, work opportunities, transportation, child care, and other types of support (Finkel, Lennon, and Eisenstadt 2000; Forrest and Williams 2001; National Housing Law Project 2002; Kingsley, Johnson, and Pettit 2003). The physical design also differs by including mixed-income, low-rise housing, and homeownership options at some sites (Freedman 1998).

[7] While no complete listing of this population exists, I obtained partial resident lists from the Housing Authority of New Orleans (HANO) in May 2004 for my original dissertation research. The distribution of the lists was authorized by the HUD federal receiver, who was managing HANO at that time. The resident lists included a roster of residents relocated from the Desire public housing site and a roster of approximately one-third of all dislocated families from the St. Thomas community, equaling 694 heads of household in total. A supplemental list of forty St. Thomas families was also received following the storm from a social service provider with long-standing connections to the community. Only women were considered for an interview due to the fact that fewer than 10 men were among the entire sample frame.

[8] Since my apartment was undamaged and I did not move residences, I did not qualify for any long-term rental assistance, despite the fact that my source of employment—teaching adjunct classes at Tulane—was unavailable. By contrast, I know some other people who moved across town and received 12 months of aid because they moved, yet they retained their jobs. Some five months after returning to the city, FEMA called to say I was eligible for a trailer, which was ironic given a FEMA inspector visited my apartment to see it wasn't damaged and denied me the rental assistance in the first place.

[9] MRE = Meals Ready to Eat.

[10] Lacking a refrigerator meant I had to shop for perishables and ice every other day and wait in the long line even if I needed only a few items.

[11] Unlike many landlords, mine were fantastic. Since they were unable to begin repair on their own flooded home on the Northshore, they went out of their way to quickly replace my refrigerator within 2 days in order to feel productive in the face of such loss. Aside from discarding a 40-gallon fish tank covered in live maggots, cleaning out the refrigerator in a failed attempt to salvage it, and removing leaves, limbs, and debris from the yard, my return home was simple, as my apartment was in near perfect condition. By contrast, the emotional work of recovery was, for me, a process in which I am still actively engaged.

[12] Bonner 2007/2011; Pardee 2007/2011.

[13] It was also economically unfeasible. Adjunct work dried up in my home department, and given the option to earn a regular salary with medical insurance, or to borrow more in students loans to live in a city where most everyone with whom I interacted had moved away, the idea of leaving a second time by choice grew in attractiveness. By May 2006, nearly half of all faculty in my home department had found other jobs, and three-quarters of remaining graduate students had transferred departments as well. I was among the last to receive a Tulane Sociology Ph.D., my degree program being another casualty of the storm.

[14] Nock, Sanchez, and Wright 2008; Sanchez et al. 2001.

[15] The sampling design is a purposive sample. Due to the incomplete nature of the sampling lists and the massive displacement of the target sample, locating a randomized sample was not feasible. In fact, locating a non-random sample was still quite difficult under these circumstances.

[16] Looking back, I should have interviewed every low-income public housing woman I spoke with, regardless of which development she lived in, and created a comparative study. However, the offer of funding came with rigid sampling requirements, and it was the close-ended items that were of interest to faculty with whom I was initially working. As the composition of my dissertation committee changed and the project took shape, it became clear that the qualitative data were by far the more interesting and sociological relevant side of the study.

[17] It was my belief that a personally addressed letter would be more likely forwarded by the then over-taxed postal service in New Orleans.

[18] Women who received the letter would call my New Orleans cell phone number if they were interested in the study. I then offered to call them back if they had a landline, or in some cases arranged a time to talk when it would not cost them precious cell phone minutes. I only acquired cell phone numbers

when women contacted me from the letters, or a referral by another respondent. I cannot estimate what proportion of women used cell or landlines.

[19] One fifth of women were in the pretest sample. The "pretest" sample refers to interviews gained early in the process, prior to the securing of any type of funding. The final survey is a modified version of the Neighborhood Change Survey, a NSF-funded project to understand the evacuation and recovery experiences in selected New Orleans neighborhoods. Combining this research with the larger project allowed participants to receive a twenty dollar gift card as compensation.

[20] ACORN is the Association of Community Organizations for Reform Now. Their mission is to promote stronger communities through petitioning for affordable housing, better schools and serving as a watchdog for fair housing law violations. Following Hurricane Katrina, ACORN was one of the few agencies fighting on behalf of the displaced homeowners, many of whose homes were going to be bulldozed before they were even allowed to return to the city to see them or retrieve any remaining possessions that they could. Similarly, they were supporting homeowners against talks of reclaiming low-lying land in New Orleans through the use of eminent domain. Sadly, they did not have any services for renters, whose housing rights were unprotected after the storm.

Bibliography

Abt Associates. 1996. "An Historical and Baseline Assessment of HOPE VI." Volume I. Cross-Site Report. Washington, D.C.: U.S. Department of Housing and Urban Development.

Adams, Richard E. and Joseph A. Boscarino. 2005. "Stress and Well-Being in the Aftermath of the World Trade Center Attack: The Continuing Effects of a Communitywide Disaster." *Journal of Community Psychology* 33(2): 175-190.

Adams, R.E., E.J. Bromet, N. Panina, E. Golovakha, D. Goldgaber, and S. Gluzman. 2002. "Stress and Well-being in Mothers of Young Children 11 Years after the Chernobyl Nuclear Power Plant Accident." *Psychological Medicine* 32: 143-156.

American Community Survey. 2010. Orleans Parish Poverty. Accessed online at:http://factfinder2.census.gov/faces/tableservices/jsf/pages/productview.xhtml?pid=ACS_10_1YR_S1701&prodType=table. Retrieved 6/30/2012.

Anderson, Elijah. 1989. "Sex Codes and Family Life among Poor Inner-City Youth." *Annals of the American Academy of Political and Social Science* 59-78.

—. 1990. *A Place on the Corner*. Chicago and London: University of Chicago Press.

—. 1999. *Code of the Street*. New York and London: W.W. Norton & Co..

Arena, John. 2012. *Driven from New Orleans: How Nonprofits Betray Public Housing and Promote Privatization*. Minneapolis, MN: University of Minnesota Press.

Bacon, Elinor. 1998. "Opinion and Comment." *Journal of Housing and Community Development* 55(6): 7-10.

Bankoff, Greg. 2004. "The Historical Geography of Disaster: 'Vulnerability' and 'Local Knowledge.'" in *Mapping Vulnerability: Disasters, Development, and People*. Edited by Greg Bankoff, Georg Frerks, and Dorothea Hillhorst. London: Earthscan.

Bankoff, Greg, Georg Frerks, and Dorothea Hillhorst. 2004. *Mapping Vulnerability: Disasters, Development, and People*. London: Earthscan.

Bankston III, Carl L. 2007/2011. "How I Spent my Hurricane Vacation." Pp. 20-33 in *Narrating the Storm: Sociological Stories of Hurricane Katrina*. Danielle A. Hidalgo and Kristen Barber, Eds. Newcastle, U.K.: Cambridge Scholar Publishing.

Behan, Pamela. 2007/2011. "The First Major U.S. Evacuation: Houston and the Social Construction of Risk." Pp. 176-189 in *Narrating the Storm: Sociological Stories of Hurricane Katrina*. Danielle A. Hidalgo and Kristen Barber, Eds. Newcastle, U.K.: Cambridge Scholar Publishing.

Benson, Charlotte. 2004. "Macro-economic Concepts on Vulnerability: Dynamics, Complexity, and Public Policy." In *Mapping Vulnerability: Disasters, Development, and People.* Edited by Greg Bankoff, Georg Frerks, and Dorothea Hillhorst. London: Earthscan.

Bolin, Robert and Lois Stanford. 1998. "The Northridge Earthquake: Community-based Approaches to Unmet Recovery Needs." *Disasters* 22(1): 21-38.

Bonacich, Edna. 1972. "A Theory of Ethnic Antagonism: The Split Labor Market." *American Sociological Review* 37(5): 547-559.

Bonner, Donna Maria. 2007/2011. "A Bricolage of Loss." Pp. 200-211 in *Narrating the Storm: Sociological Stories of Hurricane Katrina.* Danielle A. Hidalgo and Kristen Barber, Eds. Newcastle, U.K.: Cambridge Scholar Publishing.

Boteler, F.E. 2007. "Building Disaster-Resilient Families, Communities, and Businesses." *Journal of Extension* 45(6).

Brunsma, David L. 2007. "Preface." In *The Sociology of Katrina: Perspectives on a Modern Catastrophe.* Edited by David L. Brunsma, David Overfelt and J. Steven Picou. Lanham, MD: Rowman and Littlefield.

Brunsma, David L., David Overfelt and J. Steven Picou (Eds.). 2007. *The Sociology of Katrina: Perspectives on a Modern Catastrophe.* Lanham, MD: Rowman and Littlefield.

Callamard, Agnès. 1999. "Refugee women: a gendered and political analysis of the refugee experience." Pp. 196-214 in *Refugees: Perspectives on the Experience of Forced Migration.* Edited by Alastair Ager. London and New York: Pinter.

Cardona, Omar D. 2004. "The Need for Rethinking the Concepts of Vulnerability and Risk from a Holistic Perspective: A Necessary Review and Criticism for Effective Risk Management." In *Mapping Vulnerability: Disasters, Development, and People.* Edited by Greg Bankoff, Georg Frerks, and Dorothea Hillhorst. London: Earthscan.

Carey, Mark. 2005. "Living and dying with glaciers: people's historical vulnerability to avalanches and outbursts in Peru." *Global and Planetary Change* 47: 122-134.

City of New Orleans. 2006. "New Orleans MSA Labor Force." Online at http://cno-gisweb02.cityofno.com/recoverymatrix/viewChart.aspx?type=11. Retrieved on 10/18/06.

Collins, Patricia Hill. 1998. *Fighting Words: Black Women and the Search for Justice.* Minneapolis, MN: University of Minnesota Press.

—. 1995. "The Meaning of Motherhood in Black Culture." Pp. 201-204 in *Women: Images and Realities: A Multicultural Anthology.* Edited by Amy Kesselman, Lily D. McNair, and Nancy Schniedewind. Mountain View, CA: Mayfield.

Couch, Stephen R. 1996. "Environmental Contamination, Community Transformation and the Central Mine Fire." Pp. 60-84 in *The Long Road to Recovery: Community Responses to Industrial Disaster*, edited by James K. Mitchell. New York: United Nations University Press.

Cutter, Susan. 2005. "The Geography of Social Vulnerability: Race, Class, and Catastrophe." Understanding Katrina: Perspectives from the Social Sciences. Online at: http://understandingkatrina.ssrc.org/Cutter/pf/. Retrieved 10/11/2006.

Cutter, Susan L. and Christopher T. Emrich. 2006. "Moral Hazard, Social Catastrophe: The Changing Face of Vulnerability along the Hurricane Coasts." *The Annals of the American Academy of Political and Social Science* 604: 82-112.
Davis, Mike. 2000. *Magical Urbanism: Latinos Reinvent the US City*. New York: Verso.
Department of Housing and Urban Development. February 12, 2006. *Current Housing Unit Damage Estimates: Hurricanes Katrina, Rita and Wilma*. Washington D.C.: HUD, Office of Policy Development and Research.
Devine, Joel A. and James D. Wright. 1993. *The Greatest of Evils: Urban Poverty and the American Underclass*. New York: Aldine De Gruyter.
Domínguez, Silvia and Celeste Watkins. 2003. "Creating Networks for Survival and Mobility: Social Capital Among African-American and Latin-American Low-Income Mothers." *Social Problems* 50(1): 111–135.
Downing, Theodore. 1996. "Mitigating Social Impoverishment when People are Involuntarily Displaced." Pp. 34-48 in *Understanding Impoverishment: The Consequences of Development-Induced Displacement*, edited by C. McDowell. Oxford: Berghahn Press.
Drabek, Thomas E. 1986. *Human Systems Responses to Disasters: An Inventory of Sociological Findings*. New York: Springer-Verlag.
Drabek, Thomas E. and Keith S. Boggs. 1968. "Families in Disaster: Reactions and Relatives." *Journal of Marriage and the Family* 30(3): 443-451.
Drabek, Thomas E., William H. Key, Patricia E. Erikson, and Juanita L. Crowe. 1975. "The Impact of Disaster on Kin and Relationships." *Journal of Marriage and the Family* 37: 481-494.
Dreier, Peter. 2006. "Katrina and Power in America." *Urban Affairs Review* 41(4): 528-549.
Dreier, Peter, John Mollenkopf, and Todd Swanstrom. 2001. *Place Matters: Metropolitics for the Twenty-first Century*. Lawrence, Kansas: University of Kansas Press.
Dynes, Russell R. 2005. "Social Capital: Dealing with Community Emergencies." *Homeland Security Affairs* 2(2): 1-26.
Dynes, Russell R. and Havidán Rodríguez. 2005. "Finding and Framing Katrina: The Social Construction of Disaster." SSRC website. Online at: http://understandingkatrina.ssrc.org/Dynes_Rodriguez/pf/.
Edelstein, Michael R. 2004. *Contaminated Communities: Coping with Residential Toxic Exposure*, 2nd edition. Cambridge, MA: Westview Press.
Edin, Kathryn and Laura Lein. 1997. *Making Ends Meet: How Single Mothers Survive Welfare and Low-Wage Work*. New York: Russell Sage Foundation.
Ehrenreich, Barbara. 2001. *Nickel and Dimed: On (Not) Getting By in America*. New York: Owl Books.
Elliott, James R. and Jeremy Pais. 2006. "Race, Class and Hurricane Katrina: Social Differences in Human Responses to Disaster." *Social Science Review* 35(2): 295-321.
Enarson, Elaine. 2012. *Women Confronting Natural Disaster: From Vulnerability to Resilience*. Boulder, CO: Lynne Rienner.
Enarson, Elaine and Betty Hearn Morrow (Eds.). 1998. *The Gendered Terrain of Disaster: Through Women's Eyes*. Westport, CT: Praeger.

Enarson, Elaine and Joseph Scanlon. 1999. "Gender Patterns in Flood Evacuation: A Case Study in Canada's Red River Valley." *Applied Behavioral Sciences Review* 7(2): 103-124.

Erikson, Kai. 1976. *Everything in its Path: Destruction of Community in the Buffalo Creek Flood*. New York: Simon and Schuster.

—. 1994. *A New Species of Trouble: The Human Experience of Modern Disasters*. New York: W.W. Norton.

—. 2007. "Foreword." In *The Sociology of Katrina: Perspectives on a Modern Catastrophe*. Edited by David L. Brunsma, David Overfelt and J. Steven Picou. Lanham, MD: Rowman and Littlefield.

Federal Emergency Management Administration. 2003. "Fact Sheet: Individuals and Household." Online at: http://www.fema.gov/news/ newsrelease.fema?id=5404. Release number: 1497-01-FactSheet. Retrieved 6/18/08.

Finkel, Andrew E., Karin A. Lennon, and Elizabeth R. Eisenstadt. 2000. "HOPE VI: A Promising Vintage?" *Policy Studies Review*. 17(2/3): 104-119.

Fordham, Maureen. 2004. "Gendering Vulnerability Analysis: Toward a more nuanced approach." In *Mapping Vulnerability: Disasters, Development, and People*. Edited by Greg Bankoff, Georg Frerks, and Dorothea Hillhorst. London: Earthscan.

Fordham, Maureen and Anne-Michelle Ketteridge. 1998. "'Men Must Work and Women Must Weep': Examining Gender Stereotypes in Disasters." Pp. 81-94 in *The Gendered Terrain of Disaster: Through Women's Eyes*. Edited by Elaine Enarson and Betty Hearn Morrow. Westport, CT: Praeger.

Forrest, Ray and Peter Williams. 2001. "Housing in the Twentieth Century." Pp. 88-101 in *Handbook of Urban Studies*, edited by Ronan Paddison. London: Sage.

Fothergill, Alice. 2003. "The Stigma of Charity: Gender, Class, and Disaster Assistance." *Sociological Quarterly* 44(4): 659-680.

—. 1999. "Women's Roles in Disaster." *Applied Behavioral Science Review* 7(2): 125-143.

—. 1998. "The Neglect of Gender in Disaster Work: On Overview of the Literature." Pp. 11-25 in *The Gendered Terrain of Disaster: Through Women's Eyes*. Edited by Elaine Enarson, and Betty Hearn Morrow. Westport, CT: Praeger.

—. 1996. "Gender, Risk, and Disaster." *Journal of Mass Emergency Disasters* 14: 33-56.

Fothergill, Alice and Lori Peek. 2012. "Permanent Temporariness: Displaced Children in Lousiana." Pp. 31-46 in *Displaced: Voices from the Katrina Diaspora*, edited by Lynn Weber and Lori Peek. Austin, TX: University of Texas Press.

Frederico, Margarita M., Clifford J. Picton, Steven Muncy, Luis Ma Ongsiapco, Celia Santos, and Vladimir Hernandez. 2007. "Building community following displacement due to armed conflict: A case study." *International Social Work* 50(2): 171-184.

Freedman, Anthony S. 1998. "HOPE VI: Lessons and Issues." *Journal of Housing and Community Development* 55(4): 25-30.

Freudenberg, William R. 1997. "Contamination, Corrosion, and the Social Order: An Overview." *Current Sociology* 45(3): 19-39.

—. 1993. "Risk and Recreancy: Weber, the Division of Labor, and the Rationality of Risk Perceptions." *Social Forces* 71(4): 909-932.

Freudenburg, William R., Robert Grambling, Shirley Laska, and Kai T. Erikson. 2009. *Catastrophe in the Making: The Engineering of Katrina and the Disasters of Tomorrow.* Washington, DC: Island Press.

Fritz, C.E. 1961. "Disasters." Pp. 651-694 in *Social Problems*, edited by Robert Merton and R. Nisbet. New York: Harcourt, Brace, and World.

Fussell, Elizabeth. 2005. "Leaving New Orleans: Social Stratification, Networks, and Hurricane Evacuation." SSRC website. Online at: http://understandingkatrina.ssrc.org/Fussell/pf/. Retrieved 10/11/06.

Government Accountability Office (GAO). 2006. "Hurricane Katrina: Strategic Planning Needed to Guide Future Enhancements beyond Interim Levee Repairs." GAO-06-934.

Gladwell, Malcolm. 2007. *Blink: The Power of Thinking Without Thinking.* New York: Little, Brown & Company.

Gladwin, Hugh and Walter Gillis Peacock. 1997. "Warning and Evacuation: A Night for Hard Houses." Pp. 52-74 in *Hurricane Andrew: Ethnicity, gender, and the sociology of disasters*. Edited by Walter Gillis Peacock, Betty Hearn Morrow, and Hugh Gladwin. New York: Routledge.

Goering, John, Ali Kamely, and Todd Richardson. 1997. "Recent Research on Racial Segregation and Poverty Concentration in Public Housing in the United States." *Urban Affairs Review* 32(5): 723-745.

Goetz, Edward G. 2000. "The Politics of Poverty Deconcentration and Housing Demolition." *Journal of Urban Affairs* 22(2): 157-173.

Gotham, Kevin Fox. 2002. *Race, Real Estate, and Uneven Development: The Kansas City Experience, 1900- 2000.* Albany, NY: State University of New York (SUNY) Press.

Gotham, Kevin Fox and James D. Wright. 1999. "Housing Policy." Pp. 237-255 in *Handbook of Social Policy*, edited by Midgley, James, Michelle Livermore, and Martin B. Tracy. Thousand Oaks, CA: Sage.

Granovetter, Mark. 1978. "The Strength of Weak Ties." *American Journal of Sociology* 78(6): 1360-1380.

Greater New Orleans Community Data Center (GNOCDC). 2006. "Metro New Orleans Fair Market Rent History." Online at: www.gnocdc.org/ reports/ fair_market_rents.html. Retrieved 9/25/06.

Handmer, John. 2000. "Are Flood Warnings Futile? Risk Communications in Emergencies." *The Australasian Journal of Disaster and Trauma Studies* 2000 (2).

Haney, Timothy J. 2007/2011. "Disaster and the Irrationality of 'Rational' Bureaucracy: Daily Life and the Continuing Struggles in the Aftermath of Hurricane Katrina." Pp. 134-144 in *Narrating the Storm: Sociological Stories of Hurricane Katrina*. Danielle A. Hidalgo and Kristen Barber, Eds. Newcastle, U.K.: Cambridge Scholar Publishing.

Haney, Timothy J. and Kristen Barber. 2013. "Reconciling Academic Objectivity and Subjective Trauma: The Double Consciousness of Sociologists who Experienced Hurricane Katrina." *Critical Sociology* 39(1): 105-122.

Haney, Timothy J., James R. Elliott, and Elizabeth Fussell. 2007. "Families and Hurricane Response: Evacuation, Separation, and the Emotional Toll of Hurricane Katrina." Pp. 71-90 in *The Sociology of Katrina: Perspectives on a Modern Catastrophe*. Edited by David L. Brunsma, David Overfelt and J. Steven Picou. Lanham, MD: Rowman and Littlefield.

Harrell-Bond, Barbara. 1999. "The experience of refugees as recipients of aid." Pp. 136-168 in *Refugees: Perspectives on the Experience of Forced Migration.* Edited by Alastair Ager. London and New York: Pinter.
Harrold, John R. 2006. "Agility and Discipline: Critical Success Factors for Disaster Response." *The Annals of the American Academy* 604: 256-272.
Hays, Sharon. 2003. *Flat Broke with Children: Women in the Age of Welfare Reform.* New York: Oxford University Press.
Henly, Julia R., Sandra K. Danziger, and Shira Offer. 2005. "The Contribution of Social Support to the Material Well-being of Low-Income Families." *Journal of Marriage and the Family* 67: 122-140.
Hidalgo, Danielle and Kristen Barber. 2007, Reprint 2011. *Narrating the Storm: Sociological Stories of Hurricane Katrina.* Cambridge, U.K.: Cambridge Scholars Publishing.
Hilhorst, Dorothea and Greg Bankoff. 2004. "Introduction: Mapping Vulnerability." In *Mapping Vulnerability: Disasters, Development, and People.* Edited by Greg Bankoff, Georg Frerks, and Dorothea Hillhorst. London: Earthscan.
Holzer, Harry. 1987. "Informal Job Search and Black Youth Unemployment." *The American Economic Review* 77(3): 446-452.
hooks, bell. 1984. *Feminist Theory: From Margin to Center.* Boston: South End Press.
Huggins, Martha K. and Joel A. Devine. 2005. "New Orleans Hurricane Katrina: Natural or Social Disaster?" *Footnotes.* Available online at www2.asanet.org/footnotes/nov05/fn14.html. Retrieved 7/14/07.
Idakula, Ruth S. 2007/2011. "Cataclysm in New Orleans: Story of a Black Single Mother." Pp. 33-46 in *Narrating the Storm: Sociological Stories of Hurricane Katrina.* Danielle A. Hidalgo and Kristen Barber, Eds. Newcastle, U.K.: Cambridge Scholar Publishing.
Kates, R. W., C. E. Colten, S. Laska, and S. P. Leatherman. 2006. "Reconstruction of New Orleans after Hurricane Katrina: A research perspective." *Proceedings of the National Academy of Sciences* 103: 14653-14660.
Kingsley, G. Thomas, Jennifer Johnson, and Kathryn S. Pettit. 2003. "Patterns of Section 8 Relocation in the HOPE VI Program." *Journal of Urban Affairs* 25(4): 427-447.
Klinenberg, Eric. 2002. *Heat Wave: A Social Autopsy of Disaster in Chicago.* Chicago: University of Chicago.
Kozol, Jonathan. 2005. *The Shame of the Nation: The Restoration of Apartheid Schooling in America.* New York: Three Rivers Press.
—. 1991. *Savage Inequalities.* New York: Crown Publishers.
Kreps, G.A. 1984. "Sociological Inquiry and Disaster Research." *Annual Review of Sociology* 10: 309-30.
Lavell, Allan. 2004. "The Lower Lempa River Valley, El Salvador: Risk Reduction and Development Project." In *Mapping Vulnerability: Disasters, Development, and People.* Edited by Greg Bankoff, Georg Frerks, and Dorothea Hillhorst. London: Earthscan.
Lein, Laura, Ronald Angel, Julie Beausoleil, and Holly Bell. 2012. "The Basement of Extreme Poverty: Katrina Survivors and Poverty Programs." Pg. 47-62 in *Displaced: Voices from the Katrina Diaspora,* Lynn Weber and Lori Peek, Eds. Austin, TX: University of Texas Press.

Literacy Alliance of Greater New Orleans. 2002. Summary Report. Available online at: http://www.boggslit.org/Alliance_Summary_Report.pdf. Retrieved May 2007.

Litt, Jacquelyn. 2012. "'We need to get together with each other': Women's Narratives of Help in Katrina's Displacement." Pg. 167-182 in *Displaced: Voices from the Katrina Diaspora*, Lynn Weber and Lori Peek, Eds. University of Texas Press: Austin, TX.

Marshall, Brent K, J. Steven Picou, and Duane A. Gill. 2003. "Terrorism as Disaster: Selected Commonalities and Long-Term Recovery for 9/11 Survivors." *Research in Social Problems and Public Policy* 11: 73-96.

Massey, Douglas S. and Nancy A. Denton. 1993. *American Apartheid: Segregation and the Making of the Underclass*. Cambridge: Harvard.

Miller, Kristen and Joanne Nigg. 1993. "Event and Consequence Vulnerability: Effects on the Disaster Process." Preliminary Paper No. 217. Disaster Research Center, University of Delaware.

Miller, Lee M. 2012. "Katrina Evacuee Reception in Rural East Texas: Rethinking Disaster 'Recovery.'" Pg. 104-118 in *Displaced: Voices from the Katrina Diaspora*, Lynn Weber and Lori Peek, Eds. Austin, TX: University of Texas Press.

Mitchell, James K (ed). 1996. "Improving community responses to industrial disasters." Pp. 1-40 in *The Long Road to Recovery: Community Responses to Industrial Disasters*. New York: United Nations University Press.

Murray, Charles. 1984. *Losing Ground*. New York: Basic Books.

—. 1994. Reprint. *Losing Ground*. New York: Basic Books.

National Housing Law Project (NHLP). June 2002. *False HOPE: A Critical Assessment of the HOPE VI Public Housing Redevelopment Program*. Oakland, CA.

Nigg, Joanne M., John Barnshaw, and Manuel R. Torres. 2006. "Hurricane Katrina and the Flooding of New Orleans: Emergent Issues in Sheltering and Temporary Housing." *The Annals of the American Academy* 604: 113-128.

Nock, Steven L., Laura A. Sanchez, and James D. Wright. 2008. *Covenant Marriage: The Movement to Reclaim Tradition in America*. New Brunswick, New Jersey: Rutgers University Press.

Noel, Gloria E. 1998. "The Neglect of Gender in Disaster Work: On Overview of the Literature." Pp. 213-219 in *The Gendered Terrain of Disaster: Through Women's Eyes*. Edited by Elaine Enarson, and Betty Hearn Morrow. Westport, CT: Praeger.

NOVA. 2005. *Hurricane Katina: The Storm that Drowned a City*. Documentary. WGBH Boston Video.

Oliker, Stacey J. 2005. "Work Commitment and Constraint Among Mothers on Workfare." *Journal of Contemporary Ethnography* 24(2): 165-194.

Oliver, Melvin L. and Thomas M. Shapiro. 1995. *Black Wealth, White Wealth*. New York: Routledge.

Oliver-Smith, Anthony. 1996. "Anthropological Research on Hazards and Disasters." *Annual Review of Anthropology* 25: 303-328.

—. 2004. "Theorizing Vulnerability in a Globalized World: A Political Ecological Perspective." In *Mapping Vulnerability: Disasters, Development, and People*. Edited by Greg Bankoff, Georg Frerks, and Dorothea Hillhorst. London: Earthscan.

Pardee, Jessica W. 2012. "Living through Displacement: Housing Insecurity among Low-Income Evacuees." Pg. 63-78 in *Displaced: Voices from the Katrina Diaspora,* Lynn Weber and Lori Peek, Eds. Austin, TX: University of Texas Press.

—. 2007/2011. "Using Simmel to Survive: The Blasé Attitude as a Disaster Reaction and Response." Pp. 151-168 in *Narrating the Storm: Sociological Stories of Hurricane Katrina.* Danielle A. Hidalgo and Kristen Barber, Eds. Newcastle, U.K.: Cambridge Scholar Publishing.

Pardee, Jessica W. and Brian Barry. n.d. "After the Flood: Reconstructed Lives and World Views among Believers following Hurricane Katrina." Conference paper presented at the Eastern Sociological Society annual meeting, March 21, 2013.

Pardee, Jessica W. and Kevin Fox Gotham. 2005. "HOPE VI, Section 8, and the Contradictions of Low-Income Housing Policy." *Journal of Poverty* 9(2): 1-21.

Pattillo-McCoy, Mary. 2000. "The Limits of Out-Migration for the Black Middle Class." *Journal of Urban Affairs* 22(3): 225-241.

Peek, Lori. 2012. "They Call it 'Katrina Fatigue': Displaced Families and Discrimination in Colorado." Pp. 31-46 in *Displaced: Voices from the Katrina Diaspora*, edited by Lynn Weber and Lori Peek. Austin, TX: University of Texas Press.

Picou, J. Steven, Brent K Marshall, and Duane A. Gill. 2004. "Disaster, Litigation and the Corrosive Community." *Social Forces* 82(4): 1493-1522.

Popkin, Susan J., Bruce Katz, Mary K. Cunningham, Karen D. Brown, Jeremy Gustafson, and Margery A. Turner. 2004. *A Decade of HOPE VI: Research Findings and Policy Challenges.* Washington, D.C.: Urban Institute; Brookings Institute.

Quarantelli, E. L. and Russell R. Dynes. 1977. "Response to Social Crisis and Disaster." *Annual Review of Sociology* 3: 23-49.

Quillian, Lincoln. 2006. "New Approaches to Understanding Racial Prejudice and Discrimination." *Annual Review of Sociology* 32: 299-328.

Rainwater and Yancey. 1967. *The Moynihan Report and the Politics of Controversy.* Cambridge, MA: The M.I.T. Press.

Rank, Mark R. 2011. "Rethinking American Poverty." *Contexts* 10(2): 16-21.

Roberts, J. Timmons and Melissa M. Toffolon-Weiss. 2001. *Chronicles from the Environmental Justice Frontline.* New York: Cambridge University Press.

Rodríguez, Havidán, Joseph Trainor, and Enrico L. Quarantelli. 2006. "Rising to the Challenges of a Catastrophe: The Emergent and Prosocial Behavior following Hurricane Katrina." *The Annals of the American Academy* 604: 82-101.

Rose, Chris. 2005. *One Dead in Attic.* New Orleans: Chris Rose Books.

Sanchez, Laura, Steven Nock, James D. Wright, Jessica Pardee, and Marcel Ionescu. 2001. "The Implementation of Covenant Marriage in Louisiana." *Virginia Journal of Social Policy and the Law* 9(1): 192-223.

Seccombe, Karen. 2007. *Families in Poverty.* New York: Pearson/Allyn and Bacon.

Smith, Kenneth J., and Linda Liska Belgrave. 1995. "The Reconstruction of Everyday Life: Experiencing Hurricane Andrew." *Journal of Contemporary Ethnography* 24: 244-269.

Stack, Carol. 1974. *All Our Kin*. New York: Basic Books.
State of Louisiana. 2004. *Temporary Assistance for Needy Families State Plan*. Available online at: http://dss.louisiana.gov/departments/ofs/TANF State Plan.html. Retrieved 3/19/07.
—. 2006. *Temporary Assistance For Needy Families State Plan*. Available online at: http://dss.louisiana.gov/departments/ofs/TANFStatePlan.html. Retrieved 7/14/07.
Stephen, Linda. 2004. "Vulnerable Regions vs. Vulnerable People: An Ethiopian Case Study." In *Mapping Vulnerability: Disasters, Development, and People*. Edited by Greg Bankoff, Georg Frerks, and Dorothea Hillhorst. London: Earthscan.
Stockard, R.L., Russell L. Stockard Jr., and M. Belinda Tucker. 2007/2011. "Subverting Social Vulnerabilities and Inequalities in Disaster Survival." Pp. 62-77 in *Narrating the Storm: Sociological Stories of Hurricane Katrina*. Danielle A. Hidalgo and Kristen Barber, Eds. Newcastle, U.K.: Cambridge Scholar Publishing.
Stohlman, Sarah. 2007/2011. "My Aunt Po: Collective Memories Shaping Collective Responses." Pp. 141-152 in *Narrating the Storm: Sociological Stories of Hurricane Katrina*. Danielle A. Hidalgo and Kristen Barber, Eds. Newcastle, U.K.: Cambridge Scholar Publishing.
Tierney, Kathleen, Christine Bevc, and Erica Kuligowski. 2006. "Metaphors Matter: Disaster Myths, Media Frames, and Their Consequences in Hurricane Katrina." *The Annals of the American Academy* 604: 57-81.
Tomaskovic-Devey, Donald and Kevin Stainback. 2007. "Discrimination and Desegregation: Equal Opportunity Progress in U.S. Private Sector Workplaces since the Civil Rights Act." *The Annals of the American Academy of Political and Social Science* 609(1): 49-84.
U.S. Bureau of the Census. 2000, 1990, 1980, 1970. STF-1, STF-3. Available online at: www.census.gov.
—. Poverty Rates and Number in Poverty. Online at http://www.census.gov/hhes/www/poverty/data/incpovhlth/2010/figure4.pdf. Retrieved June 29, 2012.
U.S. Census Bureau, Current Population Survey, 1960-2003. Annual Social and Economic Supplements. Online at www.census.gov/hhes/poverty/poverty02/pov02fig1.jpg. Retrieved 7/10/03; Update online at: http://www.census.gov/hhes/www/poverty/data/incpovhlth/2010/figure4.pdf. Retrieved 6/28/12.
U.S. Department of Housing and Urban Development (HUD). 2/16/2006. "Current Housing Unit Damage Estimates: Hurricanes Katrina, Rita, and Wilma." Washington, D.C.: HUD Office of Policy Research and Development.
U.S. Department of Housing and Urban Development. 2005. "Katrina Disaster Housing Assistance Program, (KDHAP) Application. User Guide." December. Washington, D.C.: HUD.
—. 2006. "Housing Choice Voucher Program FY 2006 Appropriations Implementation." Washington, D.C.: HUD Office of Housing Voucher Programs.
Waugh, William L. 2006. "The Political Costs of Failure in the Katrina and Rita Disasters." *The Annals of the American Academy of Political and Social Science* 604: 10-25.

Weatherunderground.com. Historical weather data is available online at: http://www.wunderground.com/history/airport/KAUD/2005/9/1/DailyHistory.html Retrieved 12/22/11.
Weber, Lynn. 2010, 2nd edition. *Understanding Race, Class, Gender, and Sexuality: A Conceptual Framework*. New York: Oxford University Press.
Weber, Lynn and Lori Peek (Eds.). 2012. *Displaced: Voices from the Katrina Diaspora*. Austin, TX: University of Texas Press.
West, Candace and Don H. Zimmerman. 1987. "Doing Gender." *Gender and Society* 1(2): 125-151.
West, Darrell M. and Marion Orr. 2007. "Race, Gender, and Communications in Natural Disaster." *Policy Studies Journal* 35(4): 569-86.
White House, The. 2006. "The Federal Response to Hurricane Katrina: Lessons Learned." February. Washington, D.C.
Wilbon Hartman, Andrea. 2007/2011. "Filler Up Please: Coping With Racial Stigmas after Hurricane Katrina." Pp.10-18 in *Narrating the Storm: Sociological Stories of Hurricane Katrina*. Danielle A. Hidalgo and Kristen Barber, Eds. Newcastle, U.K.: Cambridge Scholar Publishing.
Williams, David H. n.d. "Temporary Assistance for Needy families in Louisiana." Online at www.loyno.edu/~quigley/deskman2001/booktempassist.pdf. Retrieved 7/16/07.
Wilson, William Julius. 1987. *The Truly Disadvantaged*. Chicago: University of Chicago.
—. 1996. *When Work Disappears*. New York: Vintage Books.
—. 2010. *More than Race: Being Black and Poor in the Inner City*. New York: W.W. Norton & Co..
Winant, Howard. 2000. "Race and Race Theory." *Annual Review of Sociology* 26: 169-185.
Wirth, Louis. 1938. "Urbanism as a Way of Life." *American Journal of Sociology* 44: 1-24.
Wisner, Ben. 2004. "Assessment of Capability and Vulnerability." In *Mapping Vulnerability: Disasters, Development, and People*. Edited by Greg Bankoff, Georg Frerks, and Dorothea Hillhorst. London: Earthscan.
Yinger, John. 1995. *Closed Doors, Opportunities Lost: The Continuing Costs of Housing Discrimination*. New York: Russell Sage Foundation.
Zakour, Michael J. 2008. "Social Capital and Increased Organizational Capacity for Evacuation in Natural Disasters." *Social Development Issues* 30(1): 13-28.
Zhou, Min and Carl L. Bankston III. 1998. *Growing Up American: How Vietnamese Children Adapt to Life in the United States*. New York: Russell Sage.

Index

Abundance Square, 9, 97. *See also* Public housing
Addiction, 106
Age, 5, 21
Alcoholism, 131
Anderson, Elijah, 23-24
Arena, John, 210
Assistance. *See* Survival Strategies. *See also* FEMA

Bankston, Carl, 66
Barber, Kristen, 210
Belgrave, Linda, 125
Between two worlds, 125
Bevc, Christine, 113, 153
Blockbusting, 18, 31, 194
Boggs, Keith, 39, 53, 63
Bush, George, 117
Bundling, 173

Car ownership, 20
Catastrophe, 4, 17, 51, 95-96, 124
Chapman. *See* Recovery
Charity Hospital, 11, 162, 186, 192
Childcare, 158
Children, 82, 87, 108; acting out, 142, 159; counseling, 132, 159; harassment, 181, 183, 185; missing, 111; murder, 107, 175-176; rape, 104-109, 114-115, 119, 133
Churches, 121, 130, 142, 191
Citizenship rights, lost, 91, 116, 144, 179-180, 183-184, 194
Civic participation, 19-20
Class, 28, 31, 38-39, 53, 57, 63, 66, 72-73, 94, 96, 151, 153, 157, 182, 194, 198
Classism, 96, 166, 179, 182-183
Coast Guard, 75, 82, 85, 121
Collins, Patricia Hill, 30
Contexts of reception, 129-131, 136, 156, 165, 172, 191

Cost of living, 149-150, 160, 164, 172, 176-177
Couch, Stephen, 27, 192
Counseling, lack of, 132, 176
Crime, 78, 92, 108, 153, 172, 174, 182; police committing, 93
Curfew in New Orleans post-Katrina, 100

Death, 74, 84, 110, 114, 124, 127, 134, 158, 167, 194; kin and friends, 12, 75, 92, 115, 158-159, 168-169, 175-177, 207; smell, 111; toll, 4, 25, 92, 167, 199; witnessed, 12, 70, 72, 86-87, 91, 105-108, 111, 114-116, 200
Decision making, 14, 17, 25, 38-54, 57, 66-67, 190-191; negotiated process, 10, 38, 40, 42, 45, 47-50, 53, 57, 103; statistical patterns, 12
Dehumanization, 117-118
Dehydration, 109-118, 127, 133
Denton, Nancy, 32
Department of Housing and Urban Development (HUD): rental assistance, 13, 141. *See also* Public housing
Depression, 139, 148, 168, 176, 208
Desire public housing. *See* Abundance Square
Devastation, 167-168, 209
Devine, Joel, 22
Disability, 21
Disaster, 18. *See also* Hurricane Katrina; commodification, 105-106; effects, 26-28, 189, 192; mitigation, 96; natural, 27-29, 37, 189, 194; planning, 96, 99, 120; social, 116, 120, 169, 189, 194; status, 151; survival systems, 10, 13, 40, 65; technological, 28, 86, 189, 192, 194; warning, 25-26,

223

37, 39-40, 43. *See also* Hurricane Katrina
Discrimination, 31, 153-156, 159, 164-166, 172, 178, 182, 190; class, 73, 166, 178, 182; geographical, 156-157, 161, 163-164; labor market, 153; race and ethnicity, 31-32, 73, 155; racial residential, 18-19
Displacement, 4, 14, 27, 37, 61, 106, 118, 123, 127-129, 133-138, 147-165, 172-173, 178, 183, 190, 201-202, 205; development induced, 148; extended, 13, 17, 61, 125, 128, 143-144, 146, 152-153, 171, 177, 191, 194; lived experience, 8, 55, 88, 124-125, 136, 138, 142-143, 147-165, 167, 197, 199; permanent, 171, 174
Doubling up, 135, 139-140, 142, 160-161, 173, 178, 186
Downing, Theodore, 163
Drabek, Thomas, 39, 53, 65, 107
Dreier, Peter, 33
Drugs, 105-107, 131
Dynes, Russell, 39, 53

Edin, Kathryn, 23
Education, 6, 19, 189; achievement in New Orleans, 19, 194; dropout, 18-19, 154-155; enrolling in new schools, 123, 137, 142-143, 147, 169
Elliott, James, 38-39, 43, 53
Employment, 152; after Katrina, 152-157, before landfall, 6, 11; loss, 154
Enarson, Elaine, 28
Erikson, Kai, 3
Ethnicity, 155, 157
Evacuee grapevine, 172
Evacuation, 3, 31-32, 37-39, 52, 55-67, 69, 135, 147, 190, 198-200; bathroom access, 59; challenges, 20, 80, 136; compliance, 40, 56; contraflow, 99; cost, 45, 55, 201; magnet locations, 14, 61, 129, 137-138, 143, 150, 153, 171; non-compliance, 38, 47, 50-52, 67, 92, 99; operationalized, 66,
90; post-storm, federal, 6, 12, 74, 75, 77, 82-83, 86-87, 90, 104, 106-111, 113-114, 117-118, 125, 130, 133, 141, 145, 147, 189; post-storm, self-initiated, 6, 48, 53, 56, 64, 70, 74, 77-81, 90, 136; pre-storm, self-initiated, 6, 8, 9-10, 12, 32, 38, 41, 46, 48, 50, 53, 55-56, 62, 127, 158, 197; private citizen, after landfall, 87-88; rates, 38-39; risk, 10, 37-38, 40-41; risk perception, 12, 40-42, 46, 50-51, 58, 60; timing, 38-39; traffic, 10, 56, 58, 62-63, 100; transportation access. *See* Transportation; vertical, 51, 57, 63, 71, 75-76, 83, 86, 107, 135
Eviction, 177-178, 180-186, 202

Family, 5, 90; dissolution, 18; reunion, 13, 50, 65, 84, 123, 135, 141-142, 145, 159, 191, 193; separation, 3, 12, 64-65, 84-85, 90, 106, 123, 127, 133, 145, 150, 158-159; structure, 5, 6, 9; unity, 102-103, 106-107, 111, 127, 136-138, 191
FEMA, 81, 88, 96, 120, 143, 145, 153, 157, 163, 189, 192, 211; assistance, 13, 61, 123, 128, 135, 140-141, 158, 160, 162, 186, 191; IHP, 141-142; lack of assistance, 13, 14, 175; recalling assistance, 142-143, 161, 173; trailers, 13, 29
Financial instability, 149, 152, 155, 165, 191, 194
First responders, 2; as sexual predators, 109; negative experiences, 71-73, 81, 88-89, 91, 93, 95, 114, 116-118, 189, 203, 208
Flooding, 2, 10, 11, 27, 41-43, 50, 59, 64, 70-72, 74-77, 79-80, 82, 84-87, 90, 92, 96, 99, 101, 104, 108, 114, 127, 135-136, 149, 169, 200; flood line, 10, 28, 167, 207; patterns, 17, 109
Food stamps, 13, 24, 61, 144, 150-151, 160-161, 173, 189. *See also* Survival strategies

Forced dependency, 86, 88, 119, 134, 139-140, 190
Fordham, Maureen, 26
Fothergill, Alice, 39, 82
Fussell, Elizabeth, 39, 43, 53

Gangs, 107
Gender, 18, 28-31, 39, 50, 53, 62-64, 67, 73-74, 79, 95-96, 120, 132-133, 136, 145, 151, 175, 182, 194, 198, 208; eldercare, 10, 74, 104, 117, 174-178, 191; masculinization of New Orleans, 168; men as predators, 93, 104-106, 109, 120 ; men as providers, 2-3, 10, 23-24, 48, 51, 53, 63, 95, 113, 136; men's roles, 29, 39, 63-65; mothering and grandmothering, 11-12, 23, 39, 62, 64, 77, 82-87, 95, 104-107, 111, 113, 115, 117-118, 132, 148, 150-151, 159-160, 175-176, 183-184, 191, 194; pregnancy, 39, 83; rejected, 131-133; women's roles, 24, 29, 39, 48, 71, 73-74, 87, 132-133, 169, 174
Gentrification, 186
Geography, 14, 21, 31, 66, 77, 145, 148, 151-153, 155, 157, 160-161, 163-164, 169, 192-193
Gladwin, Hugh, 38
God, 1, 49, 52, 55, 58, 62, 169
Gotham, Kevin, 19
Government mistrust, 169-171, 193
Grieving, 93
Guns, 88-89, 100, 116-118, 127, 129, 202-203

Handmer, John, 26
Haney, Timothy, 39, 43, 53, 210
HANO. *See* Housing Authority of New Orleans
Harassment, 81, 118, 170, 177, 178-186. *See also* Racism
Hash marks, 167, 207
Hate, 87, 155, 202; racial, 96, 194, 208-209
Hays, Sharon, 33
Healthcare access, 81, 160, 162, 169

Helping ethic, 1, 61, 70, 72-73, 76, 84-87, 95, 104, 107-108, 112-113, 119, 131, 133, 136-137, 184, 194
Homelessness, 128, 141, 144, 149, 151-152, 157, 172, 185, 191, 193-194; absence of, 134-135
Homesickness, 170, 203
Homicide, 100, 104-108, 115, 119, 174, 177; women affected by, 9, 77, 174-175
hooks, 29, 62
HOPE VI. *See* Public housing
Housing, 144, 169; affordable, 17, 143, 169, 183; assistance, 135, 140, 144, 164, 191; competition, 143; loss, 17, 21, 27, 74, 171-172, 192; overcrowding, 138-139, 191; projects. *See* Public housing; Stability, 10, 14, 29, 123, 128-130, 134-135, 137, 141-142, 144, 159, 184, 191, 194. *See also* Patchworking; temporary, 10-11, 129; vouchers, 14, 61, 88, 140-145, 185, 191. *See also* Public housing
Housing Authority of New Orleans, 15, 172, 184, 201, 204
HUD. *See* Department of Housing and Urban Development
Humanization of survivors, 130
Hurricanes: Andrew, 4, 38, 125; Betsy, 42; categories, 4, 41, 55, 69; culture, 41; George, 41, 49, 75, 99; Ivan, 41, 45, 49, 75, 99, 100; Rita, 133
Hurricane Katrina: damage, 3-4, 21, 28, 41, 52, 69-70, 74, 77-79, 84, 86, 88, 91, 96, 103, 127, 167, 170, 178, 199; economic opportunism, 72-73, 79, 95, 177-180, 182-185; Gulf Coast, 4, 69-70; landfall, 1, 4, 37, 55, 69-70, 75, 120, 127, 189, 199; lived experience, 1-4, 9, 14, 18, 23, 31, 33, 37, 41, 43, 49-50, 52, 64, 70-71, 73-79, 81-84, 86, 88-92, 94, 99-100, 103-118, 175, 177, 190-191; passing over, 2-4, 14, 43, 75, 78-80, 82-83, 86, 91, 103-104,

117; politics, 171; response, 73, 76, 81, 86-88, 95-96, 99-100, 120; risk perception. *See* Narratives; smell, 111, 113, 115, 140, 159; warning, 1, 4, 42, 48, 52, 64, 74
Hypersegregation. *See* Segregation

Illiteracy, 20
Implicit prejudice theory, 156
Incivility, 88-90, 107, 109, 194
Income: caps, 24; pre-Katrina, 6
Inequality, 161-162, 189, 193-194; class, 3, 9, 31; gender, 9, 29, 31, 120; race, 3, 9, 31, 120; social, 3, 17, 31, 81, 94, 102, 179, 189; systems, 26, 29, 120, 145, 172, 179-180, 184
Information control, 104, 117-119, 123
Insurance, 17, 168
Intersectionality, 18, 26, 29-31, 73, 86, 94, 96, 113, 120, 125, 133, 151, 153, 157, 179-180, 182-184, 186, 190, 194, 198

Jefferson Parish, 37

Killing. *See* Homicide
Kin caravan, 6, 12, 39-40, 45, 47, 49, 51, 55-65, 67, 79-80, 82, 102, 127, 135-137, 142, 158, 191; characteristics, 57, 59, 61-63, 65; defined, 57; shelter environments, 107, 111
Kin outsiders, 40, 46, 91, 99, 138
Kuligowski, Erica, 113, 153

Labor markets: post-storm, 14, 153; split, 154, 156, 159, 164
Left behind, 40, 46, 63-65, 91
Lein, Laura, 23
Levee breaches, 1-2, 4, 28, 71, 73-77, 79, 83-84, 86, 101, 120, 123, 135, 169-170, 189, 198-199
Liminality, 125, 131-132, 137
Literacy Alliance of Greater New Orleans, 20, 31
Litt, Jacquelyn, 65

Looting, 76, 81, 89, 93-95, 100, 112-114, 116, 118, 153, 156
Loss, 93, 134, 155, 158, 167-170, 175-176, 194, 203, 207-209; sense of community, 167-170, 172-174

Marginalization, 120, 189, 194
Marginal stability, 194
Massey, Douglas, 32
Mayor. *See* Nagin
Media coverage of the storm, 17, 85, 94, 100-101, 104, 109-110, 113-117, 120, 153, 156
Medical care: access, 57, 73, 162, 164, 169, 174-175; cost increase, 11; Medicaid, 144, 160, 162; Medicare, 144, 162-163
Methodology, 5, 8, 15, 125, 197-212; counseling access, 206-207, 209; interview structure, 205; limitations of the study, 30; locating displaced populations, 201, 204-205, 211; phone access, 205, 211; positionality, 197-199, 210; rapport, 209-210; transparency, 197, 206-207; trauma research, 207
Microentrepreneurship, 106
Militarization of disaster, 70, 76, 81, 88-90, 93-94, 96, 100, 104-105, 109, 113, 115-118, 133, 189, 202-203, 209
Miller, Kristen, 26
Mollenkopf, John, 33
Mothering. *See* Gender
MREs, 85
Murder. *See* Homocide

Nagin, Ray, 42, 171, 199
Narratives, 41-54; alternate, 44-47; collective, 42, 47-50, financial, 42, 44-47, 53; safety, 6, 42-46, 48, 51-53, 56, 58, 60, 64, 75, 80, 168, 191, 199; threat or risk, 6, 38, 41-43, 46-53, 57-58, 60, 64, 71, 91, 169, 191-192
National Guard, 12, 70, 74, 86, 91, 93-94, 96, 100, 105, 110, 114,

117, 202-203; assertiveness, 93-94, 96, 106, 116, 118
Neighborhood watch groups, 100
Networks: kin-based, 29, 39-40, 42, 46-49, 53, 55, 65-66, 73, 78-80, 107, 111-112, 118-119, 133, 141, 144, 158, 169-170, 174, 184, 190-191, 193; limitations and strain, 63-65, 73, 135, 137-141, 158, 165, 173, 177-178, 180, 184, 191; social, 38, 40, 44, 47-48, 52, 66, 76, 95, 119, 147, 159, 199, 205
New Orleans: demographics, 100, 171; geography, 25; life after the storm, 125, 127, 167-186, 201, 208; life before the storm, 99, 101-102, 110, 141, 152, 173; new normal, 168, 170, 172, 174, 176, 183-184, 186, 203; poverty, 18-19; recovery, 167-186; social inequality, 17, 94; Superdome and Convention Center. *See* Shelters of last resort
Nigg, Joanne, 26
Nock, Steven, 201
Norm maintenance, 108, 119
Norm violation, 104-105, 109, 119, 134, 168

Objectified suffering, 72, 88, 104, 117-118
Oliver-Smith, Anthony, 26

Pais, Jeremy, 38
Panic, waves, 114-115
Pardee, Jessica, 19
Patriarchy, 120, 132
Peacock, Walter, 38
Peek, Lori, 4, 29, 39, 82
Place. *See* Geography
Police, 70, 91, 94, 96, 105, 108, 115-117, 174-176; assertiveness, 87, 89, 93-94, 118, 170, 174, 208; brutality, 80-81, 89-90, 96, 170; committing crimes, 94, 171
Poverty, 42, 76, 79, 85, 91, 148, 182, 193; chronic, 17-21, 31, 42, 44, 77, 198; concentrated, 18, 32, 77; consequences, 18-19, 21-22, 28, 53, 65, 77, 193; deepening after Katrina, 149-152, 162, 164, 173, 177, 191, 195; effects on recovery, 24; extreme, 149, 165; place-bound, 19, 21, 33; programs, 33; race, 19; rate, 19, 21, 33; threshold, 22, 33; working poor, 11
Poverty survival every day, 18, 22-24, 29, 31, 38, 44, 52, 77, 82, 148, 154, 158, 164, 177, 191, 193. *See also* Survival strategies
Power, 102, 132
Powerlessness, 104-106, 120
Prejudice, 31, 81, 120, 155, 189
Private property, 95
Public housing, 5-6, 18-19, 71-72, 74, 77-78, 88, 91, 97, 128-129, 141, 150, 160-161, 169, 174, 177-179, 181-185, 207; demolition, 17, 21, 171, 184, 186; Desire, 198, 200-201, 204; HOPE VI, 5, 19, 21, 127, 169, 177-178, 182-183, 198, 200-201, 205, 210; Section 8, 129, 141, 163, 178, 201; St. Thomas, 198, 201, 204. *See also* River Garden; superblocks, 97; tenancy rules, 178, 186

Race, 29-32, 38-39, 53, 63, 66, 72, 90, 96, 120, 133, 153, 155, 157, 179-180, 182, 194, 198
Race restrictive covenant, 18, 32
Racial identity, 15
Racial isolation, 19, 77
Racial steering, 18, 32
Racism, 72, 81, 87, 94, 96, 113, 153, 155-156, 166, 168, 170-172, 189, 194, 208
Rape, 30, 93, 100, 104-106, 115, 117-118, 131, 133-134, 208; children, 104-109, 114-115, 118, 133
Rebuilding, 27, 29, 133, 141, 147, 149, 171, 177, 179, 186, 189, 191-193, 195
Receiving communities, 131, 133, 136, 157
Recovery, 123-195, 211; challenges, 20, 148-151, 158-159, 161-165,

172, 176, 178, 181-186, 189, 193; corrosive community, 28, 72, 107-108, 119, 134, 172, 181-182, 192-193, 209; disaster, 3, 9, 24, 27-29, 31, 33, 144-145, 169, 192-195; extended displacement as, 172, 184-185, 194, 202-203, 209; factors effecting, 26-27; lived experience, 93, 123-125, 172-173; low-income, 3, 9, 11, 13-14, 18, 27-28, 31, 131, 140, 143, 169, 171, 190, 192-195; New Orleans, 17, 27, 167-186; pathways, 130, 190, 194; stage model, 27, 37, 40, 192; therapeutic community, 27, 104, 112, 192

Red Cross, 61, 81, 99, 107, 133, 203
Redlining, 18, 31
Refugees, 116-117, 156
Rent, 149, 177, 202; increases, 11, 21, 149,160, 172, 176, 178, 202
Returning home, 14, 27, 125, 127, 136, 140, 144, 152, 157, 159, 161, 165, 167-186, 201-202; ambivalence, 169, 171, 174
Riot behavior, 113-114
Risk, 10, 12, 25-26, 39, 41-42, 46-48, 50, 55, 60, 84
River Garden, 112, 127, 157, 169, 177-186. *See also* Public housing

Sample, 5, 15, 18, 30, 38, 47, 200, 210-211; demographics, 7-8, 45, 54, 56-57, 70, 74, 77, 82, 102, 121, 128, 135, 143-146, 149, 152-154, 160-161, 169, 187, 190, 202, 205-206, 212; recruitment, 203-206
Sanchez, Laura, 201
Scholar-survivor, 8, 15, 210
Segregation, 19, 33, 193. *See also* Discrimination; de facto, 18; dimensions, 18-19; hypersegregation, 18-19; racial, 17, 19, 25, 77, 194
Self-empowerment among survivors, 17, 42
Self-sufficiency, 87, 91, 119
Sexism, 96, 113, 153, 168, 208

Shelter, 14, 31, 77-78, 82, 86, 101, 110, 124, 127-145, 160, 171; churches, 136-137; evacuation, 106-107, 123, 125, 127-130, 133, 135, 137, 141, 143; hotels, motels as, 60, 62, 123, 127, 129, 133, 135-137, 158, 163; kin offering, 10, 42, 59-60, 62, 66, 71, 73, 77-79, 82, 112, 123, 127, 135-140, 142-143, 158, 161, 180, 191; population, 90; rental, 135, 143
Shelters of last resort, 99-121, 191; Convention Center, 56, 100, 109-115, 118, 141; Superdome, 51-52, 56, 86, 93, 99-110, 117, 199
Smith, Kenneth, 125
Sniper fire, 100, 106, 108, 116
Social capital, 39, 49, 53, 66, 95, 119; situational, 6, 10, 59, 62, 66, 79, 174. *See also* Networks
Social control, 108, 116-118
Social justice, 3
Social security, 144, 160, 163
Spaces of fear, 131
Split labor markets, 154, 156, 159, 164
Stack, Carol, 22-23, 39
Starvation, 105-106, 109-111, 113-118, 127, 133
Stephen, Linda, 26
Stigmatization, evacuee, 87, 90, 153, 155-157, 164, 190
Stranded, 14, 17, 31, 56, 70-120, 132, 139, 141, 168, 190-192; hollering out, 84; lived experience, 1-3, 10, 12, 15, 71, 82-83, 87, 89-90, 99-111, 208; rescued, 2, 6, 12, 70-75, 77, 84, 86-87,110; spatial entrapment, 104-106, 110, 112-113, 117-118
Strip-searching, 118, 131
Suicide, 100, 105-107, 117, 157
Superdome, *See* Shelters of last resort
Survival compromises, 94-95, 116
Survival strategies, 3, 9, 11, 18, 22-24, 31, 40, 105, 125, 128, 149, 169, 174, 194; assistance-based, 11, 13-14, 23-24, 61, 106, 128-131, 134-135, 140, 142,144-145, 148, 151-152, 157, 160, 161-165,

171-172, 180, 184-186,190-193; dismantled, 46-47, 128, 138, 140, 144-145, 151-160, 162, 165, 169, 171-172, 180, 189-190, 192-193, 195; network-based, 10, 13, 22-23, 38, 40, 47, 49, 52, 55, 57-65, 73, 78-80, 82, 95, 109, 112, 118, 128-129, 134-141, 145, 147, 157-160, 164-165, 184-186, 190-191, 193. *See also* Networks; network drain, 24, 40, 73, 157; Patchworking, 106, 127-128, 134, 137, 139, 142-143, 164, 202; Transferability, 125, 128, 147-148, 152, 150, 163-165, 169, 180, 185-186, 190-192, 195; Work-based, 13-14, 23, 36, 47, 51-53, 58, 144, 148, 151-157, 160, 164-165, 176, 185, 190, 193
Swanstorm, Todd, 33
SWAT, 100

TANF, 24, 33, 144, 160. *See also* Welfare
Terror, 82, 92, 99, 102-109, 113, 117, 133, 175
Theft, 131-134
Theory, 18-35
Thomas, Oliver, 85
Threat legitimation, 48-49, 51-52, 64
Tierney, Kathleen, 113, 153
Toxic soup, 28, 77, 79, 82-84, 94, 111
Transportation: access, 6, 19, 38, 54-56, 90, 136, 158, 191; evacuation, 20-21, 42, 80, 88, 136; lack of access, 21, 38, 43-44, 47, 52, 92, 149, 155, 175
Trauma, 3, 12, 70, 73, 77-78, 81-82, 85-87, 89-90, 92, 101-109, 113-115, 117, 120, 124, 127, 129, 131-133, 139, 158-159, 167, 169-170, 175-177, 199, 205, 207

Unemployment, 18, 20, 144, 164, 169, 171; individuals experiencing, 9, 155, 157, 169
Urbanism, 135

Victimization, 78, 92, 94-96, 104-106, 133-134; first responders causing, 88-90, 94, 96, 105, 116, 118-119, 134; victim-blaming, 102, 156, 168, 194
Violence, 3, 18, 70, 77-79, 81, 86, 88-90, 92, 94, 96, 99, 104-108, 111, 114-115, 118-120, 127, 140, 153, 156, 169-170, 172, 194, 203; applied racial, 94; domestic, 132; sexual, 131, 133. *See also* Rape; Children
Vulnerability, 25-27, 39, 72, 120; development-induced, 25-26; geography, 21, 25, 160; hazard, 26; physical, 25,103-109; predictors, 24, 132; sexual, 93, 104-105; social factors, 25-26, 70, 115; structural factors, 25

Weber, Lynn, 4, 29
Welfare, 20, 32
Wirth, Louis, 134
Work, 58, 74, 83, 88, 127, 176, 179, 198; access, 20, 142, 160, 164, 172; illegal, 23; income, 23; loss, 44-47, 52-53, 154, 171, 193, 202; post-storm, 13-14, 123-124, 142, 152-157, 185; sense of duty, 12, 45, 47, 91-92, 190, 200, 202
Wright, James, 22, 201

About the Book

Jessica Pardee documents and examines the experiences of low-income African American women during Hurricane Katrina to uncover the ways that race, class, and gender shape the experiences of disasters. Drawing on intimate interviews to explore the complex challenges that these women faced in the course of the hurricane and its aftermath, Pardee reveals how, with so few material resources, they survived the storm and began the process of rebuilding their lives.

Jessica Warner Pardee is assistant professor of sociology at Rochester Institute of Technology.